# ROUTLEDGE LIBRARY EDITIONS: 19TH CENTURY RELIGION

Volume 3

# THE WORK OF T. B. BARRATT

# THE WORK OF T. B. BARRATT

T. B. BARRATT

Routledge
Taylor & Francis Group

LONDON AND NEW YORK

First published in 1985 by Garland Publishing, Inc.

This edition first published in 2018
by Routledge
2 Park Square, Milton Park, Abingdon, Oxon OX14 4RN

and by Routledge
711 Third Avenue, New York, NY 10017

*Routledge is an imprint of the Taylor & Francis Group, an informa business*

© 1985 Thomas Ball Barratt

All rights reserved. No part of this book may be reprinted or reproduced or utilised in any form or by any electronic, mechanical, or other means, now known or hereafter invented, including photocopying and recording, or in any information storage or retrieval system, without permission in writing from the publishers.

*Trademark notice*: Product or corporate names may be trademarks or registered trademarks, and are used only for identification and explanation without intent to infringe.

*British Library Cataloguing in Publication Data*
A catalogue record for this book is available from the British Library

ISBN: 978-1-138-06800-1 (Set)
ISBN: 978-1-315-10089-0 (Set) (ebk)
ISBN: 978-1-138-06988-6 (Volume 3) (hbk)
ISBN: 978-1-138-50521-6 (Volume 3) (pbk)
ISBN: 978-1-315-11522-1 (Volume 3) (ebk)

**Publisher's Note**
The publisher has gone to great lengths to ensure the quality of this reprint but points out that some imperfections in the original copies may be apparent.

**Disclaimer**
The publisher has made every effort to trace copyright holders and would welcome correspondence from those they have been unable to trace.

# THE WORK OF
# T. B. BARRATT

Garland Publishing, Inc.
New York & London
1985

For a complete list of the titles in this series
see the final pages of this volume.

The facsimile of *In the Days of the Latter Rain*
has been made from a copy in Central Bible College.

Library of Congress Cataloging in Publication Data
Barratt, Thomas Ball, 1862–1940.
THE WORK OF T.B. BARRATT.

("The Higher Christian life")
Reprint (1st work). Originally published:
In the days of the latter rain.
Rev. ed. London : Blim Pub. Co., 1928.
Reprint (2nd work). Originally published:
When the fire fell,
Olso, Norway : T.B. Ball, 1927.
1. Barratt, Thomas Ball, 1862–1940. 2. Pentecostalism
—Apologetic works. 3. Pentecostals—Biography.
I. Barratt, Thomas Ball, 1862–1940. When the fire fell,
and an outline of my life. II. Title. III. Series.
BX8762.Z5B37  1985    270.8'22    85-6786
ISBN 0-8240-6404-6 (alk. paper)

The volumes in this series are printed on
acid-free, 250-year-life paper.
Printed in the United States of America

# CONTENTS

*In the Days of the Latter Rain*

*When the Fire Fell and
an Outline of My Life*

PASTOR T. B. BARRATT

# IN THE DAYS OF THE LATTER RAIN

# IN THE DAYS
## OF THE
# LATTER RAIN

BY

THOMAS BALL BARRATT

*Revised Edition*

LONDON:
ELIM PUBLISHING COMPANY, LTD.
Park Crescent, Clapham S.W. 4.
1928

First Edition - - 1909
Revised Edition - - 1928

Made and Printed in Great Britain
by the Elim Publishing Co., Ltd.

# PREFACE

DEAR READER,—It is with much prayer and with thankful hearts we again reprint this book and issue a new edition. The former edition was issued not many years after the commencement of the Pentecostal Movement or Revival. This edition has been revised, but holds on to the great truths advocated in the former.

The chapters of this book were first printed as *separate pamphlets,* and were then collected and issued as *a book.* There may therefore possibly be very little logical order in their combination as chapters, but we trust, nevertheless, that THIS edition will prove to be as great a blessing to the readers, as we have reason to believe the first was.

It was written mostly during travel in India and England, when occupied with the strain of conducting missions, and attending to an ever-increasing correspondence.

It is possible that repetitions may be found, and those wishing to criticise may no doubt find occasion to do so. But we are seeking no reputation for well-formed essays. The chief thought in our mind is that of honouring Christ, and awakening a desire in all hearts for a deeper work of grace *through the Atonement and by the Power of the Holy Spirit.*

We have tried to *meet some of the criticisms of the day* concerning the Pentecostal Movement or Revival, in as straight, open, and fraternal spirit as possible. We have no desire to engage in *strife,* and will not do so, but being questioned as to our *faith,* we have tried to state it in as clear terms as possible. And we trust that when the *truth* is known to all, prejudices will fall, and numbers hail with joy this mighty outpouring of the " *Latter Rain.*"

Yours in *the Redeemer!*

T. B. BARRATT.

OSLO, NORWAY.

# CONTENTS

### CHAPTER I.
A CALL TO PENTECOST . . . . *page* 13

### CHAPTER II.
A FRIENDLY TALK WITH MINISTERS AND CHRISTIAN WORKERS . . . . *page* 25

### CHAPTER III.
TONGUES OF FIRE . . . . . *page* 43

### CHAPTER IV.
MORE ABOUT THE PENTECOSTAL OUTPOURING . *page* 81

### CHAPTER V.
PENTECOST WITH TONGUES FROM HEAVEN NOT FROM BELOW . . . . *page* 95

### CHAPTER VI.
THE PENTECOSTAL VISIONS OF TO-DAY . . *page* 99

### CHAPTER VII.
THE GIFT OF PROPHECY . . . . *page* 107

## CHAPTER VIII.

THE TRUTH ABOUT THE PENTECOSTAL REVIVAL, OR MOVEMENT . . . *page* 143

## CHAPTER IX.

THE BAPTISM IN THE HOLY GHOST FOR CHILDREN . . . . . *page* 179

## CHAPTER X.

TO SEEKERS AFTER "THE PROMISE OF THE FATHER" . . . . . . *page* 187

## CHAPTER XI.

A SPIRITUAL UNION OF FIRE-BAPTISED SAINTS *page* 217

## CHAPTER I.

# A Call to Pentecost

"THE PROMISE IS UNTO YOU AND YOUR CHILDREN"
(Acts ii. 39).

THERE are, in our day, so many claims made on the members of the different churches and Missions, calling for support and active work, that some of the most vital interests are often thrust aside, or only occasionally touched upon.

I refer especially this time to the little thought given to the necessity of being *endued* with

### "Power from on high."

There are church members who, when merely reading that statement, are apt to say: "*Nonsense! what do I care about such high-toned phrases?* That may do for ministers, but it is completely outside my sphere!"

And still, without this power, all the other interests of the church drag on, drag on—and become a drudgery instead of a delight.

Those Christians who have not quite closed their ears to the voice of the Holy Spirit, as He points to the dead state of numerous church members, are getting alarmed, and are beginning to see that the

### Supreme Need

of the Church to-day is not any got-up *man-made* revival —but a mighty outpouring of Pentecostal power. It finds expression in many ways. Prayer-circles are being formed, and prayers are constantly being offered up in churches and elsewhere for a general Pentecostal Baptism of the Holy Spirit. Leaders of the various churches and denominations are complaining of the spiritual dearth prevalent in so many communities, clogging the wheels of the church and preventing the onward march of the great kingdom of Christ.

It was said of John the Baptist that "*he was a burning and a shining light.*" Both are necessary, not only to shine, but also to burn. There is much would-be Christianity in our day, but it has only an outward brightness, there is *no fire within.* I was surprised one day to see the bright light in the windows of a house on one side of the hills close by Oslo. It seemed as if the house was on fire, but it was only the reflection of the sun. Some Christians reflect the glory of Christ, others have it *within,* they both *burn and shine.* They have Christ and His Holy Spirit within them.

God be praised, the cry is constantly growing more intense: "*Oh, that the fire of heaven might fall with all its refining and strengthening power on all Christians.*"

It is very easy to see that the churches are *not reaching the masses* as they ought to. Crowds surge by their doors without ever a thought of entering.

Then, in order to reach them, all kinds of devices are resorted to, with the cry: "Let us reach the people by all means!" And many a time the Church has adopted methods that cannot possibly be blessed by the Holy Spirit, to save the world. What is the good of getting a crowd into the church for a "*special occasion*" unless there is Pentecostal *power* in the pulpit and in the pew? Do you think the "secrets of the unbeliever's heart will be made manifest; and so falling down on his face he will worship God, and report that God is in you of a truth?" (I. Cor. xiv. 25).

There are even revival meetings held that seem to leave a very weak impression on the community. A very influential and wealthy layman in America said to me in answer to my question: "Don't you have revival meetings in your church?" "Yes, but they do not revive! They are more a financial operation than anything, for clearing church expenses." Now just fancy that—a revival that can only pull the people up to the level of giving a little more than usual to the cause of Christ! On what level do that class of people generally stand during the rest of the year? I will tell you. They attend church just when it pleases them, just to keep up the appearance of being members, or not to offend the Pastor, or because they have some general interest in religious work. They have associations there, and like to appear in stylish or attractive dresses, of course "in proper keeping with the surroundings." They give their pastor a good salary (*perhaps?*), and are interested in his high-flowing rhetoric and proud of his popularity (and I would not disparage this for a moment, but he himself will one day find out that souls have to be won by another power than that, and give up his seeking for reputation and honour! Then what oratory he may be master of will have another effect on his hearers); they are interested in philanthropic work, or may merely come and go as members without burdening theirs hearts with any of the claims of church members save living a moral life, attending services and the ordinary routine of church life. They, *many of them,* have no evil conscience because of supporting theatres by their presence there, or leading the minds and hearts of their children away from vital religion and personal communion with God by card-playing and dancing. They will merely laugh you to scorn if you, "in this intelligent age," should mention it in so many words.

Can you expect a *revival,* a genuine, heart-searching, lasting revival of grace, where *such a state of things exists, in any general way?* Should a real

### Holy Ghost Revival

strike such a church by some kind of a miracle, it would either sweep away all the vain idols of these would-be members and humble them in the dust before the Lord, revealing to them their lukewarmness and worldliness (I. John ii. 15-17), and bring them out on the resurrection side of the Cross of Christ—washed and cleansed in His atoning blood, or it would make them ask for their certificates of church-membership, and seek another church as dead as themselves. "Birds of a feather flock together."

The real facts, when known, are these, that a number of church members have

### Never been Saved!

They have been received into membership merely on a general confession of their acceptance of Christ and Christian principles, and the doctrines of the church. But they have never experienced *a change of heart, and therefore know nothing by practical, personal experience* of being *justified* through the merits of Christ by faith, and *regenerated* by the power of the Holy Spirit (Rom. v. 1; John iii. 8). Much less do they know anything by experience of the blessings of *sanctification* and the *baptism of the Holy Ghost.* There are, nevertheless, some of them, having heard about this blessing—*the full Pentecost*—seeking it, but *vainly,* because they have not yet *entered in by the door* to the kingdom of Christ. We have *really met cases where people are seeking this Pentecostal power who have not yet been saved.* How so? Simply because they have claimed that *church membership* is sufficient to make them Christians. What stupendous blindness! How often have I, on asking people if they were Christians, been met with the answer: " Oh, yes, I belong to the —— church " or, " Yes, sir, I go to hear Dr. —— " And they seem stupefied if you reveal to them that the Church cannot save, or that church-membership is not enough. " Protestants! do Protestants live in such blindness? " Yes, by the thousand, I am sorry to say.

Do not suppose that I disparage church-membership. It is a matter of your own conscience to which church you will belong. But, for God's and your own sake, see well to it that you *do not put your salvation in that*.

How can we expect any other state of things in the churches, when they are so full of nominal Christians?

The work must, naturally, be hindered from progressing. The pastor weeps and prays, and plans and studies the best methods of work (the sincere pastor does), and many of the sincere members do so too, but something is in the way. What is it? Ah, friend, there is " death in the pot." Not one, but *many* Achans, even on the Official Boards. They have touched the forbidden and condemned thing. They have hid it in their hearts.

Now, you may be perfectly assured that *if this is tolerated your church will not prosper*. It may keep up an outward appearance for a time, so long as you have an attractive, unsanctified orator in the pulpit, but the deep work, that *lasts for eternity,* and for which the

B

church is supposed to stand, *will not be done.* You have lost your first love! (Rev. iii. 17). But,

### A Revival is coming!

Praised be God! There are many praying and waiting souls, both among the ministers and the laity. They have already heard the sound of many waters. The revival is coming, it is coming! Hallelujah! But when it does come, many of those who prayed for it will be surprised, Ah, it HAS ALREADY COMMENCED and the surprise is seen, the consternation, yea even the doubt and opposition of many, because it came in a way they did not expect or care for.

To be candid, dear reader, *I do not believe that anything now, short of the same Pentecostal power that fell on the disciples at Jerusalem will suffice;* but when that once falls on the Church as a whole, we will witness the same demonstrations as recorded in the Acts, and the same, yea, *even greater results,* because the Church is more extensive now than then.

You may be prepared for any marvellous exhibition of the " power from on high " in these days. So do not be surprised. If you want to be in the fray when the blessing comes, if you want to see the glory of the Lord as He demonstrates His mighty power to save sinners and sanctify and empower His people with His Divine strength, then you must fall into line with *His* claims.

Oh, let us take this matter seriously! There is no time for *man-made* schemes and proud and haughty attempts to do the work that

### God alone can do.

When will you get to see that *our* plans, ideas, theories and schemes, that we are asking God to bless, are only a hindrance to *His* cause—so much rubbish that fills the track where the Gospel train is to roll by. The sooner we get it out of the way the better. We have to get there where we ask God, " What are *your* plans, *your* interests? What kind of work is it *you* have in store for me? " (Eph. ii. 10). Anything else must be doomed to destruction, but if we go where God wants us to go and do His will, endued with Pentecostal power— spiritual *dynamite*—we will be surprised to see the wonderful success God gives us.

But ere it comes to this, something

**will have to die** (John xii. 24),

and that something may be *you*. You must die to *self,* the *world,* and all your un-Christlike motives and pride, and make a *complete surrender* of yourself to God.

And ere this revival can enter the *Church* of Christ GENERALLY, and in its FULL POWER, the Church must have its *bochim* (vale of weeping, Judges ii. 1-5). Its pride and formalism, its self-seeking spirit, its bigotry and worldliness, must be blotted out through the blood of Christ, before it gets the power. The Church has

**sinned**

and polluted its ways by touching the unclean thing. *The Holy Spirit has been grieved* and all the leaders of the churches, in all the denominations, ought to cry out to the people of God, as they confess their *own* sins, and call them to repentance. The *constant covering over of sins and weakness,* making excuses for impurity and lukewarmness will never satisfy the Holy Spirit. The time is come for the Church to *shake off its fetters,* and break away from the yoke of formalism; and its arrogancy and half-hearted fight in the interests of Christ must be publicly confessed and forsaken. There *ought to be a general season of prayer and fasting throughout all Christendom.*

The appeal made by the Rev. Dr. Daniel Steele to the Methodist Episcopal Church applies to all the Churches: "*Cease living on the heroism of your fathers; quit glorying in numbers, sacrificing to statistics, and burning incense to general minutes; down upon your knees, and seek and find yourself the secret of the power of the fathers,—a clean heart and the endowment of power from on high; and then arise and unfurl the banner of salvation free and full, and a common sense theology.*"

God *must* have the right of way in the Church!

But in speaking to the Church collectively, do not let us forget that the needed blessing must be accepted by the *individual* member. Therefore if the Church *as a whole* is too dead to rise out of the dust, let not that prevent *you* from seeking your *personal* Pentecost.

Be subject to the conditions laid down in God's Word. Claim, as you fully surrender yourself, a perfect *cleansing* in and through the *Atonement* by *faith* (Acts xv. 9; II. Cor. vi. 11-18; vii. 1; i. 21, 22). Then *receive* the gift of the Holy Ghost.

As the power strikes you, do not ask God "*to stay His hand.*" Many have done this as they felt the power entering their physical being, and have been unnecessarily anxious. Does not the Almighty know what you can stand? It is merely His Holy Spirit taking full possession of your whole being, and is desirous to give you the *same blessing as that received by the first Christian Churches* (comp. Acts x. 46 and xix. 6 and Mark xvi. 17).

When the Holy Ghost floods and fills you *through*

*and through, as He filled the disciples on Pentecost,* you will begin to praise and magnify God *in tongues,* as the Spirit giveth utterance. It may not be the *" gift of tongues "* you receive, spoken of in I. Cor. xii., but snatches of various languages, or some celestial language that the angels and God will understand (I. Cor. xiii. 1; Eph. iii. 10). It may not mean that you are to become a missionary, although you are, of course, willing to become anything for Christ. It was not received by Cornelius and his friends in order for them to go out as missionaries, it was a *proof and sure evidence that they had received their Pentecost* (Acts x. 46). And besides this, your soul becomes so filled with the glory of God, that you will wonder how the Church could live on regardless of this wondrous miracle of grace.

Numbers—thousands upon thousands round about the world—are now rejoicing in the experience of Pentecost and the new and wonderful light it fills their lives with. I thank God that I may testify to this fact by personal experience. (Read *" When the Fire Fell and an Outline of My Life."*)

You become lifted to a higher plane in your spiritual life. This is not the culminating blessing, but it makes your heart a hot-bed for all the fruits of the Spirit (Gal. v. 22), and ought, therefore, to be attained when we start out on our spiritual " race " (Heb. xii. 1), enabling us to be victorious always. It does not imply that we receive other supernatural gifts, such as the gifts of healings, casting out demons, or miracles. All the " gifts " except tongues and interpretation, were in the Church of God before Pentecost, and practised by the disciples themselves. But you may *seek* these special gifts as led by the Spirit.

Pray, do not mix things! Just at this point I find

now that mistakes are being made. Some suppose that they have the *special* gifts because they have received the Baptism in the Holy Spirit, and become discouraged when the supposed results do not follow. Some, even ministers, are apt to condemn the movement and say: "Pentecost is not come," because those who say they have obtained it *do not perform miracles.*

We would say that it is a miracle that they have received their Pentecost. It is a miracle, too, to speak in tongues. Good Matthew Henry said that tongues belong to the "*greater things*" promised by Christ. The prophetic message delivered is also a miracle, and no less a miracle is the interpretation. We might speak of visions and wonderful healings that have taken place as real as those spoken of in the Bible, that have attended this wondrous Pentecostal Revival, but the *greatest miracle* is the transformed life and the new and great spiritual results in the life and work for the Master of that person who receives his Pentecost.

If the world is to be saved and made better, it will be by Spirit-filled men and women!

With this *full* Pentecost, your heart and life becomes entirely changed. In a truer sense than ever before it may be said: "*All things are become new!*"

Praised be God, it is for

### all His people.

Christ did not die for a nation, a church, or a sect, but for *all the world,* and purchased the same blessing for all. On His way back to heaven through Gethsemane, Calvary, and the earthquakes and revelations of Easter morning, He left the door open to Pentecost for *all* who would enter in (Acts ii. 1-4, 39).

"*Ask,* and it shall be given you; *seek,* and ye shall

find; *knock,* and it shall be opened unto you!" (Luke xi. 9-13).

*Lastly*: You may possibly know all this, but when, dear reader, will the time for *action on your part* come? If you *sin* any longer against the light, is there not a danger that God will " remove your candlestick out of His place " (Rev. ii. 5), and leave you to your own slothfulness of heart and mind?

Go down at the Cross at once. Put everything else aside. Get the matter settled NOW, for your own sake and for the sake of Christ and His kingdom.

---

CHAPTER II.

# A Friendly Talk

### with Ministers and Christian Workers.

" HE SHALL BAPTISE YOU WITH THE HOLY GHOST AND WITH FIRE " (Matthew iii. 11).

IT is not my intention to present any new methods or discuss the general equipment necessary for ministerial work. I merely want to have a friendly talk with you about what to me is the most vital point in all our work, and without which, whatever our ability or education, we will never reach satisfactory results. This is, to my mind, the very best equipment for the high office to which we are called. I refer to the need of

#### Pentecostal Power,

" the promise of the Father " to the disciples and servants of Jesus Christ.

Have we not been disposed to enter our ministerial labours without preparation? We have, of course, prayed and earnestly asked the Lord to baptise us with the Holy Ghost, but have we *tarried* UNTIL WE HAVE RECEIVED the power? We may have had some precious foretastes of what God can do for us, and seen considerable success attend our efforts; but have we received the *power* promised us by our Saviour, enabling us to fill our place as we are expected to do by Him?

Now, let us be perfectly honest. We cannot conceal anything from the Almighty, and He will judge us according to the light which He has given us. We are so used to putting the searchlight on the lives of others and on the community at large, that we scarcely get time to examine our own hearts and the motives that dictate our own life work. Is it not time for many of us to draw aside, and let the searchlight of God's Word fall on our own hearts and lives? Just get away from the rush and whirl of our everyday life, and, alone with the Holy Spirit, penetrate into the deepest cavities of our being, and weigh our motives, thoughts, actions, plans, methods, studies, public connections, ministerial responsibility, social relations, and everything that goes to make up our life, and ask ourselves: *Where* am I? *What* am I doing? Am I *satisfying* my Master's claims to the best of my ability? Am I working in the *right* spirit? Have I the *necessary* power to deal properly with the questions that arise in my work, to save souls and build up the kingdom of God? Or am I doing only *half* or a *quarter,* or *not even that,* of what I could do, if endued with power from on high? Elderly ministers may smile at the idea of raising such questions as these. They consider themselves as having passed through all those ordeals of self-examination, and look forward to the quiet of a happy old age. I certainly wish them every possible blessing in the evening of life, and thank God with reverence for every stone they have laid in the temple building, be it small or great; but I am sure that many of the old ministers are " giving up " too soon.

In passing through the Methodist Book-room in New York, the ex-president of the preachers' meeting stopped me and said: " I have just been telling my friend here of your experience, and remarked that the other day a friend of mine said that he did not believe in any such thing. I told him," the president continued, "that this, according to my mind, *was what every preacher stood in need of, and that all may have this baptism of the Holy Ghost,* and that the old preachers would then be able *to hold on to the day of their death."* I of course, fully agreed with him, and said that this was certainly the great need of the ministers in our day. There seemed to be nothing wanting in other respects, but the *very chief thing* necessary to work the first-class machinery our modern life has produced was absent. I remember I likened it to a street-car in perfect working order, standing on the rails, but dark and unable to move. Why? **Because the connections were not made with the copper wire overhead.** The moment the long arm touches the wire the car is flooded with light, and by a turn of the switch is able to move. Thus with the ministers, and in fact every Christian. There is power and light enough to be obtained; it is just waiting to be "let on."

You may have a superior education, great oratorical or administrative abilities, a wonderfully attractive personality, and by your popular style of speech, your high-toned lectures, or your popular methods, draw great crowds and gain general reputation, but are you

### winning souls?

THAT is the vital point! Without the power from on high, no matter what your qualifications, you cannot do so. You are merely gaining renown for yourself, and obtain your reward *here,* but you will get none at the hands of your Master. You have been seeking your *own* glory and *not His*—that is the reason! His Father will not honour you, because you have not honoured Him.

Make the connection with the " power house." If

you by faith have touched the wire of mercy, there is light within: you are His. But "turn on the switch" until the power goes through your whole being, and takes every ability God has given you into the service of the divine Master—then you will move and move others in the right direction. And, thank God, there is *power enough*—the resources of the Holy Spirit are unlimited—and all you need is at hand; all you have to do is to *meet the conditions*.

I expect this book will fall into the hands of men with directly opposite views. Some by training and culture are only in sympathy with the methods so predominant in cathedral work or 'neath the domes of old church structures, whose very appearance call for a stately and imposing ritualistic service; or more generally, it may be, read by men whose work requires the "rough and ready" style, as they deal with the problems that arise in the slums and on the streets of our great cities; or it may be glanced at by the busy pastor of a large church, almost rushed to death in the incessant duties of the society and the many lines of work that claim his zeal and interest "if things are to go"; or perhaps some quiet-going country pastor, with "no great plans or any big pretentions," "just jogging along in time with folks around him," may read it; or (who knows?) some "red-hot evangelist" or Salvation Army officer may get hold of it. No matter who, or what their position may be. I fully believe that the Lord has faithful workers in every church. But the question is—Do we measure up to the possibilities provided for us? Are we, in other words,

**Spirit-filled workers?**

If not, *why not?*

There is no reason in the world why we should not be. We have the *promise!* Then if we are not reaching out as we should, and obtaining the results we might, the fault *must be ours.* I know well enough from my own personal experience, that it is hard for a preacher of long standing to get *down to the point* where he sees he has been losing time and not had the success he *might* have had. I do not say that you have not been a magnetic preacher or a good pastor. It would be wrong, probably, to say that you have not been fraternal in your relations to other preachers, even preachers in other denominations. The Temperance cause has received your unqualified support; the other institutions, within and outside your church, have been helped greatly by your talents as a lecturer, writer and preacher; *but have souls been won for Christ, and the people of God been sanctified and baptised in the Holy Ghost?*

The great social problems of the day may even in you have had their most ardent advocate; *but have souls been saved, cleansed and filled with God? Have the sick been healed?*

I know full well, too, that all this outside work has given you great confidence among the people, but have you used this confidence to *bring men to Christ?* or has your self-consciousness and pride grown with your growing reputation, making it difficult or impossible for you to take the humble position of inviting men *to break off from the sins of the world and accept Christ?*

Oh, I know these questions are harrowing and painful; but your hearers have to stand many cutting questions at your hands, so be calm. I have been testing my own life along these lines, at any rate, and do not impose on you anything I have not been willing to bear myself.

And then, again, what have been your *motives* in preaching? Have you never found out that " the old Adam " in you was seeking, somewhere back at the root of things, to gain reputation, honour and a name: " What a splendid preacher ! " Have you never found out that pride that can even twine itself around the actions performed in the most holy ministries? It is so, nevertheless !

So what has been your *real* standing in the sight of *God* all these years and what is your standing now? Get down on your knees and pass through the testing fire of the Divine presence ! Do not spare yourself in the least. In your " zeal for the Lord " you have not spared others, so go under the fire yourself now and be resigned to the will of God. Let the " still small voice " of the Spirit test you, and be obedient when you hear it. Do so, brother, for your own sake and for the sake of Him who died for you, and for the sake of the people among whom you labour.

Another thought suggests itself here. What is there that divides the Church in our day more than the struggle about *theological problems,* especially as presented by the " *higher critics.*"

Brethren, these problems are no doubt very *important*. But *the problem that ought* to stir every fibre in our being now and bring us on our knees in humble supplication, and stir up ministers and church-members alike is this supreme question about the

### Baptism of the Holy Ghost.

Then let me entreat of you to lay aside every other question until *that* is settled. It will not hurt anybody if they rest awhile. Where *self* has been seeking renown, drop it, stop it! Where motives have been pure, let nevertheless all your theories and systems be hung on file *until this matter has been settled.* Whatever ideas or views you may have adopted, or systems you may have formed, you surely are aware that YOUR *conceptions of God and His dealings with man are not absolutely perfect.* I concede to that at once myself. But there is one thing on which the Bible is perfectly clear in its statements, and that is *the necessity of " power " in our spiritual life and work.* And do you not feel the want of a more complete work in your soul and victory over self? Then, friend, with all your learning and research you will acknowledge that you have *but one way to go, the way of full surrender to God.*

Lay those ideas and systems you have coined on the shelf awhile. If they are worth anything, they can well afford to wait, and in the light of the holy fire God will impart to your mind and heart, you will understand them better *after* the baptism than before. And should the fire consume them, neither you, the Church or the world will be any the poorer for it. If they are of value in God's sight, they will emerge from the flames as pure gold.

So get down on your knees, brother, if you have not done so, and surrender self and all to Christ! Take it very simply. You are so used to gigantic tasks and mighty problems, you have always revelled in doing such great things that you don't seem to know how to " become as a little child." Is not that your difficulty? So used to great things that the simplicity of a child can scarcely be attained. But that is your way, friend! It is the royal road to success—eternal prosperity.

Will you not offer some such prayer as the following:

"Lord, I intend now to rest my mind and heart simply on Thee, in perfect obedience to Thy will and at whatever cost. I may have been mistaken and deluded in many things, although my motives have been pure. I am determined by Thy grace to seek the purity of heart and life Thy Word teaches and Thy mercy provides. I surrender all, no matter what the consequences may be to my reputation, my social influence and standing in the church and in the community, I seek **Thy glory alone!**

**Let Christ be my all!"**

I have merely touched some of the chords in a prayer of that kind. But make your own prayer.

Then *down at the old cross,* no matter who you are, just accept by child-like faith the cleansing power of the atonement. The pure life you are seeking, the perfect rest, the experience of full communion with the Master will be yours. A life of purity, holiness in all its spotless beauty, through the perfect work of love that was revealed on Calvary, garments whiter than snow are waiting for you down at the foot of that old despised cross.

But why speak more about it? You know the old story well. Perhaps *holiness* has been the chief theme in your catalogue of subjects during the years that have rolled by. You have preached about it perhaps, without the experience, but kept up the preaching and discussed the subject at conventions and preachers' meetings with interest. No matter. Let the whole bent of your life reach its goal now. Claim the promise and God will cleanse your heart and give you the witness of the work done within.

Then abide at the Cross and await the

### Infilling of the Holy Ghost.

He may come immediately or delay His coming some little time (comp. John xiii. 10; xvii. 6, 16, 22; xx. 22; Acts i. 8, 14; ii. 1-4; x. 44-46); but He *will* come and fill you with "power" to live that pure and humble, but glorious and effective life of a Spirit-filled Christian and minister of the gospel.

Do not rest until you have received the full and glorious baptism of fire from on high—*the same kind of baptism as that received by the 120 on Pentecost* and as that received by the little crowd in the home of Cornelius (Acts x.).

What a revolution it caused in their lives! what a wonderful change it will make in yours! You will be strengthened as by nothing else, it will make you bold and strong, progressive and successful, because being fully sanctified you have no plans but those *God* calls you to execute, and with His power nothing will be impossible. Oh, what an outlook! What hope and joy, what victory *through Him* who has obtained full and perfect control of your life—Hallelujah!

You wish to partake *in the world-wide revival?* Then be prepared. We have so often seen that where a revival *does* come in answer to prayer it may come in a *different way* than was expected. Then some are apt to be disappointed. But there is no reason to be so. God knows what is best and what means and methods are best able to further *His* interests. The Holy Ghost may upset all your plans, dear friend! And if they in any way are at variance with His will, the sooner that takes place the better. But if you are sanctified and baptised by His power, you are prepared for any emergency.

If we expect a *genuine revival*, we must ever remember, that it is NOT learning, culture, oratory, splendid intellectual outbursts or arguments, systems or even *revival methods* that are to bring it. All these will have their place if they are consecrated to the will of Christ, *but they will never bring about the revival,*

#### the genuine revival.

We may have the best church machinery in the world, but it is of no good without power to work it. The locomotive is of little good, however modern in its construction, however polished and even *clean* it may be, unless there is *fire* in it.

Don't let us put the cart before the horse. Let us ask God to surcharge us with His Divine power. Then we ourselves will be the centre of a revival constantly taking the fire with us, " turning the world upside down " and hastening on the kingdom of our glorious King and Redeemer.

Oh, when once the ambassadors of the Lord seek this supreme blessing and get hold of this secret of power in their work, what a revelation it will be to them!

There is *our friend in the cathedral.* His training from childhood has stamped him as the ritualist. Let us suppose he is really honest and has attained to a personal communion with God by faith. He may in his worship, mid the sweet strains of the organ and the trained voices of the choir, and all the paraphernalia of the cathedral service have longed for and found that sweet joy, that faith in Christ alone can bring us. The Lord knows how to find the secret passage to the heart. And now his eyes are opened to see as never before the responsibility of being a minister of the Gospel. If he surrenders and meets the conditions, for him as for all there is that same way to tread. *Surrender all and claim a full cleansing through the blood of Jesus Christ;* if he fully gives way to the Divine leading, his soul and life will be sanctified and filled with a peace and joy hitherto unknown. Being cleansed by faith he will wait for the "promise of the Father." His colleagues will already have noticed a great change in his life and in his whole attitude to his surroundings. The old bigotry is gone, his relations to the ministers of other denominations are become fraternal and as becometh a Christian. A greater earnestness infuses his ministry, and his character has received a vivid touch of the Divine Spirit.

But as he waits for *the full Pentecost,* the Spirit suddenly one day comes to the cleansed temple and fills it with that same Divine power and glory that fell on the waiting disciples at Jerusalem. And with what *results?* I really cannot say. The workings of the Spirit are not always similar in their outward demonstrations. But of one thing I am certain, that should his colleagues hear him speak in " tongues " and see the glory of the Divine light shine forth from that heaven-turned face and hear him prophesy as with loosened tongue of the wonderful works of God, or see him prostrated by the power, and for some time unable to tell of the unspeakable peace within or the visions he has received, or see him leap for very joy as the power strikes him, they will possibly suppose him *crazy.* But he himself will be perfectly regardless of their opinion. He KNOWS *he has at last* obtained what *gold cannot purchase* and has entered as it were *a new world.* If his relations to his surroundings had become changed before, they will be more so now. You may depend upon it, that whatever special ability or gift the Lord has given him will now find expression in some powerful form. He is ready for persecution too, yea, even the martyr's cross. He has but one object in view, and that is to *honour his Lord and Master.* And the church must either bear with him, and *submit to the revival he brings about by the new power within,* or close its doors against him. Ah, it is hard to say, but that is generally the case. When the fire falls and there comes a stir—when the *real* thing takes place, nominal Christianity closes its doors against God. But wherever the transformed minister comes, he will in life and word and deed be an exponent of the power of God to save,

### through the Blood of the Lamb.

Then there is *our brother doing good mission work* in the slums and on the streets. What a change will be seen in him when the power comes upon him! He, too, will be a marvel to his friends and co-workers from that hour, and the results of his work will be far deeper and greater. People have possibly already wondered at the consecrated zeal and self-sacrifice he has shown in his Master's service, but a new force will mark his course now. He will himself be surprised at the great difference in his new life. An unusual calm will settle down over his heart and work, not the calm of indifference, and indolence, but the calm that marks the progress of the deep river, the majestic calm of heaven, in which the forces of the Godhead display their energy, not in spasmodic outbursts and frenzied attempts to do God's work, coupled with the underlying hope to obtain prominence for the heroic work done; but in the settled purpose, the harmonious motives of his life work, the deep love to God and man that stamps his every step, rolling on like a river, sweeping away the smaller difficulties without a frown, and cutting its way through the spiritual filth and mud of vice and poverty of the city, making its bed deeper and broader annually and daily, bringing life and prosperity with it everywhere. For " by the river upon the bank thereof, on this side and on that side, shall grow all trees for meat, whose leaf shall not fade, neither shall the fruit thereof be consumed; it shall bring forth new fruit according to his months, because their waters *they issued out of the sanctuary;* and the fruit thereof shall be for meat and the leaf thereof for medicine . . . And it shall come to pass that everything that liveth, which moveth, whithersoever the river shall come, shall LIVE—*and everything shall* LIVE *whither the river cometh* (Ezekiel xlvii.).

But what about the *busy pastor* in the large church? Well, if anybody in ministerial or mission work needs the full Pentecostal power *he is the man.* I feel like writing a little book about all the difficulties of the pastor in a large city. But that is not needed. The thing needed is, if he does not yet understand it—and there are many who, whatever their abilities and reputation, have not yet discovered this secret—*his supreme need is the*

### full baptism of power from on high.

I agree that there are men who seem to have a special call to evangelistic work, but I am perfectly sure *that any pastor,* who gets Pentecostal power, *will soon have a revival in his church.* A holy determination will seize him. He cannot be content with half measures. He will first of all try to get *his official board* to fall in line with his plans, and urge them to seek the blessings he himself enjoys, and then with them and other warm-hearted members of his church he will steadily but firmly arouse his church, until all have felt that he means business. Then from that awakened church will go forth a thousandfold shout of triumph that will startle the world around, and the people will cry out:

**" Men and brethren what shall we do? "**

And if *the members of the board* will not support any attempt to awaken the sense of holiness within the church, and not seek the blessings themselves, he will appeal to others within his church, who will side with the Lord and him in this, and there will surely be someone. We can scarcely imagine a church so worldly or formal but that a few *real* Christians will be found in it. With these he will form a league of prayer and launch out in the name of the Lord, whatever the dead or half dead officials or members of the church will say. And if he should be left standing alone, he will either determine, like Dr. Goodell, of Calvary M.E. Church, New York, if the Spirit leads him that way, that there shall be victory for his Lord and Master in the church or a " funeral in the parsonage," or *he will have to leave them and shake off the very dust of his feet against them,* as a testimony against their ungodliness. But it shall be more tolerable *in the day of judgment* for the harlot and the publican *than for that church!*

It may mean much self-sacrifice for a pastor to take his stand thus. But the *" funeral in the parsonage "* had really taken place before he received his Pentecost. It was when the old man *Self died* (John xii. 24) that prepared the way for Christ and His glorious Holy Spirit.

A Pentecostal pastor knows that he is a pastor *in order to win souls for Christ and build up the Church*

**in holiness and the fear of the Lord.**

He has not received his *Pentecost* unless he knows that and acts accordingly.

If filled with the Holy Spirit, he will draw all the lines of the various institutions within his church towards that point. " But that will cause antagonism on the part of some wealthy members," it is said. It may or it may not. There is often a stupid fear of the rich supporters of the churches exhibited by some pastors. If they had the courage of their convictions and spoke in a straightforward, manly way concerning these vital truths in the Bible, without compromising with the world and the devices of Satan, they would gain the respect more generally of their rich supporters. As it is now they allow the money question and the social privileges they enjoy in the homes of the rich to dominate their preaching and relations to them. But when Pentecost comes that is done away with. With gentleness and love, but with all the firmness of a conviction that fears nothing, they proclaim the glorious promises of the Gospel and condemn the sins of their day, making Christ so attractive in their preaching and lives that rich and poor alike will claim him as their Lord or reject Him. *And thus the dividing line will be clear and comprehensive,* and that is just the want of our day.

And as regards the pastor himself, the new power will be a revelation to him. The worry and fuss, the constant anxiety, as to the outcome of his services and work, will be gone, because *now* he rests perfectly in the Lord. It is not *his* service, or *his* revival campaign, but *the Lord's!* It is not *his* honour that is at stake, if that of anybody, but the *Lord's,* and there need be no more fear about His honour. He knows how to move things. The pastor has merely to be

**obedient to His will,**

and he will bear fruit as naturally as the branches of

the purified vine. The power is not the pastor's but the Lord's, that is the difference now. Oh, Hallelujah! When you get that vision clear to your heart, it will revolutionise both you and your work completely.

And the quiet *young country pastor* will get his vision too. Perhaps he will find out that his easy going life is not of the Lord. For with all the inner calm of that strong life which the Holy Ghost imparts, it is directly opposed to laziness and the " don't care " style of some preachers. I would not be misunderstood as saying that the " don't cares " are merely in the country villages. But I do mean to say that when the country parson or preacher has received his Pentecost, he will immediately be as a flaming fire, and there will be a stir somewhere.

The Holy Spirit is never inactive, and if you have received the fulness of the Spirit you will be sowing the good seed by all waters and the results will be sure. The mere fact that you have become a changed man (I. Sam. x. 1-12; Luke ix. 54, 55; Acts viii. 14-17) and have a " passion for souls "—not as the fruit of zeal merely, but of *love,* or speak in " *tongues* " or *heal the sick,* will make the people desirous to know something about the new power that fills you. This spirit of inquisitiveness drew surging crowds around Christ. People will feel you have imbibed His Spirit, and as they listen to the burning message you bring them from Him, of full and free salvation, they will be saved in numbers.

The mistake of your life has been this, *that you have not tarried until " endued with power from on high! "*

A man once stood on a hill-side in the harvest season and noticed a group of men busily at work mowing down the long sweet grass. Some stopped very often to sharpen their scythes, the others worked on energetically, but very seldom attended to the sharpening of their scythes.

He went down to see the results of their work and found out that those who took time to sharpen their scythes right often, did their work better, easier, and quicker than the others.

When Luther was hard pressed with work he prayed more than usual. Take time to pray, friend, and pray until you get your Pentecost. This applies to the " red-hot evangelist " as well as the Salvation Army officer, and every worker in the Lord's great harvesting field. We may be " red-hot " without the Pentecost. It may be the red heat of zeal and enthusiasm, but you want

### The White Heat of Pentecost.

Here are *two pieces of steel*. Their weight, shape, appearance, length and breadth are just the same. You cannot at first observe any difference. But place one of them in a heap of iron nails, filings, and needles. The influence exerted is very apparent. The whole heap seems to be alive. Every bit of iron there starts out towards it.

Now take it away and put the other piece of steel in its place. There is no stir at all. There it lies quite inert and ineffective.

How do you explain the difference? Simply this. One has been magnetised, the other not. One surcharged with power, the other not.

And this is the difference between Christian workers. Some are filled with Holy Ghost power, the others have failed to obtain it.

Oh, friends, do not let us make a mistake in this most vital point. May the Lord be able to use us all as *He intends to!* For when our life work is done, it is of little importance what *men* may have to say about it, if His " well done! " is not heard. But they that be " *wise* shall shine as the brightness of the firmament; and they that *turn many to righteousness as the stars for ever and ever!* " **Amen!**

CHAPTER III.

# Tongues of Fire

" AND THERE APPEARED UNTO THEM CLOVEN TONGUES, AS OF FIRE " (Acts ii. 2, 3).

IT will certainly be a help to many to be able to compare the speaking in tongues and the prophetic speeches of to-day with those of former days.

As regards the *gift of prophecy,* we find it already in the old dispensation; whereas the first record of *speaking in tongues* is in the New Testament.

*Jesus* had said that believers should " speak with tongues " (Mark xvi. 17), and the first fulfilment of that prophecy took place on the Day of Pentecost at Jerusalem.

The prophet Joel had prophesied that the Spirit should be poured out " upon ALL FLESH, and your sons and your daughters shall *prophesy* " (Acts ii. 17).

The most remarkable thing is that the Apostle Peter makes use of this in connection with the *speaking in tongues* heard at Jerusalem.

The mode of speaking in tongues heard there must have had the character of prophecy—that is, *they spoke* of " THE WONDERFUL WORKS OF GOD." There were then in the messages, given in tongues, truths full of " edification, exhortation, and comfort." This is evidently the idea conveyed by Peter, when quoting Joel concerning PROPHECY (I. Cor. xiv. 3). But there was no doubt also much adoration and praise, especially when they were in the " upper room " (comp. Acts x. 46; xi. 15).

Men and women of the different nationalities, present in Jerusalem on that occasion, could at once distinguish their own language, when the disciples came down to the crowd from the " upper room," and the messages brought to them through it. But they only understood what was said in **their own tongue.** There was therefore considerable speaking in tongues not understood by all the people.

Possibly those who spoke in tongues did not understand what they were saying. We have very often cases in our day, where direct messages have been given to someone present, who knew the language, and was stirred by the message, although the speaker did not know what was said. The Holy Spirit gave the utterance.

God's *chief idea* with this miracle seems to be that of revealing divine power through His disciples, giving them authority—His own divine seal—in the presence of all the people. Not so much that of reaching them with the gospel in their mother-tongue, as it seems very clear that the crowds attending the Jewish festival were generally acquainted with the Aramaic or Greek language. There was therefore no necessity for them to have the Gospel preached to them in their own language. The *miracle* was to call their attention to the wonderful revelation of Divine power in connection with these despised followers of Jesus Christ. And as such it worked, causing surprise, amazement and wonder, and open ridicule from many, unwilling to see the Divine power in it, and ascribing it to *natural* causes. Just as in our day!

The disciples, it seems, understood what was said when the astonished people asked, " How hear we every man in our own tongue wherein we were born?" And when Peter stood forth all the people clearly understood his sermon. This proves satisfactorily to our mind that the tongues were not necessary as a means of communication on the Day of Pentecost. Still, about 120 men and women *spoke in tongues.*

Possibly not all of them received the " GIFT " (I. Cor. xii.) enabling them to control a language, but no doubt several did. All spoke under the POWER OF THE HOLY SPIRIT, as all do, more or less, when speaking in tongues.

Although, as we have pointed out, the chief aim with this miracle was to give the disciples and the preaching of the Gospel the background of Divine support, it also opens up the possibility, when God sees fit, of giving Gospel messages in this way. Dr. A. B. Simpson concludes from this miracle that God will yet bestow "MISSION TONGUES," in order to hasten His work among the heathen.

That, then, means to say, that Spirit-filled people may obtain perfect control over a language—or, rather, the Holy Spirit gets such perfect control over them that He will be able to address the heathen through them—without their having to study the language spoken. We have already cases in our own day of this kind. But the Spirit does not always speak in the same language, so our call to any field among the heathen must not be guided by the language given; the Holy Spirit decides that for us in other ways. At least, this is the experience we have had. Perhaps there may be more regular developments later on in God's own plan.

But *tongues,* no doubt in many cases in *rhapsodic* sentences with short messages and words of adoration and praise, were given to ALL; for they were " all filled with the Holy Ghost (all the ' about 120 '), and began to speak with other tongues, as the Spirit gave them utterance" (Acts ii. 4)—some possibly speaking more clearly than others; some in short sentences; some with a most perfect address, having the " gift " of tongues to perfection; some possibly only in one tongue, others in several tongues, judging from present-day experiences.

In the house of Cornelius there was no need of the Word of God being proclaimed in tongues, in order to be understood. All present evidently understood Peter. And it is not stated that *he* spoke in tongues, but those on whom the Spirit fell, and it " fell on *all them which heard the Word* " (Acts x. 44).

Peter said they " have received the Holy Ghost *as well as we* " ("*Even as on us,*" Acts xi. 15). Both he and those who came with him were convinced of this, " FOR THEY HEARD THEM SPEAK WITH TONGUES AND MAGNIFY GOD)" (Acts x. 46).

That then is the way in which it took place on Pentecost, similar to that in the house of Cornelius; and Peter and his company would not have believed that the Spirit was given to the heathen, unless they had heard the *tongues and praises.* It gave the whole occasion this indescribable and remarkably SUPERNATURAL stamp.

What language the Spirit-filled worshippers spoke there it is not possible to say; and we do not read any statement concerning the language spoken at EPHESUS by the twelve men on whom the Spirit fell there (Acts xix). All we read is, that " when Paul had laid his hands upon them, the Holy Ghost came on them, and they *spake with tongues and prophesied.*"

Those who cannot understand the profit of speaking in tongues when the fire falls, because it is a foreign language that is spoken without interpretation, will be at a loss to answer when we ask, What profit was it at Cæsarea, at the house of Cornelius, or at Ephesus with the twelve men? If they had lived then, they would have said, "*But, dear Peter (or Paul), what is the good of people talking what others do not understand?*"— because that is the way they ask now.

They forget to distinguish between the first outburst of tongues on receiving the Baptism in the Holy Ghost, and a *later, more mature state of things.* That is, they fail to distinguish between *tongues,* as the Spirit giveth utterance, when we are baptised in the Spirit, and the " *gift* of tongues" which remains and is to be used according to apostolic instructions.

Whatever may take place during the first joyous moments or days of the great outbreak, *when " the fire falls,"* under the *ordinary* conditions of the Church, it is right to claim that the language spoken, if not understood by those present, SHALL BE INTERPRETED, either by the person himself, or by another who has received the gift of interpretation.

We will, in this little HISTORICAL summary, make use of some extracts from what the great divine, *William Arthur, M.A.,* well known within the Wesleyan Methodist Church of England, and throughout the English-speaking world, both as a writer and preacher, and by his holy life, has written on the subject; the extracts are from his *The Tongue of Fire.* Likewise some extracts from the *Church History,* by *Fredrik Nilsen;* and some articles written by *Pastor Ernst Lohman,* of Germany, in a German paper. As Pastor Lohman has not placed himself definitely on the side of those who support the present revival that is now sweeping over the earth, his historical account will be all the more interesting.

### The Outpouring at Jerusalem.

*William Arthur* says, in the chapter on "The Fulfilment of the Promise": "After ten days have elapsed, their patience is not exhausted. Did He not say, 'Not many days?'"

"No Thomas absent now! Not one heart has failed! 'They are *all* in one place.' It must have been very early; for after they received the baptism, and filled all Jerusalem with the noise of their new powers, Peter reminded the multitude who came together that it was only the third hour of the day (nine o'clock in the morning). We know not how long they had that morning urged their prayer, nor whose voice was then crying to Him who had promised . . . But 'suddenly there came a sound from heaven as of a rushing mighty wind.' Not, mark you! a wind; no gale sweeping over the city struck the sides of the house and rustled round it. But 'from heaven' directly downward fell 'a sound,' without shape or step or movement to account for it— a sound as if a mighty wind were rushing, not along the ground, but straight from on high, like showers in a dead calm. Yet no wind stirred: as to *motion,* the air of the room was still as death; as to *sound,* it was awful as a hurricane."

"Mysterious sound, whence comest thou? Is it the Lord again breathing upon them, but this time from His throne? Is it the wind of Ezekiel preparing to blow? Shaken by this supernatural sign, we may see each head bow low. Then timidly turning upward, John sees Peter's head crowned with fire, Peter sees James crowned with fire, James sees Nathanael crowned with fire, Nathanael sees Mary crowned with fire, and round and round the fire sits 'on each of them.' The Lord has been mindful of His promise."

"The instantaneous effect of the descent of the Spirit on the first Gentile converts in the house of Cornelius was that they began to '*magnify God.*' The effect would be the same in this first case. That bosom has yet to learn what is the feeling of moral sublimity, which never has been suddenly heaved with an emotion of uncontrollable adoration to God and the Lamb—an emotion which, though no voice told whence it came, by its movement in the depths of the soul, farther down than ordinary feelings reach, did indicate somehow that the touch of the Creator was traceable in it. *They only who have felt such unearthly joy need attempt to conceive the outburst of that burning moment.* Body, soul and spirit, glowing with one celestial fire, would blend and pour out their powers in a rapturous ' Glory be to God ! ' or ' Blessed be the Lord God ! '

"The fire is not a shapeless flame; it is not Abram's lamp, nor the pillar of the desert, nor the coal of Isaiah, nor the unfolding flame of Ezekiel; it is a tongue, yea, cloven tongues. On each brow glows a sheet of flame, parted into many tongues. Here was the *symbol* of the new dispensation. *Christianity was to be a tongue of fire.* Blessed be the hour when that *tongue of fire* descended from the Giver of speech in a cold world ! ''

William Arthur has written much in his book that would be worth while to cite, but our space is limited. What Christian is there who, when he considers the possibility of such a Pentecostal experience, would not desire to have it? But, sad enough, it has all been looked upon as a great occasion that could not be renewed; whereas God desires all His children to have *the same power and experience* as that enjoyed by the disciples on that wonderful Day of Pentecost at Jerusalem.

The gift was not, as some have supposed, confined to the apostles. William Arthur rightly says: "The tongue of fire rested upon *each* disciple, and *all* spoke with a *superhuman utterance*. Not the twelve only, the Lord's chosen apostles; not the seventy only, His commissioned evangelists; but also the ordinary believers, and even the women. The baptism of the Spirit fell upon *all*, and the spiritual gifts were imparted to *all*—not equally, for the expression, ' As the Spirit gave them utterance,' seems to indicate a diversity of gifts, which accords with other passages in the New Testament. It is not probable that *each one* could speak *every* language, for St. Paul says of himself that he ' *spoke with tongues* more than they all,' clearly implying a limit in that gift, and a different limit in different persons."

It is interesting to notice how one, who probably never had the gift of tongues himself, could enter so clearly into the question as does Mr. Arthur. The edition of his book that we have before us was issued in America in 1856. It was already then, no doubt, well known in England.

There are several remarks in it that we may differ in, but in the main we agree with him.

As to the *miracle* itself, he says it was " a miracle in a very amazing form; perhaps, as to its form, the most amazing of all miracles."

In order to prove this, he shows how matter is of less importance than *mind*. Those are mighty miracles that are wrought in seas, mountains, the firmament, or the human body, that display a power which rules the frame of nature or the frame of man; yet all these may be called the PHYSICAL MIRACLE. " But beyond this lies a *higher* miracle, of which the sphere is MIND, and which, therefore, we may call the MENTAL MIRACLE."

"Of this order two forms had been witnessed previously, *inspiration and prophecy;* but now a **new** miracle was to challenge the belief of all Jerusalem. This miracle, as to its *moral* impression, differed totally from all physical miracles—even from that complex and most peculiar miracle, *the raising of the dead* . . . That miracle stands alone; yet the chief impression which it makes, and certainly the impression which all purely physical miracles make, is the POWER."

"In *inspiration,* we see *the mind of man* enabled to sit down among the morning mists of things, and to write a book which will stand while the world stands. In *prophecy* (foretelling) we see *the mind* enabled to look through a thousand years, and describe what lies beyond so plainly that, when it is unfolded to ordinary sight, it shall at once be recognised. Both these miracles bring us, not so much into the presence of a Ruler, *as into the presence of a Spirit.*"

"As however, we watch the MIRACLE OF TONGUES, a strange solemnity falls upon us; we feel as if we had left the region where mind slowly and dimly learns through sense, had crossed some invisible line into the land of spirits, and were standing before the *Original Mind.*"

"What knowledge of *mind* so minute as that which scans every sign whereby every mind expresses its ideas "—that can make use of the expressions by which man makes his thoughts known to others!

And on those who heard it the influence was convincing, as they heard the SAME message through all these speakers. The men who speak, too, are unschooled peasants, yet all gifted with the same unheard of power.

The tongues are different, but " the impulse is one, and the message one! From *what centre* do all these languages issue?" The answer leads us back to the presence of the Central Intellect of the Spirit which "formeth the spirit of man within him"—of *the Supreme Mind,* to which all *mind* is common ground—of the Father of thought!

### God had spoken!

All doctrine is not therefore the thoughts of man or his work, the product of thinker, or the juggling of priests! No! now GOD HAS SPOKEN DIRECTLY THROUGH HIS FIRE-BAPTISED SERVANTS!

In answer to those who believe that the miracle did not consist in the SPEAKING in other tongues, but that the miracle was one of HEARING rather than speaking, Mr. Arthur says: "Had it been as here supposed, the symbol of the miracle would not have been cloven tongues, BUT MANIFOLD EARS. The double declaration of the narrative corresponds with the symbol. As regards the *speakers,* it says that THEY 'spake with other tongues'; as regards the *hearers,* that they heard every man in his own tongue.

"When Paul finds fault with the use of the *gift* of tongues in Corinth, he does not blame the hearers for lacking an ear that would interpret their own tongue into foreign ones, but blames the speakers for *speaking* with the *tongue* words not easy to be understood 'by the unlearned,' not being interpreted. This proves that a foreign language was used as the instrument of *speech.*

"If," Mr. Arthur continues, "the supposition of the miracle in hearing, instead of in speech, has been resorted to with a view to simplify the miracle, *it defeats its own object;* for, to sustain that supposition, the miraculous influence must have been exerted on a number of persons as much greater than in the other case, as hearers were more numerous than the speakers. At the same time, the nature of the miraculous operation would be in every respect equally extraordinary."

We believe, with Mr. Arthur, that those who spoke made use of the languages well known by the foreigners present. Their own statement concerning this is decided and clear.

It has, as already stated, happened at several times at the meetings in Norway, Sweden and Denmark, and other countries, that those present heard the Word of God spoken in their own language, or languages well-known to them, by persons influenced by the Spirit, who did not themselves understand these languages.

As regards the gift of *prophecy* (forthtelling), Mr. Arthur considers it to be of greater practical value for the " *unlearned* " than the gift of tongues. And of course, we may easily understand, *if the tongues are not interpreted,* that the hearer, especially if he has come to make fun of the meeting, might feel inclined to say that the speaker had " gone mad " (I. Cor. xiv. 23). But it must be remembered that where the *miracle of interpretation* accompanies the miracle of speaking in tongues, the " tongues " are *equal in value to the gift of prophecy.* When Paul says, in I. Cor. xiv. 5, " greater is he that prophesieth than he that speaketh with tongues," he adds, " EXCEPT HE INTERPRET," thereby signifying that the speaker in tongues in that case edifies the Church, just as much as the prophets. In fact three miracles are then combined: the message, the foreign tongue, the interpretation.

It has also very often happened at meetings, that people present have not only understood the foreign language spoken, but have attested to the fact that the *interpretation given* was also perfectly correct.

THE GIFT OF PROPHECY (I. Cor. xiv. 3) has much in common with the Gift of Tongues. It is born of the same Spirit. The words spoken may be simple, as were Peter's on the Day of Pentecost, consisting of a number of passages of Scripture. BUT THERE IS HOLY FIRE IN THEM! That is why they cause conversions and life, where human eloquence could not do anything. Paul says, concerning the power of prophecy, " if there come in one that believeth not, or one unlearned, he is convinced of all, he is judged of all: and thus are the *secrets of his heart made manifest,* and so falling down on his face he will worship God, and report that *God is in you of a truth."* *The same takes place where the tongues are interpreted* and even where no interpretation has taken place sinners have been stirred up to seek God, impressed by the divine power glowing in the " tongues " and the heavenly light in the face of the speaker.

Oh, that the hearts of God's people were burning with this holy fire, so that words of fire might burn on their tongues and proceed from their lips!

### At Corinth.

The Apostle Paul's relation to the GIFT OF TONGUES has been stated at some length by *Pastor Ernst Lohman.* We cite the following statements: " We notice in the first chapter of the First Epistle to the Corinthians, that the special gifts were very prominent in the Church there.

" Although the Church was scarcely five years old, and most of its members were saved from the worst heathendom and its sins, the apostle says, nevertheless, that they were ' enriched in everything,' and as compared with other churches, ' came behind in no gift.' The new spiritual life had here obtained a mighty outbreak.

"The apostle does not doubt at any moment that these marvellous revelations were the result of God's Spirit dwelling in the Church. The gifts were genuine. As he himself had the gift of tongues in an exceptional degree, he is able to speak from personal experience. It is far from his intention to act in a preventative or quenching spirit. Instead of that he considers these gifts not only as a matter to be borne with, but as being very desirable. He exhorts the Church to 'COVET' these gifts 'EARNESTLY'; it is his prayer, his exhortation that all may obtain them. '*I would that ye all spake with tongues*' (I. Cor. xiv. 5). We remember that he on one occasion wrote to his friend and co-worker, Timothy, whose gifts of grace were evidently waning :' *Neglect not* the gift that is in thee, which was given thee by prophecy with the laying on of the hands of the presbytery' (I. Tim. iv. 14). But the apostle does not over-estimate these gifts."

Pastor Lohman then gives his views as to the proper relation of the Gift of Tongues to Christian work and experience. But in this book we wish more expressly to prove the presence of these gifts in the Church from its very commencement, in a greater or less degree.

We have already mentioned the well-known places in Acts ii., x. and xix., and need not touch on them any further now. They speak for themselves. It is impossible to be an honest student of the Bible and pass them unheeded. The same may be said of the three chapters in the First Epistle to the Corinthians (xii.—xiv.).

And the fact that these gifts were not merely intended for the first Christian Church is shown us by Church History and the experiences made during the times of great revivals.

### Testimonies of the Church Fathers.

In Fredrik Nilsen's *Church History* we read (page 78), concerning *speaking in tongues* (Glossolalia) *and prophecy*. " The right to speak belonged to all who had anything to say. The gifts of this apostolic age made this freedom in teaching possible, *viz.* : The Glossolalia and prophetic gifts, which both issued from the same source and had the same object—to serve the Church.

" The one who spoke in tongues was in a state of semi-consciousness,* in which he by the Spirit spoke " mysteries " (I. Cor. xiv. 2), especially to *personal* edification, and only serviceable to the Church when an interpreter was present. The speaking in tongues was songs of adoration in the spirit, not with the understanding*; but in prophecy both the spirit and the understanding were active.†

" Whilst the *apostles* themselves were a new ' gift, to which there was no equal in the old dispensation, the *prophets* exerted a gift that had existed formerly in Israel with great power.

" The prophets were of less importance than the apostles, who were *always* under the direct influence of the Spirit,‡ whilst the prophets were only occasionally ' in the Spirit ' and received revelations.

---

\* We would add, not always.
\* They might also contain *messages* to those present.
† Let us remember, nevertheless, that prophetic messages may come *direct* from the Spirit through the human agency and bearing no doubt the stamp of man, but giving the *real thought* of God (Numbers. xxiv. 13; I. Kings xxii. 14; Acts vii. 31; xi. 27, 28; xxi. 11).
‡ We think it best to say: the apostles were equipped for a *higher service* than others, but there were occasions when they also seemed to be more " in the Spirit," or " under the power," than usual (Comp. Rev. i. 10; Acts iv. 31; iv. 8; xiii. 9; II. Cor. xi. 17; I. Cor. vii. 12). In the last two cases the apostle gives his own judgment, not directly inspired by the Spirit.

" The apostles not only laboured among believers, but also among the Jews and heathen, whilst the prophets did their work *only amongst and for the believers.*\*\*

" There were apostles, as John and Paul, who also had the gift of prophecy and received great revelations, and prophets, as Barnabas (Acts xiii. 1), who might be elected as apostles.

" At Jerusalem, we meet with prophets such as Stephen and Agabus (xi. 28; xxi. 10); at Antioch others are mentioned, besides Barnabas; and PROPHETESSES are also mentioned, such as the four daughters of the evangelist Philip (xxi. 9).

In the *Doctrines of the Twelve Apostles,* which Professor C. P. Caspari, according to Fredrik Nilsen, calls " The oldest church regulations," we find the following statements. The Church father, Irenæus, born in Asia Minor, about the year 130, died a martyr in 202, or 203, was a disciple of Polycarp, and says, after quoting I. Cor. ii. 6: " I have also heard many brethren in the churches who, by the Spirit, SPEAK IN ALL KINDS OF TONGUES, and to the edification of others bring WHAT IS HID IN MAN TO LIGHT AND REVEAL THE SECRETS OF GOD."

" The gift of prophecy (I. Cor. xiv.) had its place in church worship a considerable time," says Mr. Nilsen. *Other gifts,* as in our day, were conspicuous. We find statements

**concerning power over unclean spirits.**

In the Second Apology of Justin, at the close of the sixth chapter, we read: " For there are many of us

---

\*\* This is not correct, as will be seen from I. Cor. xiv. 24, 25, and from what the writer states about Stephen and others.

Christians who, in the power of the name of Jesus Christ, who was crucified under Pontius Pilate, *have healed many*, all around the world, who were possessed with unclean spirits, also in your city."

Irenæus, Tertullian, Origen, Cyprian, Augustine and others, all speak about *the casting out of demons*. Read the 23rd chapter of Justin's First Apology. In this you also find statements concerning order of worship (chaps. lxv.—lxvii.). As to the necessity of

### keeping the holy flame

of the Spirit burning within, they referred to I. Thess. v. 19; II. Tim. i. 6; I. Cor. xii. 31; xiv. 1, 39.

" In the days of Justin, there were especially *two gifts of the Spirit* that were of importance at the services of the church—THE GIFT OF TONGUES AND THE GIFT OF PROPHECY."

In the book entitled, *The Teaching of the Apostle Addais* (one of the seventy who went to Syria), we find some words of great interest: " Ye shall not ponder over the secret things and ask questions concerning the hidden things of the holy books that ye have. Ye shall not judge the words of the prophets; remember and understand that they are spoken by the Spirit of God, and he who censures the prophets censures and judges the Spirit of God.

Let that be far from you! " because the ways of the Lord are right and righteous, walk ye in them without blame." Of course, this does not take away the right of the church to *try the spirits if they are of God*. But we are not allowed to judge the work of God. "Unbelievers stumble over them because they have not the HIDDEN EYE of the hidden mind, that needs not ask questions in matters that do not profit, but cause loss. Remember the THREATENING JUDGMENT OF THE PROPHETS, and the Lord who zealously watches their words, that the Lord JUDGES BY FIRE, and by that He tries ALL men."

"The hidden eye of the hidden mind," says A. H. Gjerve, "means the enlightenment that comes with Jesus and His Gospel," but the "HIDDEN EYE" seems to mean something deeper still, especially *the light that comes with faith in Christ,* besides the God-sent gift both to see the truth and accept it. In the Epistle to the Ephesians i. 18, we find the "hidden eye."

This book of Addais was written, either at the close of the first, or at the commencement of the second century, according to learned writers such as Dr. Alishan, Dr. W. Eureton, and Dr. George Phillips.

In the time of Justin the Martyr (A.D. 168) the Church service consisted of two special parts: A service of Scripture and prayer, and the communion service. He says: "On the so-called 'Sunday' (the Lord's Day) all come together from town and country at the same place, and, as far as time permits, the writings of the Apostles are read, or the writings of the Prophets. After this, when the reader has finished, the one standing gives an address, in which he encourages and exhorts to obey these good things.

"After this we all stand and pray, and when, as already stated, the prayers are ended, bread, wine and water are brought in, and the leader prays and praises *with all his strength,* and the people give an approving 'Amen!' After this the distribution takes place, etc."

Chapter x., in the book *The Teachings of the Apostles,* closes with the following: "If any are holy let them come, if not, let such be converted. MARAN-ATHA (The Lord cometh) Amen! But as concerns the prophets, let them offer thanksgiving *to their heart's content."* Professor C. P. Caspari says that "the prophets were accordingly allowed time *for free speech* after the communion service."

Origen (A.D. 254) says "The CONDITIONS necessary, in order to obtain the gifts, involved that they had cleansed their souls by the word and live according to the will of logos" (The Word, or Christ).

Professor Nilsen says, "The greatest personages in ancient times testify to the fact that the gifts of grace continued in the churches. THEY DID NOT SPEEDILY DISAPPEAR WITH THE APOSTLES. Irenæus, (A.D. 202), Origen (A.D. 254), Tertullian (A.D. 220), (African and Montanist), Justin the Martyr (A.D. 168), Ignatius (A.D. 115) (read his letter to Polycarp), Polycarp (A.D. 166), *all* mention them.

Ignatius exhorts Polycarp very strongly, in his letter, concerning several things; amongst others he says, in the second chapter: "Be in all things wise as a serpent and harmless as a dove. That is why you consist of both body and spirit, that you should correct whatever appears before you and pray that the unseen may be revealed (that is to say, correct the mistakes you see and ask God to reveal to you those you do not see), that you be behind in nothing, but have all the gifts of grace in abundance. The times need you in order to partake of God, just as a steersman needs the wind, or those who are in a storm need the harbour. Be watchful as a warrior of God; life eternal is the unfading prize, of which you also are assured."

Irenæus writes, according to Tischendorf (see his book *When Were the Gospels Written?*): "*Others mock the gifts of the Spirit,* which during *the last days,* according to the Father's will, were poured out upon the human race, and of the four forms we have of the Gospels, are not willing to accept the form according to John, in which the Lord has promised to send the Comforter, *but they renounce both this gospel and the prophetic Spirit.* Just as the Liberal theologians of our day.

" They are in very truth unhappy, as they willingly agree, that there are lying prophets, but will not accept the gift of prophecy in the Church."

This is the state even some Christians are in now, concerning *this present revival of grace and power.* They have seen or heard, they say, that the unclean spirits have spoken, but are *not willing to accept the prophetic gift of God's Holy Spirit.*

Irenæus continues to say: *" It is with them as with others, in order to get rid of false brethren, they deny the whole brotherhood."*

Those who evidently retained the gifts longest were the Montanists.

In Tischendorf's book (p. 56), we read: " One of the most important factors in the ancient Church, with lasting influence, was Montanism. It tried to counteract GNOSTICISM which, with its fantastical productions of philosophy, was *overwhelming the simple faith of the Church.* Montanism, on the other hand, sought *salvation* in a straightforward, deep and hearty acceptance of the truth."

I wonder if it may not be rightfully said, that this same thing is taking place in our day. THE PRESENT REVIVAL IS SENT OF GOD TO COUNTERACT the rationalism, formalism, and materialism that in many places is sapping the heart-life of the Church.

The Montanists disappear from history about one and

a half centuries after the Christian religion had become the state religion of the Roman Empire.*

From these quotations we see that tongues and prophecy existed in the Church, right up to the second and third centuries, and possibly it also existed in the fourth.

It met with opposition as we have seen, although the apostles and Church fathers considered it *to be of use to the Church and very desirable.* One, Miltiades, wrote a little book against these gifts at the close of the *second* century.

When the Christian Church became a *Church State* and Popedom developed itself, every influence that did not give way to that was suppressed by might, and every mark of such influence was entirely wiped out, if possible.

It is from *that reason,* as Pastor Lohman says, that " the knowledge of *movements of this kind* has reached us very sparingly during the intervening centuries, until the days of the Reformation. But we may fearlessly conclude that among the thousands of so-called *'heretics'* who were burnt or tormented to death by the Church there were numbers who were filled with the Spirit and enjoyed His gifts.

As soon as the

**Reformation**

brought about more freedom, some of the gifts have appeared in *almost every great revival, also the gift of tongues."*

Let us now quote freely from Pastor Lohman's in-

---

* The Carmisards, the first Quakers and Methodists, and others, were considered fanatical by many, because of their strong belief in Divine gifts and spiritual power. But where are *we,* and what is *our* spiritual standing when untouched by these? The Bible and the whole Christian religion is full of it.

teresting account: " When the edict of Nantes in France was recalled, and a season of great persecution came upon the ' Evangelicals,' the spiritual life increased among these persecuted people in intensity. The life in the deserts had often an apostolic character.

" Under the Carmisards, the stubborn ' evangelists of the Cevennes, a great revival broke out. We find the GIFT OF TONGUES here, side by side with the PROPHETIC GIFT.

" We have a German account of this revival entitled: ' The revivals in the Cevennes with the extraordinary gifts of the Spirit, the so-called *inspiration.*'

" The account reads as follows: ' In this place, during religious exercises, an extraordinary gift appeared, a PROPHETIC TEACHING, inasmuch as *children* as well as adults got up and *preached mighty sermons whilst their bodies shook violently.*

" This gift exerted a great influence and attraction, and THE CHURCH INCREASED.

" The Church authorities and the secular powers opposed it, but could not by

**murders, imprisonment, or torments,**

stop it.

" The King had to come to an agreement about everything, even as concerned the free emigration, *viz.,* the removal of these people from the country.

**A whole regiment**

of inspired soldiers went over to the army of Holland."

Mr. Lohman continues: " According to faithful accounts it happened that Spirit-filled people, who only knew how to express themselves in the ordinary dialect of their people, *spoke the French language to perfection.*

"In or about the year 1701 there were about 8,000 inspired people in the Cevennes.

"From this place the revival found its way to England and Germany in the eighteenth century.

"In England it became connected with the '*Philadelphia Church*,' which was founded in the seventeenth century by Jeane Leade, a church that declared it had heavenly visions and revelations. This Philadelphia Church spread also to Germany. A similar movement commenced in Germany through the theologian, Petersen, who was born at Osnabrück. The so-called

**' Inspiration-movement '**

reached its height at Wetteren and in the country of Witgenstein amongst the ' separated ' groups, who came from various countries, especially from Wurtemberg.

"Besides other manifestations we also find the GIFT OF TONGUES in this movement.

"In one account we even find several examples of speaking in tongues. Some words sound like Hebrew. The first line reads thus:—

" ' Schetekero, olahamanu alasch schemene tekora, Rischema, schetebirekora.' The quotations close with the words ' alla Jesus alla.' In between we notice other words, such as ' ruach adonai.' (The Spirit of the Lord).

"This movement did not merely exist in Germany, but spread also to other countries, also to Switzerland, and wherever it came there were the same or similar manifestations.

"It would take more space than intended, to give a detailed account of all these manifestations. It is of importance that we are able to prove their existence in the

**seventeenth and eighteenth centuries.**

"In the nineteenth century we find them again, this time they lead to Irvingism.

"In March of 1830, a Miss Mary Campbell, resident in a little Scottish town, received the *gift of tongues*. She suffered from tubercles on the lungs, but was

**healed by faith.**

"Shortly after, two brethren, James and George MacDonald, living in another place, received the gift of tongues.

"Next year a Mrs. Candale, wife of a lawyer, and a Mr. Taplin, also began to speak in tongues, and thus the movement commenced to spread in real earnest far and near.

"Mr. E. A. Raptauscher says concerning these manifestations, in a book entitled ' THE CHURCH BUILT ON THE ORIGINAL FOUNDATION ': ' The speaking in tongues lasts a longer or shorter period, at the highest five minutes. Very often it is but a few words, the first outbreak of the ecstatic state. This opens the secret well of the life-stream that issues from it and refreshes the Church as it contains that part of the speech that can be understood.

"' It is always a deeply felt speech, which evidently takes hold of the whole soul of the speaker.'

"' The speech is often accompanied with tears and sighs, or joyous exclamations, even laughter.' "

We notice how perfectly similar it is to much of what we have seen *in these days*—the 20th Century.

"' It is an even, intelligent, and harmonious language. It is spoken with a more powerful and strong voice, and often much more rapidly than ordinary speech. They are sounds

**that shake your inner being**

and penetrate to the soul in a way that is *not generally the case with prophecy.* The voice assumes a worthiness and strength that it does not generally own.'

"One of the inspired ones said: 'When the Spirit comes upon me and makes me speak in tongues in the presence of God, it seems as if a veil had fallen on everything around me, and as if I only saw the object of all my longings and the way that leads me to it. I feel as if I am hid in God, kept in His tent, lifted above all the voices of the world, flesh and the devil.'

"'Another of the inspired ones expresses his experience in this way: 'The knowledge of God's presence in Christ and my own presence in Christ is united with an overflowing wealth of indescribable joy.'"

Mr. Lohman says: "In this state self-consciousness is united with the consciousness of God's presence, without being completely absorbed by that. *The inspired person has as clear a conscience of his own existence* as he has of the mighty power that lies over him.

"This state is the same, both under that part of the speech which is understood, as well as the part which is not understood." This means to say *when the interpretation takes place* as well as during the speaking in tongues.

Pastor Lohman gives us another instance of these manifestations. He cites Mr. Hohl: "Before the commencement of the speech one could notice that the person in question would sink away into himself and become introspective, which could be seen from the fact that he closed his eyes and shaded them with his hand."

We think it more correct to say that he was *sunk in God* and contemplating Him, because that is the real condition.

"Suddenly, as if struck by an electric power, a convulsive shaking passed all through the person's body, whereupon a flow of burning, pointed and foreign sounds came over his lips, which was very much like the Hebrew language, and was generally repeated three times, and with an incredibly fiery and sharp expression.

"After this flow of foreign sounds, *which were generally believed to be the proof of the* GENUINE CHARACTER *of the ecstatic state,* there always come a shorter or longer speech in English, in the same fiery tone partly sentence by sentence, or word by word, and consisting generally of very severe and earnest exhortations, at times also awful warnings, but there were also spoken very precious and divinely comforting words.

"The last part was generally a paraphrase of the first part, although the person speaking could not always detect it to be such.

"'After this speech the enthusiastic speaker sank into deep quietness for some time and came back to the ordinary state little by little after this exercise of strength.'"

We have seen several who have acted similarly to this during the present revival. But we have also heard beautiful speaking in tongues *without there being any violent shaking of the body.* And what to *outsiders* may *seem* to be an extreme "exercise of strength," which naturally would exhaust the body, is only caused by the Holy Spirit's influence living within. *The body is not weakened, but strengthened!*

But to return to Mr. Lohman's account. He says that "there was, some years ago, before there ever was said anything about speaking in tongues among us, similar manifestations in the Orient." And this is a fact.

It is his opinion that all must acknowledge that this gift has again and again appeared during the different epochs, ever since the days of the apostles, until our own day.

We have been told that when the Quakers, the Methodists, and other great denominations commenced, there were several cases of speaking in tongues, and we are constantly receiving information from various sources, proving that the gift has appeared in several places of late years *before the commencement of the present revival*.

The MISTAKE, according to Mr. Lohman, has been this, that on the *official* side (the Church), attempts have been made to quell these manifestations by force, whilst on the other side one has been apt to overestimate the real worth of the " tongues."

And we would say that this is a danger that must be guarded against also in our day—*as far as " gifts " are concerned*. We must define between the " gifts," that are *retained* by those who receive them, and the rhapsodic speaking in tongues when we are baptised in the Spirit for the first time.

We must remember that there are other and precious gifts that the Lord has for His people. Their *value* will be determined largely by the use the Lord is able to make of them at the time. They become the *external* channels through which God's blessings are to flow to others.

The most important of all is, as Paul says, to be FILLED WITH THE LOVE OF GOD! or, as one has said, that the " gifts spoken of in the twelfth chapter of I. Corinthians be dipped in the thirteenth chapter, in order to be used according to the instructions of the fourteenth chapter."

There is a great truth in what Mr. Lohman says, that it is possible for Satan to counterfeit the gifts, but *not the love of God poured forth in the soul.*

At the same time we would remark that what has appeared to some as counterfeits were *no counterfeits at all*. Their *preconceived ideas* concerning God's way of work, were so entirely foreign to the new manifestations, *that they were unable to judge them with unbiassed minds*. But THAT does not prove they were unscriptural or a work of the enemy.

We know that some people quote Mr. Robert Baxter, a Scottish lawyer, who had something to do with the Irvingite movement, but later on turned around and condemned it, as saying that the whole movement was of the enemy. And they very rashly conclude that the present revival must THEREFORE also be a work *of this evil spirit*.

Mr. R. Baxter gives his reasons, as stated by Dr. Schofield, for this " right about face " of his. Perhaps HE was deluded by Satan, but that gives him no right to act as judge in the case of all the rest. Others might also have been deluded, but we have NO RIGHT TO SUPPOSE THAT ALL WERE. Numerous testimonies from other sources proves that this was not the case.

*We do not agree with all the teachings of the Irvingites.* Every denomination has some doctrine and teaching peculiar to it that caused its separation from other groups of believers.

But some people *seem led by the evil powers in our day,* to pick out cases here and there, where there may have been some fleshly or even diabolic touch, and after enlarging on these they hold them up to the world, and say, " Look here, this is the result of the movement." But the CHURCHES abound with miserable, and at times, AWFUL, COUNTERFEITS : surely the churches, as such, are not to be blamed for them all ! It is therefore *dis-*

*loyal to truth,* to judge a whole revival from separate cases where evil may have been done. We are to find out what GOD IS DOING and follow the light thus given us, and oppose with wisdom and much grace the evil influences around us. If the numerous writers, now occupied in tearing down God's work, would be THUS employed, we would not have found so many Christians involved in doubts and fears, as is now the case. This latter fact shows that the opposition has been UNFAITHFUL TO TRUTH and given the evil powers tools to handle that IMPEDE THE WORK OF GOD.

Let us first of all get CLEAN HEARTS and receive THE FULL BAPTISM OF FIRE, then LOVE will burn within, and if we only give God's Spirit an opportunity, He breaks forth in these days of the " latter rain " as on the Day of Pentecost, in seraphic or ecstatic speech, and lifts one's mind into the highest form of worship and praise that it is possible to reach on earth.

That is how the matter appears to us. When God's holy fire penetrates the WHOLE BODY, as well as soul and spirit, the speaking in tongues, *when it is not prevented,* comes as a matter of course.

I am aware that this opinion is not accepted by all and will not condemn them on that account. The value of " tongues " and that of prophecy is clearly seen in the Word of God, and if those who have another view knew the holy joy that accompanies the speaking in tongues, they would surely not oppose them, but rejoice at the possibility of attaining them. Besides the edification and joy that accompanies them, they are, when wrought by the Holy Spirit, a *sure evidence of His indwelling presence.*

We do *not over-estimate* " *tongues,*" but merely desire to let them have their proper place in the kingdom of God.

The *"Inspiration Movement,"* says Mr. Lohman, "that went all through Germany, France, England and Holland, had these extraordinary gifts. One could hear the instrument (the person) in enthusiasm, whilst the body shook, emit spiritual words in perfect keeping with the Scripture, that *did not proceed from the person's own spirit,* but were caused by another Spirit."

We see accordingly that all that has been said concerning a divinely supernatural power, working in and through man, is

**not a loose speech.**

We are standing face to face with FACTS, and we merely make ourselves the objects of derision by denying them.

Even Hedora writes in his book, *The History of Pietism from the* 18*th Century,* in connection with his statements concerning the Inspiration Movement: "We must acknowledge that the adherents of the movement exhort to repentance, conversion from sin, faith and holiness, and what they gave us "—evidently through the speaking in tongues and the prophetic speech—" *surpassed many sermons.* We cannot, without feeling greatly moved, read, or listen to, these earnest and pure testimonies.

" And it is impossible to believe these remarkable motions, these oftentimes abrupt sentences, often spoken with sighs or with jubilant voice, *are got up.* These people stood really *under a higher power,* a Spirit, that was foreign to them, when they were not in the ecstatic state."

This last statement though misrepresents the case

somewhat. This Spirit was *not* " foreign " to them, nor is it to us. It is

### the Spirit of God,

who dwells IN us and works THROUGH us, although He does not always work in the same way through all. And all those who have spoken in tongues when they were baptised in the Spirit, are *not* always moved by the Holy Spirit to do so again; whereas those, who have the GIFT OF TONGUES, seem to be able to speak in tongues more readily at will.

### In our day,

as in days gone by, the speaking in tongues and prophecy move on together. Both these gifts have appeared very extensively in connection with the present revival. It is now, as on the Day of Pentecost, when the mighty fire of the Holy Ghost gets the right of way, and permeates body, soul and spirit, then *"tongues"* and *prophecies,* and *shouts of praises are heard.* God gets the glory!

God, we find, is not limited by methods or any set time for pouring out the " promise." What He waits for *is the willing and consecrated heart,* that He may sanctify and cleanse it by the blood of the atonement, and fill it with Pentecostal glory, as the Tabernacle, when completed and set apart to the worship and service of God, was fully taken possession of by Him.

The act of *preparation* may take place very speedily, when there is simplicity enough and perfect consecration on the part of the seeker. It may cost severe struggles, and at times violent scenes have been witnessed as the old Adam has been nailed to the Cross. But there is *always victory* for those who are willing to accept the Cross and the sprinkling of the blood of Jesus.

Sometimes the fire falls on the prepared sacrifice during church service, sometimes in the home, sometimes when many, or few, or none are present. People have received the Baptism in the Holy Spirit at the wash-tub, when scouring the floor, down in the mines, when at their outdoor or indoor work, on the streets and market-places, in the tramway-cars and trains, in their beds, in out-of-the-way places, all alone on the mountains, when sick at the hospital, and sometimes just before going down the valley of death. One Bible woman told me that she received the Baptism as she was crossing the market-place in Christiania, and people turned around surprised to hear her speak in tongues. Some have been awakened by God in the middle of the night and have immediately received their baptism.

At times it takes place with the laying on of hands, but the results are just the same: *They get filled with God's Holy Spirit,* and show in

**their lives**

that *God Himself* has revealed Himself to them and has come to stay.

The fire has fallen on some when listening to a sermon, and they have at once begun to praise God in tongues. The SINGING IN THE SPIRIT, that often accompanies the baptism, is at times perfectly seraphic and impressive. Some have been baptised *the very moment* hands have been laid on their heads in prayer, others shortly after. On some, hands have been laid two or three times before the fire fell.

In some cases there have been much shouting and rejoicing, in others you have seen the radiant face, as an angel's, with the folded and extended hands, while "the tongues have been heard, but sweetly, beautifully, gently and harmoniously. Perhaps temperament has something to do with it, and God speaks differently through the different vessels, but it is nevertheless *His* voice, speaking through lips of clay. We have this glory and the Divine presence in " earthen vessels " (II. Cor. iv. 7).

Some do not speak clearly in tongues at the commencement. It sounds as if one were trying to form words, but failed. But at last the pronunciation becomes distinct and clear. We know of several such cases.

The prophesying also takes place very often in broken sentences. But there are numerous cases in which the speaker rolls forth as it were an incessant strain of gospel truths, with a clearness and, not seldom, with a choice of words far above the intellect and culture of the speaker, proving that the Divine power is at work, illuminating the mind and giving words to express the thoughts arising there, that the speaker, without the power, could not have used. *This is the more perfect way of delivery* that ought to be sought by all who prophesy. And it has been simply marvellous to hear what penetrating depth into the Word of God there has been, by people whose minds had not been trained to ponder and study its sacred pages, showing that the gift of wisdom and knowledge had also been given them to a certain degree, reminding you very forcibly of I. John ii. 20, *" And ye have an anointing from the Holy One, and ye know all things."*

I have seen several preachers of various denominations and some missionaries baptised with the Holy Ghost, and the joy and glory of such an hour is indescribable. How much it means for the cause of Christ! How their hearts burn for the salvation of the lost, for the glory of Jesus and the purifying of His Church! How Jesus delights to see His people go forward in His grace and power.

As in the days gone by, these " TONGUES OF FIRE " are causing a stir wherever they come, and meet with opposition too in every land.

It has been a marvel to see the crowds in Scandinavia thronging the largest halls obtainable, and the crowd outside unable to get in, often discussing religious matters with Bible in hand. There has been a great sale of Bibles and many people have begun to study its sacred truths as never before.

The TOPICS that in former years have caused dissensions and divisions have been laid aside at the Pentecostal meetings and gatherings, and many preachers and church members of various denominations, and such as belong to none, have been melted together by the Pentecostal fire, not by giving up their connection with these, although some are being forced to do so, but by the mutual love and bonds of fellowship that the Holy Ghost has formed between them. And this fellowship is getting strengthened as the fire increases and tribulation and opposition become more general.

The SECULAR PRESS generally *has been trying to explain away every vestige of divine power that has appeared,* just as it has been trying *to divest the Bible of the supernatural revelations and accounts that it contains.*

The COMIC PAPERS have made fun of the leaders and the meetings. Scenes have been acted out in theatres from these, lecturers have used all their wisdom to make the people believe " there is nothing in it "; rich people have expended considerable money for printing and distributing literature: books, pamphlets, circulars, tracts, etc., denouncing the revival; the matter has been discussed from the King's palace down to the poor man's hut, *but the work still goes on with unabated force,* deepening, broadening as a river each month that passes by.

There has been much misunderstanding too in THE RELIGIOUS WORLD concerning this work. God does not always work along the lines some people have thought were right and proper. He breaks away *into new forms* and *methods* in order to prevent stagnation and formalism among Christians, but the change *always meets with opposition* even among His own people. The fact is that God is bringing His people back *to the simplicity and the unembarrassed methods of earlier days,* showing us plainly that *the old Gospel has not lost its power,* and that He is willing to prove the strength of His arm, through *believers,* if they only will be faithful to Him.

He wishes to fill our hearts and touch our **tongues** with His holy fire. And this LATTER RAIN REVIVAL has become a mighty exponent of the will of God.

Many doubt that statement, we know, but *the transformed lives of thousands of human beings* around the world *is the infallible proof of* GOD'S *approval,* and confirms the revival TO BE OF HIM.

Some have considered it to be merely a matter of *promoting* " tongues " or " prophecy." There never could have been a greater mistake.

This revival promotes

### vital, living, burning Christianity!

IT IS GOD'S SPIRIT, awakening, quickening, and reviving His people, and through them reaching out in power to the lost and blinded world around them. The " tongues " come in as a matter of course, because GOD has appointed that they shall. But they merely bear witness of the inner fire and grace, and, as other gifts of the Spirit, become the outward means of communication to others.

---

This short review of God's work during the ages will have proved that *tongues* and *prophecy* have existed from time to time, *ever since the first mighty outpouring of God's Spirit on the Day of Pentecost in Jerusalem*, and many will, in reading it, have arrived at some of the following conclusions:

i. That there is a wonderful similarity between all these manifestations and those we have seen in our day.

ii. That they are caused by one and the same Spirit —the Spirit of the living God.

iii. That they follow deep and mighty revivals, no matter what country these may arise in.

iv. That it is possible to quench God's work in the life of others, and wholly stop it in our own lives by unbelief, unwatchfulness and worldliness, wherefore it is necessary above all things to seek and be kept in LOVE, and allow every gift of grace to have its place in the life of the Church.

v. That Satan will try by violence and might to stop this work of God, or by shameful counterfeits try to throw his shadow over it.

vi. That we, as sure as we allow Christ to rule in all things as Lord and King and keep to His Blood and Word, HAVE NOTHING TO FEAR. The Lord hides us in His strength and everlasting love!

vii. That what the people of God in our day need is to get as close as possible to the childlike life of faith that was seen in the first apostolic Church and be filled with

**the same power**

that helped them to such mighty and glorious victories.

viii. That we may reach this, *not by going back* (the Church had been going back enough), but by GOING FORWARD to Christ, as *they* went forth to Him, and allowed His rich and mighty Spirit-life to flow through them to others.

May I again quote some striking sentences from Mr. Arthur's *Tongues of Fire*. " They *all* began to speak. This shows that the testimony of Christ was not borne by the MINISTRY alone . . . The multitude of believers were not *mere adherents,* but living, speaking, burning agents in the great movements for the universal diffusion of God's message . . ."

" On the Day of Pentecost, Christianity faced the world, *a new religion*—without a college, a people, or a patron. She had only her two sacraments and her *tongue of fire*. All that was ancient and venerable rose up before her in solid opposition. No passions of the mob, no theories of the learned, no interests of the politic, favoured her; nor did she FLATTER or CONCILIATE ANY ONE OF THEM. With her tongue of fire she assailed every existing system and every evil habit; and by that tongue of fire she burned her way through innumerable forms of opposition. In asking what was her power we can find no other answer than this one:

" **The tongue of Fire!**

"Religion has never, in any period, sustained itself except by the instrumentality of the tongue of fire . . . In many periods of the history of the Church, as this gift has waned, *every natural advantage has come to replace it:* more learning, more system, more calmness, more profoundness of reflection . . . everything in fact, which, according to the ordinary rules of human thought, would insure to the Christian Church a greater command over the intellect of mankind—yet it has ever proved that the gain of all this, when accompanied *with an abatement of the fire,* has left the Church less efficient."

It is but right to say that Mr. Arthur does *not suppose the speaking in tongues to be* the only tongue of fire. As already stated, his view points to the PROPHETIC GIFT as being the most serviceable for the spread of the gospel. But the first miracle, *that of tongues,* had and has its place and mission. "The effect was," Mr. Arthur says, " a general impression *in favour of the Divine origin of the message,"* the prophetic message given by Peter.

Thus we see how these two gifts *work together* in perfect harmony, both caused by the same FIRE; and without this Holy flame, burning within and touching the tongue, the CHURCH IS HELPLESS in all its work, whatever be the beauty and harmony of its systems and organisations!

Only a change in the direction of *" degeneracy, not improvement,"* would, as Mr. Arthur says, be involved if our Lord had intended to leave the Church *without any manifestation of the Spirit."*

As we close we would say that the Church needs as much in our day as in former days both these manifestations of the Spirit : *The gift of tongues and the gift of prophecy.*

Some have said the " Church is not ripe for them," but God is *not dependent on Christians* who have not cared to enter into the subject. He will ever be ready to bestow on waiting and willing hearts His blessing, and *touch their hearts and tongues with His holy fire.* Then BE willing to say to the Lord,

" Here am I, send me! "

CHAPTER IV.

# More About the Pentecostal Outpouring

SINCE writing the short historical summary, "Tongues of Fire," I have read some articles by a writer in a current magazine, in which I find support for the thought I offer in "Tongues of Fire," that the worshippers at Jerusalem on Pentecost were acquainted with the language spoken by Peter.

He asks: "What was the condition of the known world at that time as to language?" His answer is:

"The conquests of Alexander and of Rome had brought about such a change in the languages of the world, that all nations were able to understand each other in both Greek and Latin. As it has been remarked, "Aramaic, Greek, Latin—the three languages of the inscription on the Cross—were the media of intercourse throughout the empire. Greek alone was sufficient, as the New Testament shows us, for the Churches of the West, for Macedonia and Achaia, for Pontus, Asia, Phrygia."

"That being so, the necessity for such a gift would not exist"—the gift of tongues, he means, in order to preach the gospel to the Jewish worshippers at Pentecost.

"The sermon Peter preached on the Day of Pentecost was spoken, it would seem, in Aramaic. It was addressed *chiefly* to the *permanent dwellers* at Jerusalem —to those amongst whom our Lord had wrought His miracles, and by whom He had been crucified (Acts ii. 22, 36). It was natural, therefore, that he should speak in Aramaic, and *the Jewish strangers* who were present on that occasion would THOROUGHLY UNDERSTAND WHAT WAS SAID." He quotes Dean Alford as saying that the message by Peter was delivered either in the Aramaic of Palestine or, more probably, in the Greek language, " which was the common medium of intercourse for all Eastern subjects of the Roman Empire."

It matters very little we think. The facts are clear; that *those present understood Peter's sermon.*

The writer then cites the late Professor Plumtre to prove that the gift was not connected with the work of preaching or teaching the gospel, but with that of praise and adoration. Let us read the Scripture text: " How hear we every man in our own tongue, wherein we were born . . . *speak the wonderful works of God. And they were all amazed* " (Acts ii. 8-12). If this *only* means praise and adoration it is doubtful. It means that although praise and adoration were evidently prominent (this we readily conclude from present-day experiences) there is good ground to suppose that addresses were given (such as is often the case in our day) in other tongues, extolling the glory of God and the power of the Cross.

He goes on to prove that all the speaking in tongues *took place in the upper room.* I do not think the Scripture bears out him, or Dean Farrar, whom he cites, in this. He says, " Reading the passage carefully makes it clear, first, that the disciples were not then speaking to the people, and, secondly, that they were not engaged in the work of preaching at all. They were by themselves—they were all believers—there were none present who needed to have the glad tidings proclaimed to them.

The multitude *outside overheard* the disciples worshipping God inside ' the house where they were sitting.' What the crowd heard was not a proclamation, a warning, or an exhortation, but a *doxology.* When the work of preaching began before the people outside, the utterance of tongues had *ceased."*

In order to make a correct statement one must know where the upper room was, and what access there might have been to it, or near it, for the people.

I agree that the fire fell when *they were alone,* and that the *first* speaking of tongues took place then. And if they all burst forth, as there is every reason to believe (comp. Acts x. 44-47; xi. 15) *simultaneously* under the power, it must have been heard some distance. The experience we have from similar outbursts in our day go to prove this. Nearly 120 people *filled with the Holy Ghost* praising and adoring God in tongues IS NO QUIET AFFAIR. The " *order* " spoken of by Paul in I. Cor. xiv. was not enforced, and *does not apply to the first outbursts of Pentecostal power* when we receive our baptism, but to a more mature state of things. It is probable too, that the " sound " of the mighty rushing wind had first of all drawn the people together, followed as it evidently was, by the " sound " of 120 fire-filled men and women, praising God *simultaneously!*

*How many languages* were spoken we do not know and not all present knew all the languages spoken. *Perhaps each Spirit-filled person had a different language* or several at the outburst. The foreigners present could each detect *theirs* (Acts ii. 9, 12). But how? Surely not when that band of worshippers were in the upper room. Perhaps occasional words might have reached their ears of the " doxology," but on seeing the crowds the disciples evidently *went out amongst them,* led by the Spirit, and spoke as *He* gave them utterance about "*the wonderful works of God.*" And as the crowds surged around them, some heard their language spoken and others theirs, and so on. There have been meetings in Scandinavia, where people have surged around those speaking in tongues in that way. Some of the languages have been understood, some not, by those present. Of course it caused surprise and amazement.

Evidently, when speaking, the disciples acted somewhat strangely, as people do at times, when under the power, speaking in tongues. Their demeanour was such that some mistook them to be "DRUNKEN" and "FILLED WITH NEW WINE."

It is easy to see how the whole thing worked. No matter what their demeanour might have been, there was the *fact that languages were spoken* by these people that they did not know themselves. *How* could it take place? *What* was the cause of it? And the crowds felt they stood before supernatural forces that they could not explain.

Now was the time for Peter's sermon. And it came! *Miracles never save people,* but are the means of leading their thoughts to supernatural things—to GOD. Then the STORY OF THE CROSS looms up with intensified authority and power. And so it is in our day. The miracle has drawn the crowds together, and then the gospel has been preached. That is at any rate our experience.

Another point in which I differ somewhat from the writer is his remark that Peter's quotation of the well-known passage in Joel had nothing to do with *tongues.* It " does not contain *the remotest hint of foreign languages,*" he says. " Hence the fancy that this was the immediate result of Pentecost *is unknown to the first two centuries,* and only sprang up when the true tradition had been obscured."

But *we must* abide by *the Bible statement.* The speaking in tongues had brought the excitement to its highest tension, as verses 12 and 14 prove. THEN Peter stood forth with the eleven, and referred immediately to the scenes going on around them, rebuking the scoffers for their coarse insinuations: " THESE "—who? Those speaking in tongues, of course. *"These* are *not* drunken, as ye suppose, seeing it is but the third hour of the day. But THIS IS THAT which was spoken by the prophet Joel." What? *This outpouring of the Spirit, accompanied with speaking in tongues.* Nothing else is recorded as having taken place so far, so *it must have been* THAT. Accordingly the messages given were *prophetic.* When therefore the Spirit spoke through those men and women they were *prophesying* in the Spirit in *foreign* languages, and, as we have seen in a former chapter, it WAS *a well-known fact* during the first centuries (I. Cor. xiv. 5).

The writer wards off, very decidedly and ably, the attempts made by many, to prove that the speaking in tongues on Pentecost was merely the result of NATURAL causes, and quotes Dean Alford to prove his statements. He says:

"I believe the event related in our text (Acts ii. 4) to have been *a sudden and* POWERFUL INSPIRATION OF THE HOLY SPIRIT, BY WHICH the disciples uttered, not of their own minds, but as MOUTHPIECES OF THE SPIRIT, the praises of God in various languages hitherto . . . unknown to them."

He then quotes from Bishop Ellicot's *New Testament Commentary for English Readers.* We cite the following:

"There is no evidence that that power was permanent. It came and it went with the SPECIAL OUTPOURING of the Spirit, and lasted only while that lasted in ITS FULL INTENSITY."

"There are no traces of its existence in any narrative of the work of apostles and evangelists. They did their work in countries where Greek was spoken, even where it was not the native speech of the inhabitants, and so would not need that special knowledge."

"The utterances of the disciples are described in words which convey the idea of rapturous praise. They speak the 'mighty works,' or better, as in Luke i. 49, the *great things* of God. Doxologies, benedictions, adoration, in forms that transcended the common level of speech, and rose, like the Magnificat, into the region of poetry—this is what the word suggests to us.

The writer then says, if this interpretation be correct, "what warrant is there for seeking the 'gift of tongues' as a means of evangelising the heathen?"

One thing, at any rate, becomes very apparent to us: The writers quoted allow that the speaking in tongues took place as a RESULT OF THE MIGHTY INFILLING OF THE HOLY SPIRIT. It is when under the supernatural and Divine power the disciples speak. The speaking "came and went with the *special outpouring* of the Spirit . . . in its *full intensity*," the Spirit using whatever language He chose.

We see very clearly therefore that it is not the person speaking who decides which language is to be spoken, BUT THE HOLY SPIRIT. How vain and thoughtless then to criticise, as it is often done in our day, the choice the Holy Spirit makes of languages. We speak as the "Spirit giveth utterance," that is *our* spirit speaks, mightily impressed by the Holy Spirit.

On the other hand, although it does not seem to be proved from Scripture, that this supernatural gift will do away with the ordinary study of languages, it can be proved, we think, from Acts ii., that God may, when He finds the time appropriate, make use of this gift *to hasten His work.* It may not have been the rule, but cases are known in our day where the gospel has been preached in that way, making it very apparent that it took place at times in the first Christian Church.

And then again, how is it possible to say that there are no traces of it in any narrative of the work of the apostles and evangelists? *The Book of Acts*, and the Epistle to the Corinthians DISPROVE that statement. It was surely *the general rule,* that *tongues* were heard *whenever the fire fell* (Acts x. 46) in the days of the apostles.

We have a case in Southern India from our day, of two Indian women proclaiming gospel truths in Hindustani to the people, although they had not acquired that language before. One of them had even been deaf and dumb from her birth, but could nevertheless speak under the power of God. She has not spoken in Hindustani for some time now, but speaks fluently in the Telegu language, which is her mother tongue, but which her deaf and dumb state has prevented her from acquiring; *she has received it supernaturally.* I have this from a missionary, who wrote to the pastor at the mission station where she lives, in order to obtain information.

Mistakes have been made by some, supposing they had received the language of some heathen people, and they have gone out to these only to be bitterly disappointed. They have supposed the language they received *to be constant,* whereas it was merely the wondrous outburst, " as the Spirit gave them utterance." But the time MAY COME when the use of the "tongues" may become more general as a channel of communication to heathen nations.

In speaking of Chrysostom, the writer says that he speaks of tongues " as one who feels the whole subject to be obscure," and then remarks that 'THE WHOLE TENDENCY OF THE CHURCH AT THIS TIME WAS TO MAINTAIN REVERENCE AND ORDER, AND TO REPRESS ALL APPROACHES TO THE ECSTATIC STATE," and this is certainly the truth. It is so in many churches *in our day*. The cry is " REVERENCE!—ORDER! " And this means generally the suppression of the Holy Spirit's work through the gifts He has appointed to His Church (I. Cor. xiv. 26). Paul speaks of " order " too, but he does not suppress the " gifts "—he bids the Church to " COVET " THEM.

As to the word " UNKNOWN " languages I think there is some misunderstanding. Even if, as the writer puts it, the word *" unknown "* is an interpolation of our Authorised Version in I. Cor. xiv. 2, the term in itself is not quite out of the way. The apostle intimates clearly that a language may be spoken, *unknown* to those present, and advises, therefore, that prayer be offered for an INTERPRETATION (xiv. 13). In xiii. 1, he intimates that even an ANGELIC tongue may be spoken. What, therefore, in Irving's day, might have appeared to outsiders "a jargon of mere sounds" or "gibberish," was nevertheless a real language, spoken somewhere, but interpretation was necessary in order to appreciate it This experience all have passed through, who have travelled among foreign nations or among heathen nations, whose language they have not known. It sounded often like " gibberish " to them.

The writer takes a very decided stand against those

who condemn *everything*. He says, " whatever explanation may be given of the facts, *there exists no ground for imputing a deliberate imposture to any of the persons who were most conspicuous in a movement.*" He refers to the Irvingite movement.

As we have seen, there must have been, besides "doxologies, benedictions, adoration," also some feature in the speaking of tongues that reminded Peter of the words of Joel concerning " PROPHECY," which, according to Paul, implies *" speaking unto men edification, and comfort, and consolation "* (I. Cor. xiv. 3).

In this case it needed no interpretation, as the different nationalities present discerned their own language. But in places where the Holy Spirit uses the miracle of *tongues*, making use of a language not known to persons present, it is necessary to obtain the interpretation, in order to edify, instruct, or comfort the " church.' It may then have the character of *prophecy,* as on the Day of Pentecost. But very often the tongues are great anthems of praise to God, that " transcend the common level of speech and rise, like the Magnificat, into the region of poetry," or as another has said : " Pentecost is a baptism of praise, coming over the balconies of heaven from the glorified presence of our Saviour, having an unmistakeable relation to His glorification, fills us with His glory, striking up chords of praise we never dreamed existed in our soul, and finding adequate expression only in the tongues, which come with it from the scenes of heavenly praise and adoration above. It is the earnest of our inheritance of eternal praise and worship. It is the preliminary notes of that ' new song,' as it were, ' which they sung before the throne.' "

We have personal experience of both of these forms of

speaking in tongues, and have heard them extensively used by the Spirit at our meetings.

When, therefore, the writer draws a line between ' Pentecost and the peculiar manifestations at Corinth," we see no necessity for doing so. He does not think the disciples on Pentecost were " in an ecstatic state," in the sense of being " *beside* " *themselves*. " It seems safe to assume," he says, " that they were in the highest possible *mental* and *spiritual* condition, when they were thus filled with the Holy Ghost." As if those who spoke in tongues at Corinth were not in this condition.

We believe that the mental and spiritual state of the speakers was equal in both cases, and that the speaking was a work of *the same Holy Spirit* through the human agencies employed.

It appears very plain that the disciples on Pentecost spoke ecstatically. The taunts of the crowd prove this clearly : " They are filled with *new wine* "; and so does Peter's answer : "These are not *drunken* as ye suppose."

The idea conveyed is, that the old bottles could not contain the new wine (comp. Luke v. 37). The old tanned hides would not be serviceable, Christ said, to put new wine in. They could not resist the pressure of the fermenting liquor, but would burst and the wine would be spilled. Now the marvellous flow of speech, the radiant face, the whole demeanour of the disciples was such, that outsiders could not explain it, save by some wonderful infilling that made them act differently to ordinary human beings.

But the old bottles had been specially prepared by our Lord for the occasion. He had cleansed and renewed them. Still the mighty power within taxed their utmost capacity. If there ever was ecstatic speech and worship, it was on the Day of Pentecost in Jerusalem.

Their mental abilities were nevertheless *perfectly normal!*

A great theologian in Sweden said lately, *that Paul spoke in tongues because he was an epileptic.* What an idea! But anything rather than accept facts. If that were the reason, then all the disciples and apostles in that " upper room " on Pentecost were epileptics. But such arguments have no weight with us. It is not even proved that Paul was an epileptic.

The fact is that the Holy Ghost, when giving the outward symbol of His presence, the cloven tongues of fire, ACTUALLY FILLED THEM, and made use of every God-given faculty to produce speech, without their mind having anything to do with it, save as a channel. How could their mind make use of a language that they knew nothing about? We have decided proof in our day, that the speakers may know nothing of the language they speak, have never heard it, but the message they bring has nevertheless a direct object in view, an appeal to someone present, or an instruction, showing that some great master mind, behind the speaker, was using him or her as an instrument. In most cases the speaker did not even know what had been said, unless the interpretation was given. The mental abilities of the speaker were not impaired, but merely held in abeyance under the Divine will.

I take exception to the contention that the tongues at Corinth " were not languages, but sounds." The apostle Paul did not thank God for emitting more " sounds " than the others, but because God had given him to speak more " tongues (languages) than they all" (I. Cor. xiv. 18), and if he did not always understand the tongue, he asked God to give him the interpretation, judging from his advice to others (*v.* 13). Now we surely cannot suppose that the apostle wants us to ask the Lord to interpret "gibberish." The very word "interpretation" refers you to a reasonable language, either earthly or celestial, that may be re-given in a language understood by the hearers. In Conybeare and Howson's *Life and Epistles of St. Paul,* on pages 401-2 (Vol. I.), we read: " Besides the power of working miracles, other supernatural gifts of a less extraordinary character were bestowed upon the early Church. *The most important were the gift of tongues and the gift of prophecy."*

As to the gift of tongues these divines do not consider it *" a knowledge* of foreign languages," expressly intended for the conversion of foreign nations. It was *" the result of a sudden influx of supernatural inspiration, which came upon the new believer immediately after his baptism,* and recurred afterwards at uncertain intervals." " Under its influence, the exercise of the *understanding* was suspended while the *spirit* was rapt into a state of ecstasy by the immediate communication of the Spirit of God. In this ecstatic trance the believer was constrained by an irresistible power to pour forth his feelings of thanksgiving and rapture in words; yet the words which issued from his mouth were not his own; he was even (usually) ignorant of their meaning." These statements strengthen the views we have presented: " The speaking in tongues was the *result of a sudden influx of supernatural inspiration."* But the expression *" irresistible "* is we think, too strong. The Divine power *may* be resisted, and the " gift " is under the control of the speaker (I. Cor. xiv. 32). The words " ecstatic trance," too, may be misunderstood. Many have trances, it is true, as did Paul (II. Cor. xii. 1-5), *but it is not necessary to be in a trance to speak in tongues.*

In closing, I would say, that whilst I, in these chapters, have shown the *similarity* of the various religious movements during past ages, *along the lines of ecstatic worship,* I have not identified myself with *all* that has been done and taught in connection with each movement. I have merely proved that ONE AND THE SAME DIVINE SPIRIT has been speaking in this miraculous way, wherever He has found open and willing hearts and lips, through whom He might speak. It has not been within my sphere to consider doctrines and systems in connection with each movement.

Our prayer is that God may have the full and perfect rule among all His people, that this poor, lost world may feel, as never before, the *wondrous and saving power of our Lord and Master*—JESUS CHRIST!

CHAPTER V.

# Pentecost with Tongues
## From Heaven, *not* from Below

"If Satan Also be Divided Against Himself, How Shall His Kingdom Stand?"—Luke xi. 18.

IT is NOT of the DEVIL, because those who HAVE received their Pentecost:—

Love Christ more;
Love their Bible more;
Love everybody more;
Long to bring Christ to lost souls;
Hate all that is of the Devil;
Are more on their knees, not as a duty merely, or for seeking any merits, but because they *love* to commune with God.

Yearn to know more of Christ and constantly grow in Him.

Feel His Spirit leading them on;
Only care to go as led by Him;
Long to be kept humble and in the dust before God.

*If* a real baptism of fire makes them better equipped to serve God and fight the Devil, then what they have received, if it is as some people say, "Of the Devil," ought to make them more useful in the *Devil's* service.

*Such* a mighty experience as this, through which they have passed, if of the Devil, *must absolutely make them* devilish, satanic, and that in a *very extreme measure*. But they themselves *find*, instead of that, that their delight is in the Lord and " His statutes are their songs in the house of their pilgrimage." They are brought *deeper down* in a full acknowledgment of their own unworthiness and constant dependence on God.

*Even* if Satan had taken upon himself an angel's likeness, and given the outward colouring a rich religious glow, they would still be able to detect if they (if only by a slight touch) had become *more worldly-minded,* more *self-conscious,* more *drawn to the lusts of the flesh,* more *prone to forsake God* and *serve the Devil;* and if *they did not see it themselves, their friends would.*

*It must* be taken as a *fact* that whatever *spirit* we imbibe and give the right of way in our hearts, minds, and bodies, that *same* spirit will exert his influence *in* us and *through* us. If it is *God's* Spirit it will be *seen in our lives,* and thus also with the Devil's spirit. "Can the fig tree, my brethren, bear olive berries? either a vine, figs? so *can no fountain both yield salt water and fresh* " (James iii. 12).

*Christ says,* " Every kingdom divided against itself is brought to desolation; and a house *divided* against a house falleth. If Satan also be divided against himself, how shall his kingdom stand? " (Luke xi. 17, 18).

It is a FACT, that people are *getting better* through this movement, are *leading purer lives,* are *paying off their debts,* are *wiping out old feuds, making restitution,* and seeking *forgiveness* for their iniquities at the hands both of God and man. They are reflecting the *image of Christ* at home and abroad. That must surely be against the interests of the Devil, upsetting his kingdom. If not, Christ and the Devil must have become united, but we have heard of no such union.

*Even if he did* try to make use of " tongues " when we, in seeking our Pentecost, are UNDER THE BLOOD, and are abiding by the Word, and have sought Divine protection against the onslaughts of the enemy, *God would be no better than the gods of the heathen,* if He delivered us to the cruel tyranny of our most bitter enemy—*the Devil.*

" If we, being evil, know better than to give our children *stones* for bread, *serpents* for fish, or *scorpions* for eggs, then surely our heavenly Father will NOT give us a devil, when we ask Him to give the *Holy Ghost* (Luke xi. 11-13).

*The Pentecost with tongues is biblical* and a gift of God (Acts ii. 1-4; x. 46; xix. 6; ii. 32, 33, 38, 39).

*The churches* are getting stirred up where this revival comes.

*The Blood of Christ* is being honoured, the *Atonement* and *Resurrection* have become living realities, illuminated and made *real* by the power of the Holy Ghost. All who are filled with the Spirit centre their faith and hope in the *finished work* of Jesus Christ.

*The name of Jesus* is constantly on the lips of Spirit-filled men and women. They love to repeat it *often,* it is the name of their heart's best friend, their beloved.

*Formalism,* materialism, rationalism, spiritualism, bigotry, and the worldly state of many ministers and divines are denounced by the spirit of this movement all over the world.

*The evangelisation of the world* becomes a necessity for *all* who get this Pentecost (Acts i. 8).

*It makes* God's people prepare for the *Coming of the Bridegroom.*

*There is nothing* the Devil and his hosts are attacking so much now as this movement, he knows his time is short and that *this* fight is real. He is using Bible, pen, papers (religious and secular), half-hearted Christians, and even honest, though *misguided* Christians, are in his service.

*The Devil* never makes us PRAISE GOD, and the Pentecostal people are a God-praising and a God-fearing people as sure as any Christian group on earth may be said to be so!

The Devil never takes us right up to heaven's gates in adoration and worship, making you feel as if the heavens at any moment could open and your spirit step right into the presence of your glorious King.

But *Pentecost* fills you with the *love of God* and gives you grace to live *normal Christian lives*—that is, lives wholly devoted to the interests of Christ, whatever position you may fill in life; it gives you *power* to go anywhere, be anything, at any time for Christ.

*Friends!* The call is going forth through all the world for whole-hearted service in the Master's Kingdom. Are you willing and have you received *power* in order to do the work in the *right spirit* and *successfully?*

Seek that *heart of hearts* (John vii. 37-39) and get your Pentecost. Not the blessing given others, but the one God has for *you—the Baptism of the Holy Ghost and Fire.*

(Matt. iii. 11)—Seek it *now.*
      Seek it *through the blood.*
      Seek it after *perfect cleansing* by faith.
      Seek it without anxiety, *trusting the Word of God* and *receive* the gift —*NOW.*

CHAPTER VI.

# The Pentecostal Visions of To-day

"I WAS IN THE SPIRIT"—Rev. i. 10.

A LETTER has been sent me, in which the "latter rain movement" seems to be approved in several respects, but it contains a general warning concerning visions, revelations, and the numerous involuntary prostrations that have taken place in this movement under the powerful influence of the Holy Spirit.

I, for one, am thankful for any timely warning against anything that might prove to be a device of the evil one, or a counterfeit of the flesh, but at the same time must confess that I heartily differ from the wholesale condemnation of visions, revelations and prostrations to be found in this letter.

In this as in all other cases we have to

### Stand by the Bible and Facts.

Hundreds of years before the Pentecost, the prophet Joel said (ii. 28), "It shall come to pass afterward, that I will pour My Spirit upon all flesh; and your sons and daughters *shall* prophesy, your old men *shall dream dreams,* your young men *shall see visions;* and also upon the servants and upon the handmaids in those days will I pour out My Spirit; and *show wonders in the heavens and in the earth,* blood and fire and pillars of smoke. The sun shall be turned into darkness, and the moon into blood, before the great and terrible day of the Lord comes. And it shall come to pass that *whosoever shall call on the Name of the Lord shall be delivered.*"

Now on Pentecost, when the Holy Ghost was given to the Church, Peter stated that the *prophetic* (I. Cor. i. 14) *speaking in tongues,* that took place there (Acts ii. 8-21), corroborated the prophecy of Joel, and was *one of the results of this mighty outpouring* of the Holy Spirit. Both the prophet and the apostle argue *that visions, dreams and signs* are caused by the same holy influence. If Peter considered the first days of the Christian Church to be a part of the " last days," then surely we, about 2,000 years later, have good reason to believe *that we are living in the " last days."* The prophecy applies especially to our time. Surely this is clear. Then accordingly *we may expect visions, signs and wonders,* in our day, without believing the devil is at the back of them all, or that they are the result of some insane freak of the mind. When these people are living under the blood of Christ, it seems much *like an insult to Him* to say that the holy visions and signs they receive, *that stimulate to purer lives and worship and service,* are of Satanic origin. If that is so, then it cannot be even safe to pray to God, as generally these visions of Christ and heaven, and other scenes, appear when in the act of worship and prayer. Then God must be a weak and feeble God, yea cruel, who, when we are invited to worship before Him, is not able to keep us from the onslaught of the devil, but gives us over to the tempter's wiles to get our minds impaired and our souls infected by the devil's own spirit.

If that is so, then we have no guarantee whatever for the genuine character of the visions of the Bible generally. The visions of the Book of Revelation might in that case be the outcome of the heated brain of the castaway on the Isle of Patmos. It ought to be remembered too, that the Christians, many of them, who profess to have seen visions in our day, *are just as real in their Christian character and have just as earnest a desire to serve God, as had the disciple whom "Jesus loved."*

Let us be careful how we treat the influence of the Holy Spirit on the spirits and minds of His people in our day. It seems strange that this also is to be traced up to Satan. It is surely wise to be on the alert against deceptions and counterfeits, but do not let us be cheated out of our rightful heritage by the devil.

The general argument used by some well-meaning people is this: that some of these manifestations are surely of the devil, then ALL must be from the same source. Why not then put Moses in class with the Egyptian sorcerers?

I beg to say that I very strongly disagree with that sentiment.

It may be perfectly true that those who have had visions have become "puffed up." I know that it is so in some cases, but it does not disprove the reality of the vision. Paul was given a thorn in the flesh *in order to keep him down, that he " be not exalted overmuch,"* but he did not contradict the possibility of " visions and revelations of the Lord " (II. Cor. xii. 1). I know personally several cases, where the visions received *have been a means of humbling the spirit and strengthening the faith* of those who received them. It would seem, too, that *they are not given to all*, or in *the same degree*. There is a great difference in that respect between Isaiah and Ezekiel, Peter and John.

It surely cannot be an argument against the possibility of *real* visions that people in the asylum may get visions, or that the devil may impose upon the minds of some, or even lead Christians astray through pride, of by making them seek visions and signs *as the only rule and guide for their steps in life.*

The thing to do is entirely different to that. As the writer himself states: " He finds numbers, who on their conversion had received the Holy Spirit and life from above, had visions." He says they were false visions, but he evidently was mistaken in several cases, especially as he seems prejudiced against them.

Visions are of two kinds: *mental* (subjective), *actual or objective.* The Holy Spirit fills the body and affects the mental elements of the system in such a way as to produce pictures in the mind, so vivid and living, that the person who sees them may think them real, whereas they are merely illustrations of some great lesson the Holy Spirit wishes to confer to the person in question, or those around, who listen to the words spoken. The person does not see anything that is really taking place at the time (as the Crucifixion, the Judgment Day, etc.), but a vivid panorama, as it were, of these events, passes by the inner eye in such a way as to make the person seeing them think them real, just as a drowning man may see his whole life pass by him in a few moments. The Holy Spirit has often, by this visionary method, wrought a great work in many hearts, as also through remarkable dreams. This should not alarm us in the least. Examples of mental (subjective) visions in the Bible are many. I just give a few: Ezek. xxxvii. 1-14; xlvi. 1-12; Acts x. 10-16.

But then, again, there are the actual (objective) visions, when the spirit is so in touch with the spirit-world that what is seen *is real,* and *is at that moment taking place* before the observer.

This cannot be doubted, as Scripture gives a clear record of such events, and the scenes and circumstances, in connection with what some people see now in our day, is so real and scriptural, that we have no reason to doubt it. Examples of actual visions: Daniel x. 3-20; Acts x. 3-6; xii. 6-12; II. Corinthians xii. 1-10.

But there seems to be a mixture of both in several cases, where the real person (possibly an angel) seen in the vision, uses the mental vision to illustrate. Compare Zech. i. 7-17; ii. 1-9; Rev. i. 10-20. It will be easy to find many other cases, both from the Old and New Testaments.

I agree that the evil one may influence the mind and cause mental visions, but that is far from saying that every mental vision is necessarily his work. If the vision comes when the soul is sunk in prayer and under the blood, and inspires to a purer life, or becomes a means of awakening the sinner, I DO NOT BELIEVE IT IS FROM THE DEVIL, he will surely not oppose his own interests (Luke xi. 17, 18).

THE MISTAKE some make is *to be constantly looking out for visions and revelations.* This cannot be healthy for the mind or the spiritual life, which *must* have its nourishment from *Christ, His Spirit,* and *His Word.* No visions can supplant or undo this fact. He alone can help and sustain us.

Then again we must be very careful not to come to rash conclusions because of the visions and revelations we think we have received. I have personally and publicly corrected those who were assured that they had received a clear statement *as to the time of our Lord's coming.* Everything like that must be checked, because it is against the Scriptures. Let us examine if the visions and revelations are *in harmony with the Word of God before giving utterance to them.* That is the safe way.

Then just a few lines concerning " prostrations." We must remember that the Bible only gives us an outline of what occurred on various occasions, but when facts are on hand in our own experience and those of others, it is right to compare them with the Bible accounts, to see if there is any clue to be obtained there concerning these special demonstrations of the Spirit.

I think the jeering rebuke of outsiders on the day of Pentecost is very emphatic: " They are *filled with new wine.*" The remark must have been so general that Peter found it necessary to explain matters. " These are not DRUNKEN as ye suppose," and the reason was given. The seeming "intoxication" arises from quite another source. " This is that which hath been spoken by the prophet Joel." It is the work of the Spirit.

It is strange that the *outward* bearing is similar in some respects between a drunken man and one filled with the Spirit, although the two powers at work, and the results, are as different as heaven is from hell. But the difference is easily seen. Both may gesticulate and speak beyond themselves, but the motive power is entirely different. Paul draws the comparison very sharply: " Be not *drunken* with wine, wherein is riot, but be *filled with the Spirit.*" In the Song of Solomon, we are invited to " drink, yea, drink abundantly." In the Norwegian translation it is rendered, " drink and be drunken." Thus speaks the Bridegroom.

A drunken man is at times very bold, sees what others do not see, staggers forth and back, or lies down under the weight of intoxication, or moves hastily about, speaks or sings, as he would not do on ordinary occasions.

Thus one who is filled with the Spirit becomes bold (Acts iv. 13), gets visions, prophesies, sings in the Spirit, staggers at times under the weight of the glory, or is obliged to lie right down on the ground, if not struck down by the overwhelming power, or may be, move about with unusual acceleration, speaking in tongues, quite oblivious of all that is going on around for a time, although not wholly unconscious. *I can find nothing to condemn in this; it is the work of the Holy Spirit, and we must let Him have His own way.* When the Pentecost comes these outward signs are very apparent. They are NOT TO BE SOUGHT. The Holy Ghost Himself is what we have to seek—the Comforter, through Christ and His precious Blood. The manifestations come with Him: that is not our business.

It is not absolutely necessary that all are prostrated, or stricken to the ground by the Spirit. I have known people who, on being filled with the Spirit, have risen quietly to their feet, with beaming faces, and testified to the power of God within; others have sprung to their feet and moved about the hall, or church, speaking in tongues and prophesying; others have acted like the man in Acts iii. 8-10, leaping, shouting, walking and praising God.

It is a mistake to say that people are not struck down by the power when they are baptised in the Holy Spirit; but it is also a mistake to say *that this is the only way* He comes.

I am perfectly sure that the *visions* and *wondrous experiences* of the prophets and apostles recorded in the Scriptures were the work of the Holy Spirit. It was when they were "*in the Spirit*" it occurred (Rev. i. 10).

They staggered, fell, as if dead, to the ground, trembled and quaked at the revelations of the Spirit. Saul lay one day and night on the ground prophesying (I. Sam. xix. 24). Many in our day suddenly see Christ, and with a loud shout fall to the ground and are soon enjoying the blessings of Pentecost, if they have not already received it.

THE RESULTS are the test. Do these people become more Christ-like, loving and good? If so, it cannot be the work of the devil or the flesh. If the work of the devil's spirit, then he must be converted, or they would at heart or in their lives be more like him. *We know the tree by its fruits!*

We have much to learn. The Church HAS SINNED GREATLY by not keeping this work in existence since the days of the apostles. It would have saved us from many doubts and spared us much trouble. But as the "latter rain" is falling, let us step out into it and be drenched. Do not put your umbrellas up! Let the refreshing rains from heaven deluge your whole soul, and may "brotherly love continue."

CHAPTER VII.

# The Gift of Prophecy

IN studying this subject we will notice two, if not three, distinct modes of prophecy used by the Holy Spirit. We lay especial stress on this last clause *used by the Holy Spirit,* because whatever may be said or done by the *prophets,* outside of the direct influence of the Holy Spirit, however acceptable it may be from a human standpoint, it has not the intrinsic value of the work done by *the Holy Spirit* through them. The apostle Paul distinguishes plainly between these two lines of work (comp. I. Cor. vii. 25 and xi. 23). There may evidently also be a mixture, that is, a working of the prophet's *own mind* in connection with the message. Chrysostom says, " He that PROPHESIETH, *speaks all things from the Spirit."* That is, of course, a very pure *degree* of prophecy. He defines also the function of a TEACHER thus: " He that teacheth, sometimes discourses also out of his own mind. Wherefore also he (Paul) said, ' Let the elders that rule well be counted worthy of double honour, especially they who *labour in the word and doctrine* ' (I. Tim. v. 17): whereas he that speaks all things by the Spirit, *doth not labour.* This accordingly is the reason why he set him (the teacher) after the prophets, because the one is wholly a gift, but the other is also man's labour. For he (the teacher) speaks many things of his own mind, *agreeing however with the sacred Scriptures.* But we have reason also to believe that prophets, when prophesying, may, where the gift is not developed to its full perfection, very often allow thoughts from *their own mind* to be mixed with the prophetic messages given by the Holy Spirit. That is evidently the reason why prophesies must be *proved* (I. Thess. v. 20, 21).

### Pure Vessels Needed.

Much will therefore depend on the vessel used—the person speaking, and the *degree* in which God's Spirit predominates.

Of course we know that God can make even *an ass* speak if necessary (Num. xxii. 21-34), and even use such a doubtful person as Balaam (Num. xxiii. 16; xxiv. 1), or Caiaphas (John xi. 49-52) to proclaim His will. In Balaam's case turning a curse into a blessing, because the curse was evidently in Balaam's heart. And in the case of Caiaphas proclaiming the most awful, but still the most glorious act enacted in the history of the world.

But this is the exception to the rule. God prefers pure and submissive channels to proclaim His will to man. Still even with the purest channels it is noticeable that the human vessel used generally imparts some of its characteristics to the message given. But this will, in such cases, not alter the subject of the message, which may nevertheless be perfectly correct, and contain the whole truth as revealed to the prophet.

### Individuality not Eliminated.

We may plainly recognise the style used by Paul, and distinguish it from that of Peter and John. So also in the Old Testament, we notice the difference between the writings of David, Isaiah, Ezekiel and others. The words spoken, or written, are truthful and reliable, but have the unmistakable characteristics of the speaker or writer.

This then seems to prove that the Holy Spirit does not break or disregard the individuality of the prophet, but *sanctifies* it, and uses it as a channel for the message to be given.

But there appear to be various DEGREES in the intensity of the Spirit's operations through the prophets. We may expect that the Spirit will illuminate the *mind*, and fill it with the *thoughts* to be revealed, and give it the *words* whereby these thoughts are to be made known to the people, and give the power to speak the words *with divine authority*. Or the Holy Spirit may even use the vocal cords *without any brain work* on the part of the speaker. This would then be a " *Thus saith the Lord!* "—Inspiration in its highest form, a case of *verbal inspiration*. But between this and the least inspired prophecy *there may be several degrees of intensity,* making it more or less a work of the Spirit through the brain or the mind, or without it. The message given need not be reckoned as a *human message merely,* because it passes through the mind. It bears a definite mark probably of the human instrument used, but the message is nevertheless *from God;* that is, *if it is consistent with the general teaching of the Bible,* and is THEREFORE NOT TO BE DESPISED (I. Thess. v. 20, 21).

We agree with Dr. Joseph Angus, M.A.,* that the *heathen* idea that *inspiration* means " possession," *to the extent of " losing self-consciousness and self-command,"* is not correct : " *the spirits of the prophets are subject to the prophets.*" Still we do believe that when the intensity of the Spirit's operations is very great, or

---

* " The Bible Handbook."

we become "possessed" by *the Holy Spirit,* then the prophetic gift *is* exercised in a *state* similar to that of people speaking *in tongues.* But this does not necessarily mean an UNCONSCIOUS state.

Bishop Westcott sums up the opinion of the FATHERS by saying, "They teach us that Inspiration is an operation of the Holy Spirit acting *through* men, according to the laws of their constitution, which is not neutralised by His influence, but adopted *as a vehicle* for the full expression of the divine message. They teach us that it is generally combined with the *moral* progress and *purification of the teacher,* so that there is on the whole a *moral fitness* in the relation of the prophet to the doctrine."

### The Spirit Works Systematically.

It is possible to discern how the Holy Spirit, who is at the back of all *genuine* prophecy, has, during the ages, been working in a systematic way, developing and spreading spiritual light according to the receptive capacity of man...*The Bible is to a great extent built on prophecy,* or is the result of this wondrous agency. Dr. Angus, M.A., shows the gradual development of the Divine messages and prophetic teaching in very clear words: "The truths and purpose of God are in themselves *incapable* of *progress;* but *not* the *revelation* of those truths. In nature, the rising sun scatters the mists of the morning, and brings out into light, first one prominence and then another, till every hill and valley is clothed in splendour. The landscape *was there before,* but it was *not seen;* so in revelation, the progress is *not in the truth,* but in the clearness and impressiveness with which Scripture reveals it."

How helpful it is to study, and how gracious of our eternal King that He has allowed us *to retain this won-*

*derful Book* in order to watch the development of the eternal light as it spreads throughout the spiritual realm, enlightening all who are willing to receive it.

In explaining his position, Dr. Angus, M.A., writes: " In the beginning, for example, *God* taught the *unity of His nature;* while the truth that there is a *plurality in the Godhead* was taught but indistinctly. In the later prophets, the truth comes out with greater distinctness; and in the New Testament it is fully revealed. In the same way, the work of the Holy Spirit is recognised in the Old Testament, and with increasing clearness as we approach the times of the Gospels. It is in the New Testament alone, however, that we have a distinct view of His personality and work. This gradual disclosure of the Divine will is yet more remarkable in the anticipations of the Christ."

As to the *prophecies in Scripture,* in which coming events are *foretold,* they are " so numerous," says Dr. Alexander Keith, " and the *proof of their fulfilment so abundant,* that instead of any deficiency of evidence, the only difficulty lies in selecting or condensing them." This applies to the prophecies concerning Christ and the Christian religion, the Jews and their history, the Egyptians, the Assyrians and Chaldeans, and so on. Tried as they have been, in the light of history, and the excavations that have been made of old historical centres, they have been proved to be correct. We may therefore with safety conclude that prophecies that refer to events that have not yet taken place *will all find their fulfilment in due time*—such as the prophecies concerning the Jews, the Lord's Second Coming, Antichrist, the Millennium, etc. Of this there should be no doubt whatever.

### The Power of Prophecy.

In the case of *forthtelling*, the spiritual *power* that attends the Divine oracles is very noticeable. The conviction, the comfort, the illumination, the guidance they bring is easily perceived and felt. *No other book* can thus be compared to the Bible. It is ever fresh and pungent in its effects, and although it has been written under conditions and in countries, and in times far different to our own, it *has not lost* any of its power, and *will never do so,* as long as there are souls found who need a light to show them the way to God.

### Methods Differ.

As we have seen, God is not committed to any one method of revealing truth. It may be delivered by verbal inspiration at times, or through the mind of man on other occasions.

Orelli considers the work of the prophet to be *twofold,* as is expressed by his two most common appellations, " seer " and " speaker "; the first name implying the *receptive,* the second the *productive* side of his attitude." " Their endowment consists chiefly in an extraordinary heightening of the perceptive faculty." He, therefore, thinks that " whether the sensuous organs are or are not concerned in this is primarily unimportant." " The contents of prophecy are, consequently, not something thought out, inferred, hoped, or feared by the prophets, but something directly *perceived.* This explains the categorical *certainty* with which they announce the oracles. They know these oracles to be independent of their own subjectivity. The revelation comes before their gaze as something independent, say, belonging to another."

It is possibly difficult to say accurately how the messages were received and delivered in *each case*. Perhaps the contents of the message itself and the occasion of its delivery had much to do with it, if it was spoken to the public or the individual, or written in the quietude of the prophet's secret chamber. God's Spirit is surely not limited to any definite and unchangeable method Nevertheless, of one thing we may rest assured—that " prophecy *came not* in the old time by *the will of man;* but holy men of God spake as they were *moved by the Holy Spirit* " (II. Peter i. 21).

Therefore, also, we know that " no prophecy of the Scriptures is of any *private* interpretation." Paul gives the rule that if any prophesy, let them prophesy " *according to the proportion of faith* " they have received (Rom. xii. 6). *Unbelief* is a barrier to all *pure* prophecy; but we know that " every Scripture *inspired of God* is profitable for teaching, for reproof, for correction, for instruction which is in righteousness: that the man of God may be complete, furnished completely unto every good work " (II. Timothy iii. 16, 17, R.V.).

### To Remain in the Church.

There seems to be no doubt in the mind of the apostles that this gift of prophecy, as all the other gifts of the Spirit, was to remain with the Church throughout this dispensation. The same arguments may be used to prove this, as those used to prove the existence and the necessity of the *tongues* and other gifts of the Spirit throughout the " last days."

### Prophecy at Times in Tongues.

On the Day of Pentecost, Peter made the statement that the speaking in tongues in Jerusalem was of a *prophetic* nature, because, as far as we can see, there was no prophetic speaking of the kind we classify with prophetic speech, but *merely tongues*. Still, he says the prophecy of Joel was fulfilled, which said: " And it shall come to pass in the last days, saith God, I will pour out of My Spirit upon all flesh: and your sons and your daughters *shall prophesy* " (Acts ii. 17).

There must, therefore, not merely have been worship and adoration in the " tongues " heard, but also *messages* to the people, similar to those mentioned in I. Cor. xiv. 3. Their character of " prophecy " arose from *this* fact, those present understanding what was said.

### Tongues and Prophecy Give Mutual Help.

Tongues and prophecy are twin brothers, and brought about by the same mighty Spirit. There was no necessity, as we have already shown, for *tongues,* as is generally supposed, on Pentecost, *in order to reach the different nationalities* assembled in Jerusalem at that time, as almost everybody knew the chief languages generally spoken, which is seen from the fact that *they all understood Peter,* without his making use of an interpreter. *The miracle of tongues* gave his message that peculiar background, that divinely supernatural stamp, without which he would have had no solicitous crowd to speak to, and certainly not the same influence over the masses that he had.

If anyone says, " Oh, yes, he would ! " I merely ask, Why then did God send His Holy Spirit to stir up all that commotion *through the tongues?* Because it is plain to every fair-minded reader of the context that it was *the tongues, and that unusual supernatural power that accompanied them,* that brought the people together and caused all the questioning and amazement and ridicule (just as in our day) that preceded Peter's message.

### Peter Prophesying.

And then it was that Peter, on fire with the *same* holy power, stood up with the eleven and spoke to the excited masses.

Here, then, we touch a point of interest, which illustrates forcibly one of the distinct lines of prophecy. The message given by Peter *was prophetic,* of the kind mentioned in I. Cor. xiv. 3: *"He that prophesieth speaketh unto men to edification, and exhortation, and comfort."* Peter spoke in the power of the Holy Ghost.

To quote the Rev. W. Arthur, M.A.,: "He had no tongue of silver; for, they say, ' He is an unlearned and ignorant man.' The rudeness of his Galilean speech still remains with him; yet, though ' unlearned and ignorant,' in their sense—as to polite learning—in a higher sense he was a scribe well instructed.

" Yet he had no tongues of honey, nor soothing, flattering speech, to allay the prejudices and to captivate the passions of the multitude. Nor had he a tongue of thunder; no outbursts of native eloquence distinguish his discourse. Peter's sermon is no more than quoting passages from the Word of God, and reasoning upon them. Yet, as in this strain he proceeds, the tongue of fire by degrees burns its way to the feelings of the multitude. The murmur gradually subsides; the mob becomes a congregation; the voice of the fisherman sweeps from end to end of that multitude, unbroken by a single sound; and, as the words rush on, they act like a stream of fire."

### The Power of Genuine Prophecy.

Now this illustrates what prophecy is and ought to be.

Paul says: "If all *prophesy*, and there come in one that believeth not, or one unlearned, he is *convinced of all*, he is *judged of all;* and thus are the *secrets of his heart made manifest;* and so falling down on his face he will worship God, and report that God is in you of a truth" (I. Cor. xiv. 24, 25).

We read that among the Carmisards, in the Cevennes, the gift of prophecy was so mighty that unlearned and simple folk delivered messages, when under the power of the Spirit, that were simply astounding. It would have been impossible for them to deliver such addresses if they had not been under a Divine influence. The thoughts were so high and beautifully expressed, *at times in the purest French,* although the speakers only knew a simple dialect of that language; and the mode of delivery was so expressive and forceful that all felt the messages came from a higher source. *Even children delivered impressive addresses* to the people.

And during this Twentieth Century Revival we have numerous instances similar to this. And it has been noticed even by the secular press. Personally I have often felt the Holy power pass through me when preaching, giving the mind a new illumination, and imparting a flow of words and thoughts and illustrations, quite outside of any line of thought prepared for the service, and this new current of thought always proves to be the right thing for the occasion, and works variously; sometimes like a two-edged sword, or as a balsam, or instructively or edifying. And this is the experience of many preachers, who are not absolutely tied down to the *written* sermon. This then is to my mind, *prophecy,* and its pureness will depend on the degree of self-resignation to God's will and the intensity of the Spirit's work.

### All Can Prophesy.

But it may take place through men and women at a meeting who *have no official standing in the Church.* Paul desires the Churches to expect it at *every meeting.* " How is it then brethren, when ye come together . . . *Let the prophets speak by two or three, and let the others discern, But if a revelation be made to another sitting by, let the first keep silence. For ye all can prophesy one by one, that all may learn, and all may be comforted; and the spirits of the prophets are subject to the prophets* (I. Cor. xiv. 26-32).

Dr. Henson says, in his book on *Apostolic Christianity,* concerning this passage : " The apostle indicates that the Church was the *critic* as well as the *recipient* of prophetic communications, and that apart from special *revelations* the prophets had messages to deliver in the assembly. By some *unmistakable tokens* the advent of a new revelation in the prophet's mind made itself known; the more normal prophesying was suspended in order that the most recent ' *Word of the Lord* ' might be delivered."

By " normal prophesying," he means the more ordinary " speaking unto men to *edification, and comfort, and consolation;* the new message, that was to engage the attention of all, was of *a more intense supernatural order.* There is the difference in this case of the *ordinary stream of prophecy* and a *revelation.*

At this point it would be wise to see *who* were called to prophesy, or made use of as channels for prophecy by the Holy Spirit.

I remember when studying the subject of " tongues " on seeking my baptism, I was considerably perplexed by I. Cor. xii. 28-31. Because I felt that the answer must invariably be *" No! "*

But then I noticed that the apostle says, in I. Cor. xiv. 24, 31, that " ALL " may prophesy, and, in verses 1 and 5, that we were to *covet* or *desire* this gift. Did then the apostle contradict himself? That could not be the case. Then there must be some explanation. And this explanation would also apply to *tongues*, and *the other gifts* as well.

It appeared plain to me then that there was *a general sense* in which *all* might be made *partakers* in these gifts, whereas there seemed to be some who were endowed with them in a *very special sense*. For instance: *All* might prophesy, " as the *Spirit* gave utterance," but some seemed to be especially called *to act as* " *prophets.*"

*All* might speak in *tongues*, " as the Spirit gave utterance," when the fire fell, but *all might not retain* tongues as a " *gift.*"

*All* might by naked *faith* in the promises move mountains and heal the sick, but *not all* had the *gift of healing.*

*All* might seek *wisdom* (James i. 5), but *not all* might have it as did King Solomon, and so on. I find now that many have this opinion.

Dr. Hensley Henson says: "The language of Paul seems contradictory. On the one hand he speaks of the 'prophets' as constituting a distinct class; both in the Corinthian and in Ephesian lists of Christian ministers they are placed *next in order to the 'apostles.'* 'And God hath set some in the Church, first apostles, secondly prophets, thirdly teachers,' is the language of the one. ' And He gave some to be apostles, and some prophets, and some evangelists, and some pastors and teachers,' is that of the other. In I. Cor. xiv. the ' *prophets* ' appear as a very well-defined group, accustomed to take an important share in the conduct of public worship, and perhaps occupying official seats in the Christian assembly. On the other hand, the apostle contemplates the prophesying of the ENTIRE CHURCH as a desirable and not improbable contingency. ' *For* YE ALL *can prophesy one by one,*' he writes, ' *that all may learn, and all may be comforted* ' (I. Cor. xiv. 31). He bids the Corinthians ' *desire earnestly to prophesy.*' "

Not even WOMEN were excluded from the prophetic gift. Nay, Paul contemplates their *publicly* exercising it : " *But every woman praying or prophesying with her head unveiled dishonoureth her head* " (I. Cor. xi. 5, R.V.). In the Acts we read of Philip the evangelist, that he " *had four daughters which did prophesy* " (Acts xxi. 2).

### Does the Apostle Contradict Himself?

In explaining this Mr. Henson says : "The contradiction is only on the surface, and arises rather from our pre-conceived notions of Church order than from any obscurity in the language of Paul."

He does not think " prophets " received any formal ordination, as did the ministry. " Moreover, the prophetic inspiration might come, and often did come, to private Christians of both sexes." *Inspiration,* he thinks, was " considered to permanently attach to whomsoever it had once been given."

There was a sense, then, in which *all* might be prepared, IF LIVING ACCORDING TO THE WILL OF GOD, to be used by the Spirit in an assembly, to the edification, exhortation, or comfort of those present; but there were also such who, *in an especial manner, were more regularly used by the Spirit as channels of prophetic messages or revelations.* Matthew Henry says that these prophets were "persons enabled by inspiration to prophesy, interpret Scripture, or *write* by inspiration, as the evangelist did."

### Foretelling.

Besides this line of prophecy, we find also that of FORETELLING COMING EVENTS in the Scriptures. As we have seen, both these phases of prophecy are found in the Old as well as the New Testament. The power of foretelling future events was indeed a mighty miracle. *Only God could disclose coming events*—the God who knew what would take place.

The truth of the prophet's statements was to be satisfied by FACTS. Death was the punishment for *false* prophets in the old dispensation (Deut. xviii. 20). The question was raised: "If thou say in thine heart, How shall we know the word which the Lord hath not spoken?" (*v.* 21); and the answer given was this: "When a prophet speaketh in the name of the Lord, if *the thing follow not, nor come to pass,* THAT is the thing which the Lord hath *not* spoken, but the prophet hath spoken it *presumptuously*: thou *shalt not be afraid of him*" (*v.* 22).

### False Prophets.

The Bible warns against false prophets both in the Old and New Testament. In I. Kings xxii., we have an interesting case of both kinds. The ungodly king of Israel is determined to war against the king of Syria. He enquires of his prophets as to the wisdom of attacking Ramoth-gilead. They, with Zedekiah at their head, agree unanimously. But Jehoshaphat, the king of Judah, who very unwisely has promised to assist Ahab, is not content with the answer of the prophets. "Is there not here a *prophet of the Lord* besides, that we might inquire of him?" he exclaims. Yes, says Ahab, "but *I hate him,* for he doth not prophesy good concerning me, but evil."

As King Ahab, so many are ever found who are more content with the flatteries and lies of false prophets than the *pure truth of God.*

Micaiah, when sent for, foretells disaster to their united campaign and the death of Ahab. The false prophet Zedekiah, who had even made him horns of iron, saying, "Thus saith the Lord, With these shalt thou push the Syrians until thou hast consumed them," smote Micaiah and said, "Which way went the Spirit of the Lord from me to speak unto thee?" But the true prophet of the Lord had even seen in a vision the LYING SPIRITS "go forth to prevail with the prophets of Ahab."

### The Faithful and True Prophet.

Micaiah was thrust into prison for *telling the truth,* and fed with the "bread of affliction and with water of affliction," but his prophecy failed not; the Lord had spoken through him.

In Acts xxi. 11, we find the prophet Agabus foretelling the persecution of Paul at Jerusalem; and, in Acts xi. 28, he foretells a great dearth, "which came to pass in the days of Claudius Cæsar."

But *much care is needed* in the use of this gift, as "lying spirits" abound just as much in our day as in former days.

### Prophecies to be Proved.

We are told, in I. Thess. v. 20, 21, not to despise prophesyings, but to "*prove all things,*" and "hold fast *that which is good."* In I. Cor. xiv. 29, we read: " Let the prophets speak two or three, and *let the others judge."* John says, in I. John iv. 1: " Beloved, believe not every spirit, but try the spirits *whether they are of God*: because many false prophets are gone out into the world."

This is very definite; and there is no doubt but what the many theories preached and imbibed by some people that do not agree with the Scriptures, *but have a religious smattering,* have been instigated and launched by evil spirits, such as Theosophy, Christian Science, Mormonism, Russellism, Liberal Theology, etc.

The other *Spirit-filled* listeners then have to " *prove* " " *judge* " or " *try* " the spirits.

This implies a " *gift of discernment,"* and of course those having this gift were best able to decide the value of the given messages.

### Is Christ Honoured?

M. Godet says, " Assuredly it is not for nothing that the apostle has begun this whole discussion on the spiritual gifts by indicating the precise *character* which distinguishes true and false inspirations, by recalling that the one have as their common character and essence this cry of adoration—JESUS, LORD! whilst the others tend to the *humiliation and rejection of Jesus.* It was sufficient then to place every prophecy in relation *with this centre* of the entire Christian revelation, THE PERSON OF CHRIST, and to see to what result the prophecy which had been heard tended to make little of Him or to glorify Him."

### The Mark of Antichrist.

This thought, we find, is supported in I. John iv.

John says, "Every spirit that confesseth that JESUS CHRIST is *come in the flesh* is of God." That acknowledgement implies the belief in *His eternal Divinity*. "And every spirit that confesseth *not* that Jesus Christ is come in the flesh is *not* of God: and this is that spirit of antichrist, whereof ye have heard that it should come; and *even now already is it in the world.*"

### Lives Speak Volumes.

Not only by their *teaching*, but also by their *lives* will it will be possible to test the false prophets. Jesus said, "*Beware of false prophets,* which come to you in sheep's clothing, but inwardly are ravening wolves. YE SHALL KNOW THEM BY THEIR FRUITS!" (Matt. vii. 15).

In the rules laid down in "The Teaching of the Twelve Apostles," it is insisted upon that a *righteous life must be the constant test of the genuine prophet*: "Not every one that speaketh in the spirit is a prophet, but *only if he have the behaviour of the Lord.* By their behaviour then shall the false prophet and the true prophet be known. And every prophet that teacheth the truth, *if he doeth not what he teacheth,* is a *false* prophet. But whosoever saith in the spirit, 'Give me money,' or any other things, ye shall not hearken to him, but if he bid to give for others that lack, let no one judge him."

This little glimpse into *the methods of the first Christians* speaks volumes. No wonder the apostles said, "*Prove! Judge!*" The heart of man was then as now prone to wander astray.

### The Sub-Conscious Mind.

Perhaps we may know more than the first Christians about the workings of the sub-conscious mind. Perhaps not. For Paul says, "The spirit of the prophets are subject to the prophets." And we do know that *the human spirit—which in fact is the sub-conscious mind,*\* may often speak its own thoughts, and we may, if not on our guard, *mistake them* for the Divine Spirit's inspiration within. Still, if we are living PURE LIVES by the power of the Blood and the Holy Spirit, and allow ourselves to be guided *only* by God's Spirit, the messages *will also be pure and reliable.*

MISTAKES made may *not always* have been the direct outcome of Satanic instigation and subtlety. So although we know lying spirits *may* influence the mind of man, the *human spirit itself may do so.* Accordingly many of the mistakes made by some people *may not have had anything to do with Satanic counterfeits at all*, but have been brought about by the HUMAN spirit.

But when the prophet or prophetess has *pure motives, and abides by the Word of God, and clings to the precious Blood of Christ, not fearfully, but trustfully,* we must be very careful what we do with the messages given. *We might come under condemnation by slighting them!*

But we have seen and heard some, possibly well-meaning, people, allow their own feelings and human conceptions, their grudges and tempers, their envyings and pride, *exert their influence in the interpretation of tongues given and in the prophecies.* Their hearts and *motives* have not been *pure.* But as the messages have been given in the form of prophecy they have done much harm, and caused schisms and distress.

*This must be withstood by the pure prophets and leaders!* Some have intimated that as

---

\* Science has thus borne its testimony to the fact of the existence of the human spirit.

### There Are But Two Masters,

that we are either serving the one or the other. That is true. But it does not imply, as they would have it, that we " are *demon-possessed,*" or " *under the devil's control,*" *because we speak in tongues and prophesy.* And, as we have just remarked, even if *mistakes* are made in prophecy, it may not be the result of *outside influences,* but caused by the human mind. It must be remembered, too, that not all seeming mistakes, as to foretelling coming events, disasters, etc., may have been mistakes. The Bible relates several cases where impending disasters foretold of God through His prophets *have been averted by intercessory prayer or the repentance of those under condemnation.* Who can say but what the intense prayers of God's people may have prevented the destruction of doomed cities *in our day?*

Still we believe it wise to

### Consult Others,

competent to judge in all such cases, before *public* statements are made. I have, as formerly stated, personally and publicly corrected those who have

### Fixed the Date

of our Lord's coming. *Lying spirits* are often deceiving by fixing dates and describing circumstances, just for the sake of sensation and fraud; and *prophets,* if any, must live very near God not to be deceived by them.

Besides, *prophecies* may be given

### A Wrong Interpretation.

How easy it was to put a false construction on the *promise to Jacob* (Genesis xlvi. 4); although the Lord said, " I will also surely bring thee up again," the

Bible states that Jacob *died in Egypt* (Genesis xlix. 33). Of course God referred to THE NATION that went forth from the loins of Jacob. That nation was to be brought up out of Egypt. And God fulfilled His word. We must also pray to get *correct interpretations* of prophecies in cases where there is doubt. Either obtaining a *clear definition* or proving that they are *false*.

We are now dealing with the case of prophecies (foretelling) by Christians, who have only *one* desire: THAT OF SERVING CHRIST. So it is not a matter of either siding with Christ or Satan. *They hate Satan and all his ways!*

But seeming mistakes have been made now and then. MUST THEY be "*possessed by evil spirits,*" having made these mistakes? No! A Christian *cannot be* if living WHOLLY for God; that is, not in his *spirit*.

### Demons

may attack his body, if he has not faith for God's preserving power *physically,* or obsess it by bringing disease and sickness, and through this try to infest the mind and spirit; but if he *withstands* in the power of the Atonement and the Name of Jesus, he will have victory over every Satanic force.

The first Church Father, CLEMENT, says that demons are only able to enter *the bodies* of men through "opportunities afforded them "—" base and evil actions." " As long as the measure of nature is kept, and legitimate moderation is preserved, the *mercy of God* does *not* give them liberty to enter into men. But when either the mind falls into impiety, or the body is filled with immoderate meat or drink, then, AS IF INVITED by the will and purpose of those who thus neglect themselves, they receive power as against those who have

## THE GIFT OF PROPHECY

broken the law imposed by God." "You see, then," Clement continues, "how important is the *acknowledgment of God* and the *observance* of the Divine religion, which NOT ONLY PROTECTS THOSE who believe from the assaults of the demon, but also gives them COMMAND OVER THOSE WHO RULE OVER OTHERS."

In exhorting the heathen to accept God, he says the *demons,* " in proportion as they see faith grow in a man, in THAT proportion they *depart* from him, residing ONLY IN THAT PART in which SOMETHING OF INFIDELITY STILL REMAINS; but from those who believe

### With Full Faith

they depart without any delay. For where a soul has come to the faith of God, it obtains the virtue of heavenly water, by which it *extinguishes the demon like a spark of fire.*"\*

We believe, then, that mistakes—if *wholehearted* Christians have made mistakes in prophecy—may have been the work of the *sub-conscious mind.* Or the mistake may have been one of

### Ignorance,

supposing *every voice* to be heard that of the *Holy Spirit;* whereas it is evident that Satan and his emissaries may SUGGEST THOUGHTS to Christians as loud as voices at times, and if people have been taught to believe and accept *every thought or suggestion,* as being from God, they would naturally be led astray although their own motives were pure; but when put on their guard, they *will easily be able to detect the voice of the enemy.*

We know also in our day how the suggestions of *men,* mind working on mind, might affect them; but

---

\* " Recognition of Clement," chap. xv.—xvii.

if keeping near God, they will be able to break through all these barriers of Satan and men, and HEAR GOD'S OWN VOICE PLAINLY.

It must be remembered, too, that a Christian may have thoughts and ideas stored up in *his own mind* that are liable to appeal to him, and *his own spirit* might take it to be *God's* thoughts and cause it to be spoken. But this is far from saying that *evil spirits* are speaking through him; it is a matter of *human* fallacy, not a Satanic product. Those, therefore, who have *spurned all because of mistakes made,* have acted very unwisely, and deny themselves the blessings they *might derive* from THIS GLORIOUS GIFT, when used in the strength of the Holy Spirit. We have then to discern what is of *God,* of *man* (ourselves or other human minds), or of *Satan.*

### In Vital Touch with God.

This may seem difficult. But when the human spirit breaks through all that is human, and trusts fully in the *power of the Blood and Name of Jesus,* losing itself, as it were, in GOD, then the Holy Spirit may work freely through the human spirit, and *clear messages will be given.* So much, then, depends on the *degree of intensity* wherewith God's Spirit may be able to work through us.

We see, therefore, that there must be discernment between *inspiration* and *fleeting thoughts and suggestions.* We are more or less free from incorrect thoughts and statements, as we are more or less submissive to the influences of the Holy Spirit.

If some people are not willing to be watchful in this respect, but accept *anything* spoken in prophecy as of the Lord,

### THE GIFT OF PROPHECY

#### We Ought Not to Work Together With Them,

when admonitions in love do not prevail. Because experience has proved CLEARLY and SATISFACTORILY that this practice leads *away from God* instead of *to God*, and dishonours the cause of Christ.

#### Not to Judge.

Especially has *harm* been done, when the prophets have *condemned to everlasting death* such as have withstood this Twentieth Century Revival, or because they have acted in opposition to *the personal desires of these prophets*. JUDGMENT is different from *discernment,* and remains with the LORD (Matt. vii. 1, 2; I. Cor. iv. 5, 6).

That the Spirit, through the prophets, will speak with awakening and quickening power is clear (I. Cor. xiv. 3, 24, 25). Many have thought the preacher was speaking directly to them, pointing out their sins publicly, although he knew nothing about them, or even noticed them. They were condemned in the spirit by the words spoken in the power of God.

It may be necessary to CORRECT SOME PEOPLE publicly. In Gal. ii. 11, it was done because of *public hypocrisy* on the part of the Apostle Peter. And we may think it possible that a person arises to speak in a meeting, or elsewhere, who is at grievous *fault* in some matter, and this being known to the public, he should be prevented from public work *until* those things are made right. Or someone might arise and teach *false* doctrine. This the Spirit will surely try to prevent. In a case as that in I. Timothy v. 20, " accusations " or *charges* have been brought against the elder, attested to by *witnesses* (*v.* 19), and if no acknowledgment of the mistake or sin takes place, then public rebuke is enjoined.

Some have, " in the spirit," so-called, in prophecies

and in the interpretation of tongues, aimed at people in the meetings, who disagreed with them or their plans, driving them and others away for good by their un-Christlike methods, causing schisms and divisions by their *harsh and judging spirit.* Surely this is NOT GOD'S WAY.

### Opponents Won.

We have known some persons, who at first hated this movement and opposed it bitterly, but have now seen their folly, and are among its *warmest supporters.* They opposed in *ignorance.*

### Harsh Judgments Condemned.

When we are dealing with the things of God, we are on delicate, yea, *holy* ground. We are very ignorant of spiritual things. And God's children, while they perhaps fail to understand—and how many of God's ways we cannot fathom!—are wise if they are sparing and careful in their words regarding them. Far better, surely, silently and prayerfully watch and wait, lest rushing on, one be found fighting even against God, and ignorantly intruding into the secrets of God. We well know what dangers are incurred in such a heedless course.

But harsh judgments, even involving eternal damnation, and forbidding to pray for the persons concerned, is quite wrong. It is another thing if the Holy Ghost definitely prevents us, or does not remind us to pray for any. If they have blasphemed the Holy Spirit *wilfully* and *willingly,* then we will scarcely be led to *pray* for them (I. John v. 16). We have evidently great need to be careful in all things.

There are people, it is true, whom we cannot commune with as *spiritual* friends, they withstand the *truth*

(II. John ix. 10, 11), but they must not be *hated* (I. John iv. 19, 20; II. Thess. iii. 14, 15). The day will prove " their real relation." There were people whom the Apostle *delivered to Satan* for *" the destruction of the flesh "* (I. Cor. v. 5). But even this took place that the *spirit* " might be *saved* in the day of the Lord Jesus." He *delivered some unto Satan,* too, that (I. Tim. i. 20) " they might learn *not to blaspheme."* But there is a great difference in this *and eternal punishment.*

In no case recorded did the apostles condemn people to eternal damnation. The Father hath given the Son that power. In the case where Peter condemned Ananias for sinning against the Holy Ghost, it was God who gave the stroke of death, and then, when Peter saw by that act that the sin was unto death, he passed sentence on the woman by the Holy Spirit's power.

*Correction* and *reproof* in the RIGHT SPIRIT—*that of love*—is in order, at proper times, and under circumstances we have already touched upon; but where prophets at every meeting are *on the look-out for someone to " cut down "* (bidding them be seated, or in other ways publicly judge them) in a *harsh, condemnatory spirit,* we may be assured that that thing

### Is Not of the Lord.

What we here state concerns the treatment given to *Christians*—not people of the *world, although they must also be treated in love.* We are assured that the condemnatory method adopted by *some* is incorrect to say the least of it.

One mistake some are liable of making at the start of their Pentecostal experience—is that of making the prophet a constant *oracle,* or *themselves,* if they have the gift; thereby trying to be guided *in all the affairs of life by that means.* Some dare not eat or sleep, save as the oracles or their own statements when "under the power," allow them.

That God is able to give messages to His people, as to the various activities in life, we know to be a fact, and cannot doubt. And it is a pleasure for a Christian to place even the trivial affairs of life in prayer before God and be guided by Him. But He can do that *without the prophets " getting under the power,"* and obtaining guidance in that way. We must remember that God has given us *common sense,* and we verily believe it is His intention we are to use it—illuminated or *sanctified common sense.*

In *more important matters* I find that God, if of personal interest to myself, gives me, if not by *revelation,* then by a decided force of circumstances, a clear understanding of His will.

If two ways are open before me, I find it best to wait until *only one of them remains.* And then I am willing to go that one way *even if it means death.*

### Not to Commune with Spirits.

It will almost be unnecessary to say that it would be *sinful* for a Christian to allow himself to be used as a kind of a Medium for communing with the other world, or with "familiar spirits." The Bible condemns such practices explicitly.

### Paul's Mode of Action.

It seems very clear that Paul and others were sometimes guided by *messages from the prophets in those early days,* when the gift was still in its virgin purity.

In Acts xvi. 6-10, we have a most remarkable account

of this: " Now when they had gone throughout Phrygia and the region of Galatia, *and were forbidden of the Holy Ghost* to preach the Word in Asia, after they were come to Mysia, they assayed to go into Bithynia; *but the Spirit suffered them not.* And they passing by Mysia came down to Troas. And a *vision* appeared to Paul in the night; there stood a man of Macedonia, and prayed him, saying, Come over into Macedonia, and help us." And he started immediately for Macedonia, *concluding that God had called him* to do so.

God's power was mightily over the first Christians, and Paul accepted this prophetic guidance in as far as he felt it was Divine.

The modern Christian, of the general type, would say, " What, guided by the talk of men and women fanatics, who believe they have the Spirit!—What, guided by a vision! "

Yes, in this age of the " Latter Rain " period, we are to expect the same mighty outpouring of the Spirit; yea, more!—with the signs following.

Still, it is interesting to note that not even in the cases referred to (Acts xvi.), did the Apostle sit down to wait for impressions or signs before acting. Supposing the Holy Spirit would check them in taking a wrong step (and He did so) they went forth boldly to the places they thought needed their services. They had gone through Phrygia; then the Holy Ghost forbade them to preach in Asia. So after they were come to Mysia they started out for Bithynia. Again the Spirit prevented it. But they did not " sit down and do nothing." They went on to Troas. There the Lord sent them definitely in a vision.

It would seem then that we have to choose and act to the best of our ability, when the matter has been laid before the Lord in prayer, not depending merely on signs and revelations. If the Lord will send us these we will thank Him.

In Acts xiii. 2 we have another case. Also in Acts xx. 23. And in I. Tim. iv. 14, we find that Timothy had received the gift that was in him by PROPHECY with the laying on of the hands of the presbytery. But Paul was not willing to go by the statements of the prophets if his own judgment determined otherwise—his own judgment illuminated by God's Spirit. No doubt he was guided by the axiom, that it is sin to do anything that cannot be done in faith (Rom. xiv. 23).

In Acts xiii., he had no doubts, and all felt that he and Barnabas were " sent forth by the Holy Ghost " (verse 4). But in Acts xxi. we have another case, giving us a sideview of this gift of prophecy. At Tyre the disciples " said to Paul, *through the Spirit,* that he should not go up to Jerusalem " (verse 4). Agabus prophesied in Cæsarea of the awaiting persecution, and all began to persuade Paul " not to go up to Jerusalem."

But Paul knew that the journey to Jerusalem would further the glory of God; and he was willing not only to be bound, " but also to die at Jerusalem for the name of the Lord Jesus."

When we consider the great importunity shown by his friends to dissuade him from going up to Jerusalem, we must admire the courage evinced by the Apostle, who was willing to die rather than seek ease and comfort for himself.

But here, then, arises the difficulty: How could the Spirit say one thing at Tyre and Cæsarea through the prophets and another thing to Paul? Possibly the four daughters of Philip, in whose home Paul was staying, also prophesied along the same lines, stating the trials to be expected at Jerusalem and trying to dissuade him from going there.

We agree to the following explanation given by some: The first part of their statements, concerning his trials, was the real message by the Holy Spirit. The second part was the fruit of their own fear of persecution and love to the Apostle. And he knew it! There was no wilful and rash conduct on the part of the Apostle. It became a battle of love. They wept and he wept. But their love to him was conquered by his love to Christ. The fourth verse of Acts xxi., according to Weymouth, reads: "And taught by the Spirit, they repeatedly warned Paul not to proceed to Jerusalem." That is, taught by the Spirit of the troubles ahead, they naturally tried to avert them by their attempts to persuade the Apostle not to go; but he was, as we read in Acts xx. 22, " *bound in the Spirit* to go."

Now some would say Paul was mistaken, but the prophets seemed to resign their position when he resolutely held on to his persuasion, and ceased their pleadings, saying, "*The will of the Lord be done.*"

We feel inclined to accept the theory that the prophets allowed their personal feelings to gain the upper hand.

If this is correct we learn the necessity of watching against personal feelings and wishes arising when prophesying, as the prophecy is apt to get mixed, and become partly human and partly Divine.

Perhaps we have a striking proof of this in the Apochyphal Books. They are not generally accepted because they, as a whole, do not appear to be Divinely inspired. They belong to the period B.C., "when prophecy, oracles, and direct revelation had ceased."[*] But there are passages where the Divine touch seems to penetrate.

---

[*] Oxford Bible.

The Book of Wisdom possesses " the highest literary excellence, and is comparable for sublimity of thought, rhetorical power, and command of language with *some of the first productions of classical antiquity."* "Some passages in *the Epistle to the Hebrews* suggest that the writer was acquainted with this book, but no direct quotation from it is found earlier than the first half of the Second Century, A.D., when it seems to be treated as inspired Scripture."† " *The foundation is laid in it* for the Christian doctrine of the existence and influence of the *Divine Word* and *the Holy Spirit."* The Re formed Church, " regarded the uncanonical books as valuable ' for example of life and instruction of manners, though *not of authority in matters of faith.* Some of them are of high value—literary, historical and otherwise: notably, I. Maccabees and Ecclesiasticus."‡

From this, one might be inclined to judge of some of the books that *there is a mixture in them of inspiration and human brain-power.* Hence, although serviceable in some respects, they are not perfectly reliable as textbooks for our faith. There may possibly in some of the present-day messages be a *similar mixture of human and Divine power.* But we believe, nevertheless, that many messages have been given, and will increasingly be so, in the Twentieth Century Revival, that are of A MUCH HIGHER ORDER.

But be that as it may—of one thing we should rest assured: *that no revelation, whoever be the seer or prophet, is trustworthy,* UNLESS IT CAN STAND THE TEST OF HOLY WRIT. *We must* CLING TO THE BIBLE *as the testing stone of all we think, say or do. And* NO PROPHECY SHOULD BE ACCEPTED ANYWHERE *that contradicts the*

---

† "Oxford Bible." ‡ "Bible Handbook," by Dr. J. Angus, M.A.

## THE GIFT OF PROPHECY 137

*Scriptures*. There can be no disagreement in the Godhead. Truth may be unveiled and opened up, but no new revelation of it will antagonise and upset the revelation given in Scripture of God's holy will.

We do not mean to say hereby, as some may suppose, that all prophecy *must be clad* in the language of the Bible, that is, by merely quoting Scripture; but that *the truths revealed* in inspired Scripture are *to be the measure applied to all prophecy in these days of " the latter rain."* If we are guided by this rule *we are safe!*

### Correctness of Prophecy is Being Proved Now.

It is so much the more necessary as rationalistic currents proceeding from Unitarianism, Theosophy, Christian Science, Spiritualism, and even from many teachers tainted with unbelief within different denominations, are trying to WEAKEN THE AUTHORITY OF THE BIBLE. In so doing they overlook the fact *that the very position they take* **PROVES** *the clearness of prophetic statement*: " In the *latter days* grievous times shall come. For men shall be lovers of self . . . having a *form* of godliness, but *denying the power thereof* . . . ever learning, and never able to come to the knowledge of the *truth* " (II. Tim. iii. 1-7). " In the *latter* times some shall *depart from the faith*, giving heed to *seducing spirits,* and *doctrines of devils* " (I. Tim. iv. 1-3). THE SPIRIT " speaketh expressly " concerning this, Paul says. And Jesus states definitely, that in those days " there shall arise *false Christs,* and *false prophets,* and shall *shew great signs and wonders;* inasmuch that, if it were possible, they shall *deceive the very elect.* Behold, I have told you before " (Matt. xxiv. 24, 25).

### The Mark of Antichrist

is being put on the foreheads of thousands in these days,

such as are not willing to accept that " Jesus Christ is come in the flesh " (I. John iv. 1-6). That is, they are not willing to give Him Divine superiority. Doubting His incarnation they also reject His atonement.

In conversing with a gentleman at an after-meeting lately, I soon found out that his theories were a mixture of Theosophy, Spiritualism, etc. He said at last, " I don't want the Blood ! " " But I do ! " I answered. " The Blood is then the DIVIDING LINE BETWEEN US ! " Opposers of the Blood, discarding the finished work of Christ, show immediately that they are influenced by Satan and his demons, and this is *a sign of the times*. The mark of Antichrist was seen even in the days of John (I. John iv. 3), but the " falling away " is increasing immensely; and the way is thus being prepared for " that man of sin, the son of perdition " himself (II. Thess. ii. 3), who will step forth amongst the nations when they have been prepared for his coming by the rationalistic teaching of our day. His coming will be *" after the working of Satan* with all power and signs, and lying wonders, and with all deceivableness of unrighteousness in them that perish; because they received not the love of the truth, that they might be saved " (ix. 10). But his reign shall be short, though awful and disastrous. *" The Lord shall consume him* with the spirit of His mouth, and shall destroy him *with the brightness of His coming! "* (verse 8).

So we see plainly how the prophecies are being fulfilled these days, and the VERY MEN AND WOMEN, who in public and private are trying to eliminate the *Divinely* supernatural teachings and statements of the Bible records, and attempting to get rid of their authority, and the fact of the incarnate and everlasting Christ, and His glorious atonement, are

### The Very People

who are fulfilling these prophecies.

How needful then that we watch against all the encroachments of the enemy! As in the case of the Book of Revelation, so also it may be said regarding all inspired Scripture: " If any man shall add unto them (the words of prophecy) God shall add unto him the plagues which are written in this Book; and if any man shall take away from the words of the Book of this prophecy, God shall take away his part from the tree of life, and out of the holy city, which are written in this Book. He who testifieth these things, saith : *Yea, I come quickly. Amen: come, Lord Jesus!* " (Rev. xxii. 18-20).

In closing, we would say that if ever the Christian Church needed the gift of prophecy,

### It Is Now!

Never was the need greater for Spirit-filled messages than *now*. And yet the Church stands aloof discarding this gift as all the rest, or it vainly tries to delude itself and others by supposing that the usual preaching and ordinary testimonies at services and smaller meetings uninspired by the Spirit, are prophecy. Generally speaking, the preaching comes more under the gift of teaching and knowledge than that of prophecy, as the teacher is more or less guided by his " knowledge " of the Scriptures (I. Cor. xii. 8, 29). The prophet or prophetess is more directly inspired by the Spirit, and, when FULLY under the power of the Spirit, *speaks in ecstasy* the truths revealed to them. *This gift seems to be acquired in a similar way as that of the gift of tongues.* We have many instances of this in our day.

Of course *teaching*, or *preaching*, may be inspired, and attain the character of prophecy, if the speaker is

under the power of the Holy Spirit, but the PROPHESY-
ING IN THE SPIRIT (outside of foretelling) is more of the
nature described in the Old and New Testament (comp.
Num. xi. 23-29; I. Sam. x. 1-11; Isaiah lv.; Luke ii.
25-38 (a combination of foretelling and forthtelling);
Acts ii. 14; iv. 8-13; xix. 6).

Oh, that the Church would now awaken to see its
privileges in Christ Jesus, by His Holy Spirit! This
gift, so highly prized by Paul, is often ridiculed by
Christians in our day. And still this is what the Church
needs and is exhorted by the Apostle to " COVET " (I.
Cor. xiv. 1).

Of course neither this gift nor any other will prove
serviceable unless the power of

### Love

is at the back and running through it. The time is
coming when *prophecies* will fail, and *tongues* cease,
and *knowledge* shall vanish away (I. Cor. xiii. 1). But
that was not to take place *before the perfection of the
eternal world* was realised, and we shall " see face to
face " and know even " as we are known " (verse 12).
THAT TIME IS NOT YET! Hence the gifts are *to continue
in the Church* until that perfection is reached. But they
are to continue *in love,* without which we are "nothing"
(verse 2). But if we are *filled with the Spirit* we are
also *filled with Love!*

What a responsibility remains with the Church! The
time is surely at hand now when I. Cor. xiv. 26-33
ought to be practised everywhere amongst God's people.
The Apostolic counsel still holds good, " DESIRE
EARNESTLY TO PROPHESY! " (I. Cor. xiv. 39). The Church
needs the edification, encouragement, exhortation and
comfort it brings, as the truth of God is revealed by

the Spirit. That is why prophecy " serveth for them which believe " (I. Cor. xiv. 22).

At the same time, we would urge those prophesying to pray for grace to deliver their messages as clearly and distinctly as possible, freed from unnecessary sounds by the lips that often attend such prophecies; and, if possible, a *ready flow of words,* instead of the broken and at times stammering utterances that are heard. When fear, anxiety, hesitation and unbelief are fully removed, we see no reason why the words should not flow freely and clearly over the lips of the speaker. Make this a subject of prayer.

May the Holy Spirit touch the *hearts* and *lips* of Christ's followers, making them as TONGUES OF FIRE! Then will unbelievers be convinced of sin as they enter the services of the saints, and falling on their faces, exclaim, " *God is among you indeed,*" and say, " *We will go with you, for we have heard* " and *seen* " *that*

**God is With You!** " (Zech. viii. 23).

AMEN!

" He that hath an ear, let him hear what the Spirit saith unto the Churches! "

———————

CHAPTER VIII.

# The Truth about the Pentecostal Revival, or Movement

THERE are very few papers, religious or secular, but what have had printed reports for or against the present revival that is now sweeping over the world. And judging from the bitter antagonism on the one hand, and the self-sacrificing enthusiasm and love for it on the other hand, every thoughtful person will come to the conclusion that the forces at work in this revival are of no ordinary character.

Personally, I claim to be in favour of this movement, and greatly indebted to it from the very first, even if in this, *as in all other revivals or movements,* there may have been made mistakes, and things arisen, here and there, that we have found necessary to check and withstand.

Numerous papers have placed my views in a false light, but I refer all to my book, *When the Fire Fell, and an Outline of My Life.*

### Personal Experience.

The first time I heard anything about this revival was in New York, America, toward the close of 1906.

I was in that country attempting to raise funds for the City Mission work of the Methodist Episcopal Church in Christiania (now Oslo), Norway. A new hall was to be erected there if I was successful. The statement made by the chief Missionary Secretary, Dr. Adna Leonard, of the Methodist Episcopal Church, that the time chosen for this tour to America was the worst we could have fixed on, proved only too true.

Although the Norwegian King allowed me to make use of his name in connection with this enterprise, which was also backed up with the endorsement of fifteen bishops and other leading men within the M.E. Church, the tour proved unsuccessful in a financial way.

But all this led to a deepening of my spiritual life. I had for twenty years taught the necessity of heart-cleansing, and the Baptism of the Holy Ghost, and had been wonderfully blessed of God in my labours. Now, I studied once more books and articles that covered the ground, especially the Bible. A copy of the paper *The Apostolic Faith,* fell into my hands, in which an account of the revival at Los Angeles was found, and the wonderful manifestations of the Holy Spirit in connection with it.

On comparing it with the Bible records, I found that the statements were correct, and that what the people there were enjoying *was the very blessing I was seeking.*

I wrote to them and received an answer from some friends there, corresponding exactly with the trend of thought in the paper. It would take too long to state all that transpired during those days in my inner life. Suffice it to say that on 7th October, when all alone in my little room in the " Alliance House " in New York, I RECEIVED THE BAPTISM OF THE HOLY GHOST, and five weeks later, at a prayer meeting with some friends, I RECEIVED the *Tongues* with an *increase of power* that convinced me I had received the Gift of the Holy Ghost as the disciples " at the beginning."

I then sailed for Norway. The account of my late experience had already appeared in *Byposten,* the City Mission paper I edited and had prepared to some extent the way for the revival in Scandinavia. It has since then appeared in a special pamphlet, entitled, " When the Fire Fell," and now the pamphlet has become a *book,* containing the story of my life, and especially God's dealings with me, after receiving the Baptism of the Holy Ghost.

When I reached Christiania I had no plan as to my future work; but I felt I must be perfectly free to be used of God and to be sent by Him to any field of labour He might choose for me. I accordingly resigned my position as *Superintendent of the " Christiania City Mission,"* and when the summer came, I asked for and obtained permission to withdraw from membership in the Annual Conference of the M. E. Church in Norway. The requests for a visit from various countries were so many, as well as from the towns and country places in Norway, that I had to take this step. I remained a member of the Methodist Church for some time, until I was baptised in water. I travelled in several countries in Europe, and visited India, Palestine and Syria, preaching this full gospel truth, until I settled down to *build up a Pentecostal Assembly in Oslo.* I have continued to help on the work elsewhere, as far as time and strength would allow, but rejoice to know, that the assembly in " Filadelfia " (the name of our hall), Oslo, is now the largest assembly of water and fire-baptised saints in Norway, and is the mother-assembly of the many assemblies that have sprung up throughout the country.

I became in this way thrust quite unexpectedly into a work that has now—over twenty years—claimed my full sympathy and labour. (Read my book: *When the Fire Fell and an Outline of My life.*).

### The Revival Spreading.

But I am only one of many, whom the Lord has led in this or a similar way. For, besides the fact that every Spirit-filled soul becomes a centre for this blessed work, there are now to be found numerous ministers, evangelists, and Christian workers, in various parts of the world, who have joined the Movement, besides the great army of preachers, evangelists and missionaries, *who have been raised amongst the Pentecostal friends.* Thousands of assemblies and churches have sprung up all over the world, and it may safely be said, that after the space of twenty years, the Movement is stronger and more effective than ever before. Hallelujah!

Mrs. ——, who wrote, at the commencement of the revival, in the *Christian* and elsewhere, denouncing it as a work of evil spirits, wrote to me personally, when I complained of her unqualified attacks, and said: "*Time will prove how true her statements are.*" But after twenty years of genuine trial, we say boldly, that time has proved that her attacks and the attacks of other leaders in Christendom, were not dictated by the Spirit of God!

In heathen lands, among missionaries, native preachers and evangelists, as well as among the people, this Holy Fire is spreading, and will do so increasingly. It may truthfully be said, that there has scarcely been any religious movement, since the days of the Apostles, that has sent forth so many missionaries, with the Gospel of Christ, within so short a time as twenty years. Surely this must be a clarion call to the world, preparing the way for the coming King!

How many have been baptised in the Holy Ghost and have spoken in tongues it is impossible to say. Thousands upon thousands of God's people, even if they have not as yet attained to their Pentecost, have been wonderfully blessed of God through this Movement. To these crowds must be added the untold thousands who have been saved. People amongst all classes of society, who no doubt would have been in their sins still, had it not been for this God-sent revival!

Countless homes have been brightened and transformed, and have become temples of the living God. And what about the marvellous miracles and healings that have taken place, and are constantly taking place. Sick people have been healed in great numbers. Old diseases have vanished before the healing touch of the Christ. Demons have been cast out of demon-possessed people, and the power of the Blood of Christ and His mighty Name have been felt by numbers of rejoicing souls as in Apostolic days. They are praising God because they are living in these glorious days, in which the *old-time Apostolic power is returning back to believers.*

Instead therefore of ruining and blighting the lives and the homes of people, as our opponents state, this revival is SENT BY GOD to promote the Kingdom of Jesus Christ.

I could occupy you with accounts from various countries of *what God is really doing,* but there will be little space for that in this book. Historical works have already been written by learned men on the subject, more or less favourable, but showing clearly the depth and breadth of this great work of God! And its saved and cleansed and baptised hosts are marching on, steadily and triumphantly, in the face of all opposition, determined to plant the banners of TRUTH wherever their Lord and Saviour sends them!

It will help you to understand the value of this work, I think, when you become acquainted with the *doctrines* taught, or the

### Teaching of The Movement.

There are of course many who still hold on to their denominations, who support it in various ways, as well as friends, who will have nothing to do with denominational life. It is not to be expected therefore, that all the friends of the Movement agree on all doctrines of religion.

But numbers have been obliged to leave their own denominations, just as myself, in order to devote themselves more fully to this great Movement. They have found, that *the general tenets of faith* (see chapter on "Spiritual Union") call for *their full and constant energy and devotion.* And having joined the Pentecostal friends, they have had to sever their connections with the denomination they belonged to formerly.

Although we thank God for the fraternal spirit shown by *real* Pentecostal friends towards other Christians, it was to be expected, that a revival of such dimensions, would lead up *to various forms of organisation.* This is a fact, and I for one, would have rejoiced to see the thousands of Pentecostal friends united on similar lines of organisation all over the world. But although that is not the case, Pentecostal friends form *one great army,* although they may be marching in different regiments. They have "ONE LORD, ONE FAITH, ONE BAPTISM."

They all believe in the authority of the Word of God, in Jesus Christ as their Saviour, Head and King. They are mostly all baptised in water, since believing, they all believe in the necessity of a clean heart and a holy life, in the possibility of being baptised in our day, as on the Day of Pentecost, *in the Holy Ghost,* and the greater number believe, that *tongues,* in connection with the baptism, is a *proof* of the presence of the Holy Ghost, and are to be expected *now* as at *first* in Jerusalem, or at least prophetic utterances and worship in the Spirit (Acts x. 46; xix. 6).

This teaching has been a thorn in the eyes of a good many teachers, not favourably disposed towards this Movement, but FACTS, as well as THE WORD OF GOD, prove the truth of it.

The *" gift " of tongues* that is to be retained, may not be given at the baptism, but marvellous utterances in tongues by the Spirit may be expected by *all.* They need not be sought, but are the natural fruit of the Spirit's presence within.

But *above all this* the NEW POWER imparted to live holy and fruitful LIVES, will be the result of the Fire falling on the altar within!

All the great truths *of any importance,* held by the evangelical denominations, are to be found in the tenets of this Movement, as well as this great truth concerning *the Baptism in the Holy Ghost,* and the signs following.

The good Lord is thus leading His people up to the position attained by the FIRST CHRISTIANS, that has been lost to a great extent during the darkness of bygone centuries. Praise His holy Name!

In the East we know there is the *" former rain," " the rain,"* and the *" latter rain."* Without the "latter rain" most of the seed sown would be destroyed, as the deluging showers of the "latter rain' are necessary to bring about the ripening of the fruit. It is this illustration the prophet Joel makes use of (Joel ii. 23), and also (Zech. x. 1), to illustrate the mighty outpouring of the Holy Ghost towards the close of this Dispensation. We believe that this is what has commenced *now*!

Of one thing we may rest assured, that is, that the human race is hastening on towards *stupendous changes* of some kind or other, and *this mighty outpouring of spiritual power ought therefore to be hailed with joy and thankfulness by* EVERY *child of God*. But this is not the case, I am sorry to say.

The same spirit of unbelief meets it at every point, as was the case with former revivals and religious movements sent by God!

The Lutheran Reformation carried the doctrine of "*Justification by Faith*" on its banner.

*How* was it met? History repeated itself. As when the disciples of Christ had to break away from much of Jewish tradition and teaching, and give a clearer definition of God and His dealings with men, whereof the Jewish Church with all its glory was but a shadow, and had therefore to force its way through Jewish hatred and Gentile scorn, so also Luther, in order to gain and restore to Christianity one of its chief doctrines, had to run the gauntlet of church hatred and the sneers of the world. But by the grace of God he conquered.

And when Wesley, heading the Methodist Revival, not only made this teaching of Luther's a reality in the lives of thousands, but with men like John Fletcher, Charles Wesley, and others, taught and sang of the

"*Beauty of Holiness*" in strong discourses and heaven-sent hymns and songs, and lived it out in their lives, *how* were they met? The churches rose against them, and the worldly masses were only too glad to be backed up by these churches in their hatred against a revival that upset the plans and devices of the Devil with such mighty power.

The doctrine of *Divine Healing,* so plainly set forth in the Bible, has also to a great extent been met with contempt by the churches, much to the delight of agnostics and rationalists.

### Attitude of the Churches.

And now, when God is teaching, or seeking to teach the Christian World, the necessity of *obtaining power for service,* through the Baptism of the Holy Ghost, and by the free distribution of His glorious gifts, *what* is the attitude of the churches? Often that of contempt and ridicule, making one of the most glorious and most needed truths in the Bible the target of derision in the world.

Of course the teaching concerning the Baptism of the Holy Ghost has won some influence in various centres in church life ere this.

Great leaders of the Christian churches, such as Finney, Edwards, Bramwell, Moody, and many others, had experienced it and spoke about it, and by some groups of Christians it was taught as a necessity for *all* who would go on with the Lord. In other circles it has been supposed to be the blessing received in *Sanctification.* Some again have taught that it might be attained without Sanctification of any degree, *opposing the possibility of attaining a clean heart.*

God has, fortunately for His Church, in great mercy done far above all that His people could think or ask for.

But the doctrine of the *Baptism of the Holy Ghost in connection with tongues and other gifts of the Spirit,* has not been so prominent in any age before, since the days of the Apostles, as it is now.

But, like every other truth in the Bible, it has to pass through the fire of criticism and scorn.

This, however, will not injure it. I feel and believe, that honest discussion about the matter cannot destroy the truth. And it is clearly seen that the very means used by Satan to stop this work of God has helped it up to a higher stage of development and strength.

God outwits the Devil always, and defeats his plans, where He can find willing and obedient hearts to follow the standard of truth.

### The Speaking in Tongues as a Proof of the Baptism.

Let me again lay stress on the fact, that although there are other evidences of the indwelling Spirit, it is clearly stated in Acts that the Apostles, when *tongues* were heard in Jerusalem and Cæsarea, considered this to be A SURE SIGN OF THE BAPTISM OF THE HOLY GHOST. No one can read the account given in the tenth chapter of Acts with a fair mind and doubt this. Still I believe that many have had, and that people may obtain in our day mighty baptisms *without this sign.* This arises then, as we have seen, mainly from *ignorance* of the subject, *prejudice, unbelief,* or some other cause. Of course, their experience will not then, as far as *this outward sign is concerned,* be perfectly similar to that recorded in Acts ii., x. and xix. And in fact we believe that the two other cases recorded in Acts of the FIRST infilling of the Spirit—at Samaria and Damascus —(there are five in all) give ample proof that *tongues were present.*

The Holy Ghost may nevertheless set up His throne within in mighty power where tongues have not been heard. This is seen from the lives and works of many. But the "TONGUES"—the *wonderfully strengthening evidence* of the Divine presence within, has then, by some means or other, been suppressed or cut off. The *assurance*, the *joy*, the *strength* that accompanies them, is indescribable. And they may evidently be expected by *all* as AN EVIDENCE OF THE INDWELLING SPIRIT, although all may not retain them as a "GIFT." No wonder they were so coveted by the early Christians.

What surprises me then is, that so many churches close their doors and their hearts against a revival *that certainly teaches what is found in the Bible, and what the first Christians thanked God for.*

If I could find that the churches of our day were *better* than the first churches, that they exhibited *more love to God, more love to men,* and *more power in their inner life* and *evangelistic work,* I should be inclined to say that we were so far ahead of the first churches, in the most important thing, that we need not consider seriously the lack of spiritual gifts, that adorned the Bride of Christ in the first Christian ages.

But this is so far from being the case, that the Christian churches of our day are *in most cases* far below the standard. There is grandeur, worldly influence, temporal power, fine culture, great educational facilities, but *where* is the power that made the preaching of the Cross of Jesus in the days of the apostles *shake the world?*

I would not discard the good that is *being done* by the churches, but generally there is a dearth and a want of *spiritual* power that is simply astounding. It has also been felt by many. Prayer circles have been formed, inspiring circulars issued, and a *mighty cry has gone forth to God for help.* His answer has been the revivals of late years, and now especially THIS REVIVAL, WHICH IS REALLY THE REVIVAL MOVEMENT OF THE TWENTIETH CENTURY. It has already belted the globe with the red light of Pentecostal glory, and kindled flaming fires in many parts of the world. But sad to say, the churches generally are opposing it. It comes with the *same signs as in the first Christian Church,* and yet it is opposed by Christians of to-day. *Where* are we? *What* is to be thought of such blindness and wondrous slowness of heart to apprehend God's call and His Day of Visitation.

Of course *we know the answer.* Fingers are pointed at the " *manifestations* " and the " *tongues* "; fingers of derision.

Learned professors try to explain away the " phenomena " on scientific grounds. Leading physicians and the directors of Insane Asylums say openly that the whole thing is an insane freak of the mind. Noted theologians tell us, unable to talk away the *fact of* " tongues " as having existed in the Church, that " tongues," as well as all supernatural gifts belong to *the inaugurating period of the Church and not to ours.* Wise heads—you would think wiser than the Holy Spirit Himself—say we do not need them in our day. *As if the Holy Spirit does not know what He is about!*

Many Christian leaders, mistaking cases of hypnotism and suggestive influence for Satanic counterfeits, have stamped the whole thing as from the Devil. Of course we allow that there have been Satanic counterfeits in this, as *in all religious movements;* but much of what has been ascribed to the Devil has been caused by *human* influence, and often by the heated brains and minds of *those condemning the work,* I mean by the would-be exorcists themselves.

Newspapers, pamphlets, tracts, have contained the most incensed condemnation of the whole thing. Theatres have acted it out; hypnotists, spiritualists, theosophists, scientists, and many other " ists " have been unanimous in their condemnation—but after all said and done *here we are* with brighter hopes than ever, with a clearer perception of the Divine leading in all this, and a *firmer assurance than ever* before THAT THIS IS OF GOD, no matter what mistakes have been made, or what excesses some have run into; " THIS IS THAT SPOKEN OF BY THE PROPHET JOEL," HALLELUJAH !

But just take an article like that written in the May number of *The Vanguard,* by Baron Porcelli. It illustrates very forcibly the lack of discrimination in the mind of some people.

The article commences thus :—

" The present wave of spiritual manifestations emanates from Los Angeles, in America, the home of all such movements. It was America that began the Spiritualistic craze, the Mesmeric craze, the Hypnotic craze, the Theosophic craze, the Christian Science craze, the Mormon craze, the Latter House of Israel craze, the Dowie craze, the Faith Healing craze, the Holiness craze, the Spiritual Gifts craze, and the Tongues craze." And we might continue and say the Finney craze, the Moody craze, the Torrey and Alexander craze, etc., and in order to give it the mixed touch of Baron Porcelli, say, the Ingersol or infidel craze, the Bible-destruction craze, etc. He mixes up things in very much the same way as do the " Humanitarians " in Hyde Park, who, on their great banner classify Jehovah, Jesus, and even the Holy Ghost with the gods of the heathen.

In that one article numerous mistakes are made, proving that the writer is not acquainted with the subject, or that he is so blinded by the *opposition craze* that he cannot see the truth. The greatest mistake of all was the statement that this revival comes from Los Angeles, whereas we all know that IT CAME FROM HEAVEN!

But we are prepared for persecution, we will delight to suffer for the Lord, who has bought us. We are perfectly assured that the teachings *being those taught by the Apostles,* our tribulations are caused by *similar evil powers that oppose them.* So we look beyond men in this warfare, and say with Paul, " we wrestle not against flesh and blood, but against principalities, against powers, against the rulers of the darkness of this world, against spiritual wickedness in high places " (Eph. vi. 12).

So when the visible agencies of the dark invisible world point their fingers at us in derision and wrath, *we* point to the Word of God, the precious Bible, and say—

YOU WILL FIND IT ALL THERE!

And we are determined, God helping us, to stand by the Word of God, even in these days, when some theologians only seem to have the coverings of their Bibles left.

### Why Oppose?

To those who are opposing the whole thing because of the *excesses of some and the counterfeits of Satan* that may have taken place here and there, I wish to put the question: Have there *never* been any excesses of *any kind in your church?* Have there been no *counterfeits* of the Devil there? And if so do you want us to discard or undervalue your church on that account?

Even Holiness-teachers are condemning this *whole movement as " of the Devil."* Surely holiness ought to teach them to obtain satisfactory proof of it before such statements are made, and if they honestly make a thorough investigation into the lives of thousands of God-fearing men and women, who are enthusiastic in their devotion to this cause, they will find that their judgment of them has *been lacking in brotherly love.*

A statement by one who has been very cautious in his relation to this revival, I mean the world-wide known President of the " Christian and Missionary Alliance," Dr. A. B. Simpson, proves what I say. In his comments on this Movement in one of his Annual Reports, he said : " We believe there can *be no doubt* that in many cases remarkable outpourings of the Holy Spirit have been accompanied with *genuine instances of the gift of tongues,* and many extraordinary manifestations. This has occurred both in our own land and in some of our foreign missions. Many of these experiences appear *not only to be genuine, but accompanied by a spirit of deep humility and soberness, and free from extravagance and error.* And it is admitted that in many of the branches and States where this movement has been strongly developed and wisely directed, there has been a *marked deepening of the spiritual life of our members, and an encouraging increase in their missionary zeal and liberality.* It would therefore be a *serious matter* for any *candid* Christian to pass a wholesale criticism or condemnation upon such movements, *or presume to limit the Holy One of Israel."*

A minister, not in favour of this revival, said to me personally, " I must acknowledge that it is generally the *most devoted and Christ-like of God's people* in the various churches who are drawn into this revival." And he was right. But why is this? Because *they find the nourishment their souls are seeking for in it*, and feel that this is *God's voice* to them and His Church in these days.

### Why Forbid Tongues? The Evidence of Scripture.

Now with regard to *tongues,* why are they to be ignored and discarded? They were reserved for the great Pentecostal outpouring in Jerusalem and this age of the dispensation of the Spirit, all the other gifts, save the interpretation of tongues, being in the Church of God before Pentecost. The *tongues* are, says Paul, for personal edification, but also a means of edification to the Church, when interpretation is given. They are a " sign " to unbelievers, they are given to " profit " thereby, they are to be " desired " and to be expected in the meetings where the Spirit has the right of way. They may be the tongues of " angels " as well as of men. Paul says all this concerning tongues, and thanks God that he was able to speak *more in tongues than they all.*

He points out, too, that they were *to remain in the Church* until the *perfection of heaven is reached* (I. Cor. xiii.), a perfection we all know is never attained by mortals on earth. The tongues were, therefore *to last continuously in the Church.*

He expresses the same thought in I. Cor. i. 7, where he commends the Corinthians for *" coming behind in no gift, waiting for the coming of our Lord Jesus Christ."* In this spirit then the whole Church ought ever to await the Bridegroom. For the " gifts," Paul says (Rom. xi. 29), and calling of God are *without repentance.*

God, therefore, having determined that these gifts should accompany the Spirit's work in and through the Christian Church, He has NEVER since altered His purpose or repented of it, and no theologian can find a sentence in the New Testament to prove that He intended to withdraw His gifts.

As they have not been in use in the Church, to the extent God intended them to be, *it is surely not God's fault;* it is caused by the unbelief and indifference of the Church. Still, there is reason to believe, that as the days of the " latter rain " have commenced, we may expect the gifts as extensively now, if not more so, than in the period of the " former rain."

Nowhere do we find that Paul ignores this gift. In I. Cor. xiv., where he says, " in the Church I had rather speak five words with my understanding, that by my voice I might teach others also, than ten thousand words in an unknown tongue," he only illustrates the necessity of *interpretation* of the tongue spoken, if there is to be any edification for the Church. He therefore says just before this : " Wherefore let him that speaketh in unknown tongues pray that he may *interpret.*"

In I. Cor. xii. *tongues* are given a place among the special gifts of the Spirit, and he commences the chapter by saying, " Concerning spiritual gifts, brethren, I would not have you ignorant."

I wonder if he foresaw the ignorance of many in this Twentieth Century concerning these gifts.

We notice also that in the sub-divisions he makes in this catalogue of gifts, *tongues* belong to the celestial gifts, linking us on as it were to heaven.

In the 14th chapter he says : " *forbid not to speak with tongues.*"

All Christian churches to-day, therefore, who are forbidding their members to speak with tongues are TRANSGRESSING THE VERY WORD OF GOD, which they say they hold so dear. Paul says, just before this command, "If a man think himself to be a prophet or spiritual let him acknowledge that the things that I write unto you, are the *commandments of the Lord.*" (verse 37).

In the 13th chapter, he speaks of Love as the necessary background for all gifts. " Love of truth, love that seeketh not her own, is not easily provoked, thinketh no evil, rejoiceth not in iniquity, that suffereth long, is kind, envieth not, vaunteth not itself, is not puffed up, beareth all things, believeth all things, hopeth all things, endureth all things, never faileth,"—with this background we are safe.

Let the gifts pass through the holy flames of this fire, and there will be no excesses, no counterfeits.

Now, if these gifts of the Spirit, as it is claimed, HAD EXPENDED THEIR POWER *in the days of the Apostles,* how is it they were found at a later period?

### The Evidence of Church History.

Church history proves satisfactorily, as we have already seen (chapter on " Tongues of Fire "), that they extended beyond the Third Century, and that it was when the churches began to attain great temporal power that the spiritual power waned, and the *real* gifts were suppressed.

The same is the case to-day. Churches have become wealthy and worldly. Christians are seeking the honour of the ungodly and unsaved people around them. The *spiritual* power has dwindled down to nothing, they have the *name of Christ* on their foreheads, but their *hearts* are full of worldliness and sin. They quite naturally *oppose all vital Christianity!* But history proves nevertheless, that there has always been a remnant that has held on to the Lord and sought His power and grace, and as a result, the spiritual " gifts " have existed up through the ages. This fact refutes the statement made, that they were confined to the Apostolic days.

We find, as formerly stated, ever since the Lutheran Reformation, that these gifts have been very prominent in some great revivals and that the peculiar manifestations, such as shakings, jerkings, twistings, tremblings and prostrations of the body were very common in the Quaker movement at its commencement, in Puritan Revivals; so also in the great Methodist Revival on both sides of the Atlantic, and in the revivals under Finney, the Irish Revival, and even in the last Welsh Revival, to some extent, under Evan Roberts. Even these manifestations are of the Christian Church.

During the revival under the Carmisards in the Cevennes, as we have seen, we find the *"gift of tongues,"* and the prophetic teaching was mighty. The people, young and old, spoke under the power of the Spirit in a way that would have been impossible for them to do, had it not been for the Divine power that filled them and illuminated their minds, as the contents of their messages and the mode of deliverance was far above their ordinary way of thinking and speaking.

Of course the Church opposed all this, and, assisted by the secular powers, tried to stop it.

But the murders committed by the authorities, the imprisonments and torments they subjected these God-fearing people to, were all in vain. Their faith in God could not be quenched. Persecution brought them nearer their Master, and made them more like Him.

The so-called Inspiration Movement, an offshoot in a way of this, swept over various parts of Germany, Switzerland, and other countries. The same manifestations were everywhere present.

We have seen then, how movements, similar to the Pentecostal Revival, especially as far as the spiritual gifts are concerned, have sprung up even after the Lutheran Reformation, and that from the days of the Apostles until the Fourth Century God spoke in THIS way to and through His people. *These are facts!*

In the time intervening the Fourth Century and the Lutheran Reformation, the genuine supernatural gifts of the Spirit WERE SUPPRESSED BY THE CHURCH. But how many of the so-called heretics during that time enjoyed the fulness of the Spirit, and were endued with Spiritual gifts? No doubt thousands upon thousands!

### Was Paul Mad?

Knowing all this and the teachings of the Apostles, especially Paul's, our opponents have had no other door of escape than by declaring Paul to be an epileptic.

But this has never, and can never be proved. The strong desire to find this weak point in the mighty apostle's career has led them to make the statement. The wish has been father of the assertion.

But of course *if that was the reason* why he spake in tongues, then *Peter, James, John, and the rest of the apostles were epileptics as well.* All, about 120, who spoke in tongues at Pentecost, must have been epileptics. And if the 3,000 were, as is believed by many theologians, baptised by the Holy Ghost, then the first great day of the Christian Church has merely recorded *an epileptic epidemic.* That is also the conclusion a writer in a Danish paper lately arrived at.

Then the marvellous outpouring of the Holy Ghost at Cæsarea merely resulted in increasing the crowd of epileptics; so also was the case at Samaria and Ephesus. And the Church at Corinth must have been crazy in the extreme, and worst of them all—Paul, the great Apostle of the Gentiles, as he thanks God in his letter to the Corinthians, *that he spoke more in tongues than they all.*

Then all the first Christian Church was epileptic or insane. But I say calmly, that men who imbibe such thoughts as that, had better examine their own bearings before they proceed further.

One writer in Denmark said that he thought it was not a subject for the Church or theologians to debate at all, but for the DOCTORS.

Well, nothing would delight me more, if they will only do it the same way as did the Apostles. *Let them have a ten-days' prayer meeting about it.* Because no one can judge of this as those who have had the *experience.* I would be delighted if all the doctors in America and England, and throughout Europe, would *get down on their knees and ask God about it.* I am sure of one thing, when they get through with *ten days of earnest prayer,* they will get a different view of the subject than many of them have at present.

Is it so difficult to suppose that the great Maker of the human harp can play on it at will, when left fully to His control?

### Is It Not Possible for God to Use Our Vocal Organs?

If we have any thought of the possibility of *God's connecting Himself with us*—God, our Maker—in any way, must it be absolutely beyond the realm of possibility *for Him to influence our bodies so as to make us speak in " tongues "?* The Bible, at any rate, sees no difficulty in this. It represents God as the supreme Spirit, able to do whatever He pleases. Of course in the case of man He has made him responsible for every action in life, and given him power even to resist His own mighty Will. But where that will is subjected to God's and the human instrument is tuned to the Divine Will, is it quite impossible to receive messages from the heavenly sphere? Who some little time ago would have thought of the possibility of wireless? Now it is an every-day occurrence.

Then cannot God in some way influence the spirit, and through that agency the human mind and body? God is not so distant and far away, as some believe!

The Bible teaches that *we* are to become temples of the Holy Spirit (I. Cor. iii.). Temples of the living God. The Spirit dwelling WITHIN US! Then, if this Spirit has taken up His abode there, as we believe, is it an impossible thought, that He might influence our inner spirit wherein He dwells, and make His influence felt, touching our soul-life, and swaying our physical being as well, which has been made over to Him?

Those who have been baptised have *felt* His inner presence, they *know* He is within! Is it then impossible for that Divine inner Being to touch our vocal cords, and make us speak words and truths He Himself desires to hear pass over our lips?

And is it absurd to suppose that He will *so fill us* with His Divine glory, joy and peace and love, that it will beam through our faces, kindle a heavenly light in our eyes, and make us burst forth in rapturous praises and adoration to our everlasting King?

Is it impossible for this glorious Being so to illuminate the mind. that it becomes lit up with new and fresh thoughts of God and His will, and receives words through this holy influence to express these thoughts in a way that far surpasses the ordinary culture and thought of the recipient?

Certainly not. The Bible attests the fact in numerous places, that this is possible, *and our* OWN *experience proves the Bible is true.* In tongues and in prophecy this has often taken place.

Why then try to limit God's influence over the mind and heart-life and body-life of the human being?

It is a false statement when Baron Porcelli says that "The essential basis root of all these manifestations is what is termed shibboleth, 'surrender of self'; or in accurate English, *the surrender of one's will to that of another.*"

*None of us use hypnotic methods* to undermine the will of another. We claim, or rather the Bible claims, the subjection of our will *to that of* GOD!

"*Yield yourselves* unto God," says Paul, "as those that are alive from the dead, and your members as instruments of righteousness unto God." *But neither God nor we ever deprived seekers of their* WILL-POWER.

In subjecting themselves to the will of God they in their heart and will-life rise against all known sin within, and seek *cleansing through the Atonement* (Heb. x. 14; I. John i. 7; II. Cor. vi. 14-18; vii. 1, 5, 14-17). They are then ready to receive the Holy Spirit within —an abiding Comforter. And this takes place *now as in the first Christian Age,* either directly as on Pentecost in Jerusalem, or by the laying on of hands, as at Ephesus. That is God's own method, and *we have no right to slight it.*

Of course physicians know that there are cases in which people have spoken in foreign tongues when delirious, or under some operation on the brain by the surgeon. Or when the speaker is under hypnotic influence. They therefore judge that this must be similar. Cells of the brain under high nervous pressure emit words or sentences, stored up there some time before.

We do not deny the possibility of this at all. But it merely proves that there is a means, a channel, in the human being, whereby God, if He chose, may speak through us. If caused by mere accident, then there would never be any order in what is spoken, the message would have *no address*. But facts prove the opposite.

### Instances of the Speaking in Known Tongues Through the Holy Spirit.

I could relate numerous cases. Take the case in India, already mentioned, which was related by several missionaries, and about which I obtained a written statement from the missionary on the station where it took place. Two native women, one deaf and dumb from childhood, often spoke in the Hindustani language perfectly, as the Spirit gave utterance, although they were perfectly unacquainted with that language, and had been taken from mission station to mission station to speak to the Mohammedans, whose language it was, in that way.

Take the case in Sarpsborg, Norway, where a lady entering the Methodist Church was spoken to in her own language by a person who knew nothing of the language in which he spoke, nor anybody else present, save the lady to whom the message was given. I have this from the pastor of the church, on whom she called the next day for an explanation, and from the man himself who gave the message. He did not even know he was speaking to her. His eyes were shut when speaking, but his hands were extended towards her.

A Baptist preacher in my hearing related, in a meeting in Norway, that a lady, not knowing the English language, had spoken perfectly in this language, and given a clear translation of what she had been speaking.

In Copenhagen, Denmark, a man who opposed this movement, was convinced God was in it, when he one day heard his sister praise God in the Spanish language, and give a correct interpretation of what she was speaking, although she did not know the language. He himself had been in Spain and knew it. He gave himself fully to God, as he understood it was God who had spoken in this miraculous way.

From America we have many well-authenticated cases. The following was given to the editor of the religious paper, entitled *The Household of God,* by Lewis Rudner, a Jew, born in Austria, and 26 years of age.

He stated that he had spoken the Hebrew language from his childhood, and had been in America six years, and was working for his rich uncle in Seattle, Washington. He said furthermore: "On a Thursday last winter, I was passing a mission building in Seventh Avenue in that city on a rainy day, and saw a sign ' *Welcome* ' over the door, and entered to get out of the rain, not knowing what was being done inside. All were kneeling in prayer. Shortly I heard a man (brother Junk, the preacher) repeating the fifty-third chapter of Isaiah in the Hebrew language. A woman (brother Junk's wife) was singing a song in Hebrew, which Jews sing on their New Year's Day. A little girl, twelve years old, on her knees, was repeating the twelfth Psalm in Hebrew, then she repeated the sixth

Psalm. A coloured woman (Mrs. Miller from Los Angeles) commenced repeating part of the thirty-fifth chapter of Jeremiah in Hebrew. A Scandinavian woman (Mrs. Olson) spoke in Hebrew, pointing at me, telling me that I was lost, and urging me to turn to God. And all this was during prayer." The Jew found tears flowing down his cheeks. After prayer they all commenced singing " The Old Foundation," which broke his heart.

Hearing all this Hebrew talk, he commenced to wonder where he was. He saw it was not a Synagogue, and the people were not Jews. Then brother Junk preached in English from the text, " His blood be upon us and upon our children," and said that great darkness fell on the earth when Jesus died on the Cross, and that the Jews were scattered throughout the world, and have had no rest since.

After preaching, Mrs. Olson testified in Hebrew, and told the Jew to read Luke xv., Rom. v. 8 and iii. 26. The twelve-year old girl testified in Hebrew, and asked him again and again where he would spend eternity. This brought him into great concern about his soul. The altar call was made, and brother Junk came to him, and taking him by the hand, urged him to come and be saved.

The Jew asked the preacher, Mr. Junk, if he was a Hebrew, to which he replied, " I am a German." The Jew asked Junk if he had studied Hebrew, and he replied " No."

" How then can you speak Hebrew? " " Did I speak Hebrew? " " Yes," said the Jew, " just such Hebrew as persons speak who are born and raised Hebrews in my country."

Then Junk told the Jew that it was God who was

speaking to him and saying what *He* wanted to say. The Jew asked who these other persons were that had spoken in Hebrew, pointing them out. He asked if the little girl was Junk's daughter, and desired to speak with her. Brother Junk called the woman to come and sit down by the Jew, and immediately the Spirit of the Lord was upon them, and they all began to speak in Hebrew, urging him to give his heart to Christ and be saved. This sudden outburst startled the Jew, and made him very nervous. They urged him to kneel down and pray. *But all spoke in Hebrew,* not knowing a word they spoke, crying to God for mercy. This praying lasted over an hour, the Jew, crying out so loud, he could be heard a block away. He was converted to God and is now a happy Christian.

Mr. Gilbert E. Farr relates that when he attended a mission in Houston, Texas, a young man spoke for five minutes or more in a foreign tongue, under the power of the Spirit. When the invitation was given for seekers to come forward to the altar, a Mexican came forward, weeping, and in broken English, said, "I sinner, I Catholic, I no Christian; woman spoke Spanish, said I sinner, no Christian, God said I repent. Pray I be saved." They prayed with the man, and he became happy, and gave good evidence of salvation.

Mr. Farr states furthermore, that he in Pueblo, Colorado, saw more forcibly the value of tongues in foreign languages than in any other mission visited. At the Bessemer Steel Mills several thousand men are employed, and more than twenty nationalities are represented among them. As most of them are Roman Catholics, the priests forbid them to attend the meetings. But they will stand on the street and listen to the workers as they sing and speak in tongues. There were Greeks, Poles, Russian, Chinese, etc., *and to each of these groups messages were given in tongues, perfectly understood by them, so that it was here as in Jerusalem on the Day of Pentecost.* These different nationalities heard the messages of God in their own language wherein they were born.

Dr. A. B. Simpson, of New York, relates a case in his paper of a lady, the wife of a Baptist pastor, who, under the power of the Spirit, was able to converse in the German language, although she had not known that language before.

In Wales a young man spoke the Welsh language fluently to a friend, stating at the same time that he was in debt, relating also all the circumstances in connection with it. He knew nothing of the language or the debt before it was revealed to him by the Spirit. Three men are witnesses to this fact.

In Sweden a Lutheran pastor lectured on his visit to Christiania, after the outbreak of the revival there. He stated that he personally heard a young woman speak the Finnish language perfectly, when she was under the power of the Spirit. He asked her several questions in that language after, but she could not understand a word, only when the power of the Holy Spirit was upon her. He had laboured several years in Finland, and knew the language well.

Thus I could go on, but if these statements do not convince it is useless to cite more; but we are perfectly assured that as the work increases, there will in all countries be abundant evidence of the fact *that the Holy Spirit knows all languages,* and is able to speak these through His believing people.

**Not Intended to Usurp the Ordinary Study of Languages.**

Still we would point out the fact that the speaking

in tongues does not seem to have been intended to usurp the ordinary study of languages. We have already seen the use they were intended for, as stated by the Apostle Paul. Their chief object on the Day of Pentecost was that of givi g Peter's sermon *a miraculous background,* and invest the disciples *with Divine authority.* This no doubt is one of the chief objects for which God uses them now. *The correct translation of the message in tongues* is also a proof of the Divine inspiration.

Many at the meetings who have heard both the tongues and the translations have given their testimony to the fact that both were correct.

### It Is Strengthening and Vitalising.

It is FALSE to suppose that those speaking in tongues, when genuine, are *weakened* by the effort. The special flow of Divine power through the body, causing the tongues, is always vitalising and refreshing.

A sudden flow of the Holy Spirit's power through the mental and physical being, as well as the spirit, is *always followed by a greater vitality and strength,* just the opposite of insane and epileptic shocks. So the doctors who talk of insanity and epilepsy in this connection do not know what they are talking about.

### Warning Necessary.

But we would have it remembered that some people are apt to run into excesses, even in connection with religious movements, not taking *necessary rest for the body.* Too much fasting, too little sleep, will soon weaken the system, and may cause physical disorder, even insanity, as may an unbiblical and a continued working up of soulish and fleshly feelings, either in company with others, or when alone, *substituting this for the won-*

*drous workings in our being by the Holy Spirit.* This we warn against!

Then we believe that EVIL POWERS are always trying to exert their influence on mind, spirit, and body, in a way similar to the Holy Spirit's work, and they are at times successful. The Bible says, "*Satan entered Judas*" (John xiii. 27). And in Luke xi. Jesus states the case of an evil spirit entering man with seven other spirits more wicked than himself, "and they enter in, and DWELL there: and the last state of that man is worse than the first."

When the MOTIVES OF PEOPLE, in seeking some special "GIFT," are *not pure,* then Satan with his awful subtlety may do much harm. Remember Simon wanting to buy the power of transmitting the Holy Ghost. Peter said, "Thy money perish with thee . . . thou art in the gall of bitterness." And when Ananias and Sapphira tried to deceive the Church by retaining part of what had been promised God, "Peter said, 'Why hath Satan filled thine heart?'" A "lying spirit" has been at work in some cases that have appeared, and when it has not been discerned, has caused scorn and ridicule.

Instead of *examining the "voices,"* and *comparing the messages heard with the* BIBLE, people have been led to do just the opposite of what the Bible teaches them.

### Let Criticism be Fair and Logical.

Our first parents fell by listening to the seductive voice of the enemy, and since their day similar cases have been "legion." But who will dare to blame Paul at Ephesus, because the demon-possessed man tore the clothes off the backs of the would-be exorcists, and drove them naked and bleeding out on the streets? As this took place in the same town and at the time of the revival there, if we are to judge cases as some do now, then Paul was to blame. No doubt many present-day opponents *would have called him insane.*

Festus, even in his day, when Paul made his defence before Agrippa, said with a loud voice that he was "*mad,*" just because he could not understand the phenomena in connection with the movement (Acts xxvi. 24-25).

But Jesus had prepared His servants for all this. He said, " the disciple is not above his Master, nor the servant above the Lord. It is enough for the disciple that he be as his Master, and the servant as his Lord. *If they have called the Master of the house Beelzebub, how much more shall they call them of His household*" (Matt. x. 24-25).

But it is nevertheless FALSE and UNJUST of the opponents to accuse honest and upright men and women as *insane* or *mad,* merely because they do not understand the phenomena arising, or accuse them of things they have never taught or brought about, but always opposed.

Who dares to blame Luther or leaders down through the ages, within the Church that bears his name, for all the fleshly excesses and cases of insanity that have taken place in their midst? Or Zwingle and his followers for similar cases within the Reformed Church? Or Wesley and his preachers for counterfeits and excesses within the Methodist Church?

And who dares to blame a Movement which strongly advocates *the gospel of goodwill and peace toward men, and brotherly love,* and *does its best to benefit mankind, with God's very best,* a movement whose *only* object is *to lift humanity to a higher level of Christ-like living and acting?* Who dares, I say, blame this movement, or its leaders, because of the excesses of some people?

Where is the sharp reasoning of our critics, who give way to such an illogical and false, and awful attack on people who are benefiting society with their prayers, their holy lives, and their burning desire to do what is right always, and in every place?

Let us be watchful against anything that cannot be supported by Holy Writ, and guard against it; but let us also be open to all the sacred influences of God's Holy Spirit.

Surely these are not times for indifference and indolence in religious matters. Enemies of the Christian religion are doing their best to undermine it. Let us not split on minor and unimportant things, but rally round the old standard of truth and liberty, the *Standard of Jesus Christ!*

**Let His Spirit Unite Us as One Great Army in This Holy War!**

Someone has said, " United we stand, divided we fall." Let then all the friends of Christ do their best to hasten on the fulfilment of His prayer *"that they may all be one,"* and the progress of His glorious Kingdom. That is the object God has in view by launching the Revival of the Twentieth Century. He desires to *raise a people* representing Christ and His principles, a people that in very truth may be the " salt of the earth."

Think of the souls saved, the numerous Christians whose lives have been renewed! The marvellous cases of Divine healing that are taking place all around the world! The *power of the Blood* and the Name of Jesus has been demonstrated right gloriously. Tongues, prophecies, have been mightily used of God. Old secret sins have been disclosed and brought to view, and sinners have confessed to the truth of the statements made.

Numbers of old backsliders have been reclaimed, and one thing not to be forgotten is the renewed preaching that is taking place in circles where this revival is not tolerated, *even concerning the subjects we chiefly preach.* There have been a far greater amount of preaching of late concerning Sanctification, the Baptism of the Holy Ghost, Divine Healing, and the Coming of our Lord, and much more written about it in periodicals and papers than formerly. This proves that this revival is stirring things to a deeper extent than people think or realise.

Our opponents are constantly underrating the " tongues " and other manifestations that have arisen in connection with the movement, and are looking out for mistakes as flies seek sores on the back of a horse. Let them do so if they will; the work goes on victoriously nevertheless.

We do not lay the chief stress on the gifts. We thank God for every gift the Bride of Christ is being adorned with, but to us the GREAT MORAL INFLUENCE of this revival, THE GREAT MIGHTY SPIRITUAL IMPETUS it gives, *is of far greater importance.* The gifts are merely the channels through which this spiritual influence may radiate to others. No wonder the Movement is hated by men of the world. The claim Christ makes *of full subjection to His will* is urged with great strength at our meetings. All forms of immorality, vice, and sin are dealt with unsparingly. Those who build their villas and palaces on the moral ruin of their fellow-men, come under condemnation, so do those whose lives are going down in a whirlpool of gluttonous and reckless living.

But the gospel of salvation is held forth with the tenderness and warmth of Christ-like love to all who are willing to forsake their evil ways, and accept redemption *through the Blood of Jesus Christ.*

It matters little that the revival is despised. *When did God ever start a great work but what it was despised* by carnal-minded men and women? It would have been the real sign of a counterfeit if all had accepted it. As it is now we see that scorn and contempt is hurled against this movement by the world. Nominal Christians, misled by false statements, and not sharp-sighted enough to look beyond counterfeits to find the *genuine* work done, are in the opposition ranks.

One brother said quite lately: " I will have nothing to do with these speakers in tongues." Poor fellow! I wonder how he would fare in heaven then if he gets there. He would not have much to do with the Apostles and the early Christians, and he would keep a good way off from Paul, who spoke in tongues *more than they all.* But such talk is the result of blindness and we forgive them willingly.

Little by little the opposition is crumbling to pieces; the work goes on, the waters are running deeper and deeper, as those in the vision of Ezekiel xlvii., " *Death is being conquered by life,* trees of life are growing on either side of the river, and the ' fruits ' are for meat, and the leaves thereof for medicine."

Let me then encourage the friends of this revival. Keep faithful to the Word of God, stand aloof from every unsound method of teaching, honour the blood of Jesus Christ, give glory to His great Name alone, then by His power victory is sure.

We are on the winning side! Our Captain is JESUS! Angels encamp around us! His Holy Spirit gives strength and grace for each day! And soon we shall, if faithful, see the King in His glory! Let us therefore keep in the Spirit of

### Love!

Every attack of the enemy will then be met with all the fortitude and boldness necessary, and our own spirits be kept pure and noble. Those who have truth on their side need not be anxious. "The battle is the Lord's!" Let us not be dismayed, but go singing to the battle, as did the army of Jehoshaphat (II. Chron. xx.) and serve the Lord in the *"beauty of holiness!"*

CHAPTER IX.

# The Baptism in the Holy Ghost for Children

"Suffer the Little Children to Come Unto Me" (Mark x. 14).

AN old Roman veteran was one day watching a great procession pass by. As the leaders of the people passed him he said to himself, "Who will take care of Rome when these are gone?" And as each separate column passed by the same thought arose in his mind, until he became quite down-hearted. Then suddenly he heard the rush of quick footsteps and happy, joyful voices, and a stream of bright-faced boys and girls went singing by him, and the old man was comforted. "Ah," said he, "there is the hope of Rome!"

The day is coming, dear children, if Jesus does not come before that, when papa and mamma, and all those you look up to now will have passed by the mile-stone of time, and entered into the glory-land, then, no doubt, many of you will still be here and must fill the empty places.

We know this to be true, and therefore we want you to be so full of the love of Jesus and His Spirit, that we may be sure you will flood the world with His light and glory.

I heard of a boy whose parents lived in one of the back streets in London, who attended Sunday School once. They told him about Jesus, washed his face and made him look tidy and neat. When he came home he didn't look like the same boy, his face brightened up the whole of that street. The mothers of other dirty-looking boys there saw his smiling, sweet face, and determined their boys should look just as nice as he. In that way, his clean-washed face lit up the homes and the street where he was living.

You don't know, dear children, how much good you can do if you get to know Jesus. Your words and your actions will remind people that you have met Him, yea, more, that He lives in your hearts.

A little girl, a long, long time ago, was captured by some soldiers and taken away from her home into a far-off country. But she never forgot her God or His prophets. She was taken to the home of the greatest general in that country, and waited on the mistress there.

She felt so grieved to think that this general was suffering from a bad disease. He was a leper. So one day she told her mistress that she knew a man who could heal him, a man who believed in God. Now just notice how far a little girl's words may reach when she loves God.

The lady of the house went to her husband, whose name was Naaman, and he believed what the girl said. She must have been a good girl, as everybody could rely on what she said. Then, if you read that story—you will find it in II. Kings v.—you will see that her words went right up to the King of Syria, from there to the King of Israel, and right away to the prophet Elisha. And it resulted in the healing of Naaman.

Now, if a little girl, in Old Testament times, could do so much for God, surely you, dear boys and girls, who have heard so much about Jesus, ought to be able to do still more. All you say and do may not reach the king's palace, but it will be recorded in heaven and do a lot of good on earth.

Let me tell you how you may reach this. First of all, be quite sure that *you*

### Belong to Jesus!

If you love Him and believe His blood was shed for you, then you are His children. He wants to make you very good, and sweet and loving. Trust Him to cleanse your heart from all sin (I. John i. 7). Just believe it, and it's done! Say: " Dear Jesus, I want to be like Thee. I cannot be so unless Thou dost help me. Oh, let Thy Blood cleanse me and make me whiter than snow! I do believe Thou didst die for me, and now I am going to give Thee all my heart, ALL MY HEART! Take it, Jesus, and put it right, and live in it for ever."

Now if you pray like that, from the bottom of your heart, He will be sure to hear you and to bless you, and He will fill you with such joy and peace that you will possibly laugh for very joy.

" I love them," the Lord says, " that love Me; and those that seek Me early shall find Me " (Prov. viii. 17). " He that hath My commandments, and keepeth them, he it is that loveth Me . . . if a man love Me, he will keep My word, and My Father will love him, and We will come unto him, and make our abode with him " (John xiv. 21-23).

But then He wants to make you as great a blessing as possible, and in order to do that, He wants you to get

### Your Baptism in the Holy Ghost.

Now don't be afraid of those words. I'll tell you what

the meaning of them is. When Jesus went to heaven, He told His disciples to wait in Jerusalem until they received power, and that this power would be received " after that the Holy Ghost was come upon them. ' And, as some of you remember, having read Acts ii. : " When the Day of Pentecost was fully come, they were all with one accord in one place. And suddenly there came a sound from heaven as of a rushing mighty wind, and it filled all the house where they were sitting. And there appeared unto them cloven tongues of fire, and it sat upon each of them. And they were all

**Filled**

with the Holy Ghost, and began to speak with other tongues as the Spirit gave them utterance."

What a wonderful miracle! But it took place very often after that. There was the case at Cæsarea, where Cornelius, " a devout man, and one that feared God with all his house, which gave much alms to the people, and prayed to God alway " (Acts x.), was told by the angel to send word to Peter. And when Peter spoke to him, his kinsmen, and near friends, about Jesus, the " Holy Ghost fell on them all and they spake with tongues and magnified God " (v. 10).

And at Ephesus, when Paul laid his hands on the twelve men who had accepted Jesus, the " Holy Ghost came on them; and they spake with tongues and prophesied " (Acts xix. 6).

So also at Samaria (Acts viii. 5-24). Although in this last place "tongues" are not mentioned, we believe it was that sign Simon " *saw* " (v. 18). And it became general in the first Christian Church.

But you see, dear children, somehow or other the Christians lost sight of this FULL Pentcostal blessing, this power and fire in our hearts that makes us speak in tongues.

But in our day people are beginning to get their eyes opened to see that it is this power all of us need, not only grown-up people, but boys and girls, young and old, not merely in order to speak in tongues, but to make us as much like Jesus as possible, and help us to win souls for Him.

On that wonderful Day of Pentecost, Peter said that it was for the children as well as for their parents. Just listen: " The promise is unto you, and

### To Your Children,

and to *all* that are afar off, even as many as the Lord our God shall call." So here, you see, we are *all* included.

It would not be like Jesus to give it only to a few. It is for all whose hearts are right with Him!

Now then, children, just talk with Jesus about it. Read what He said in John viii. 37-39: " If any man thirst, let him come unto Me, and drink. He that believeth in Me, as the Scripture hath said, out of his belly shall flow rivers of living waters. But this spake He of the Spirit, which they that believed on Him should receive."

And again in Mark xvi. 17: " These signs shall follow them that believe. In My Name shall they cast out devils; they shall speak with new tongues," etc. He will help you to understand it, even if papa and mamma, or your teachers are not able to do so.

Don't pray merely for tongues, but ask Jesus so to fill you with His Spirit that you may praise Him and magnify Him as did the people who met in the house of

Cornelius (Acts x. 46). Ask Him to give you your baptism.

I have heard many children speak in tongues when Jesus filled their hearts with His Spirit; and what good, kind, obedient, loving children they became.

All at home, and at school, and among their friends could see the change.

It was not the " tongues " that did it, but the

### Love of God

" shed abroad in their hearts by the Holy Ghost " (Rom. v. 5). The " tongues " were the miraculous proof that they had received their Pentecost.

And there is a wonderful joy, children, when the love of God wells up in the heart and you know the Spirit is come in to abide with you.

I was present when the two girls, who were

### The First Children

to speak in tongues in England in this revival, Janie and May Boddy (the daughters of the Rev. Alex. A. Boddy, All Saints' Vicarage, Sunderland), received their Pentecost. It was at the Vicarage.

The nine or ten persons present will never forget the scene. Janie received the interpretation for each sentence, and her childlike simplicity and joy, her beaming face, was wonderful to witness. The first message she received was:

### " Jesus is Coming! "

With a surprised look of joy on her face, that I shall never forget, she turned to her mother and kissed her, repeating the words: " Jesus *is* coming, mother ! "

Then her face became serious. She bowed her head a little and lifted her left hand to her cheek (she was kneeling all the time at the end of the table). Again a foreign language was heard. Then came the interpretation: "The heavens are opened!" followed by the same jubilant glee.

One message was very solemn, spoken, too, with emphasis: "The first shall be last, and the last first." Coming from such childlike lips, it made a great impression on us all.

Oh, what a joy when she said: "Oh, mummie, Jesus has come, and come to stay; oh, good Jesus, good Jesus!" then peals of joybells of laughter.

As she related her experience the next day to a large crowd of children at the Parish Hall, she said, whilst inviting them to seek their baptism, "Oh, it is so wonderful, so wonderful!"

It was wonderful, it was the Holy Spirit come to dwell within them.

May Boddy had a great revelation of God's power. She prayed so earnestly that *she might not " be left out."* It was touching, too, to see Janie, who had just received her baptism, as she laid her hand on her sister's head and encouraged her: " It's all through the blood, May, all through the blood! Jesus *is* come; He said, May too, May too!"

May spoke a long time. Some words were very clear. It seemed as if she was constantly claiming Jesus. His name was repeated time upon time. The words, " Aa, ja, Jesus! Ja, ja, ja, Jesus!" were distinctly Norwegian, with the correct pronunciation (Oh, yes, Jesus! yes, yes, yes, Jesus!). But there were many incomplete sounds in this case, words that will be clearly formed later on.

We notice that the spirit prays to God, even if the thoughts are not always clearly formed in words. But that must not cause anxiety. It is only the human ear that needs distinct words in order to understand what is said. God looks *to the heart!*

These two dear children had been kind, good girls before, and loved Jesus dearly, but now they love Him much more, and are more bold to tell others of His wonderful power to save.

Open your hearts, dear children, fully for Jesus, and let Him give you your baptism! Say:

"*Jesus, I take my baptism now from Thee, keep me under the Blood, and fill me with Thy holy fire and love; for Thine own sake!*"

Then, believe He has done it, leaving Him to give the feelings and the manifestations in His own way and time as you keep close to His loving heart and remain obedient to His Word. For, " if we know that He heareth us whatsoever we ask, we know that we have the petitions we have asked of Him " (I. John v. 14, 15).

**God Bless You All!**

CHAPTER X.

# To Seekers after "The Promise of the Father"

"BUT YE SHALL RECEIVE POWER AFTER THAT THE HOLY GHOST IS COME UPON YOU: AND YE SHALL BE WITNESSES UNTO ME BOTH IN JERUSALEM, AND IN ALL JUDÆA, AND IN SAMARIA, AND UNTO THE UTTERMOST PART OF THE EARTH" (Acts i. 8).

TWO things are requisite first of all: To know *what* we are seeking, and to be the *right kind of seekers*.

You are seeking "The Promise of the Father," you say. Then let me ask you, *"Are you a Christian?"* The question may to some seem quite unnecessary. Who would seek but a Christian?

But facts prove that there are many who have received religious training and are well acquainted with the generally accepted doctrines of Christianity, *who have not personally accepted Christ as their Saviour.* They are interested and accept gospel truth with the mind, but there has been no change of heart, and they have no inner testimony, by the Holy Spirit (Rom. viii. 16), of their regeneration and justification, through faith in the Atonement.

It happens now and then that such people, on seeing the joy and spiritual victory afforded such as are baptised with the Holy Ghost and fire, long to obtain the same blessed experience. But they must commence at the bottom of the ladder. They must become, not merely nominal Christians, but be

### Born Again!

They must, in other words, become children in the household of God before they can partake of the blessings of that household and enjoy its privileges.

Therefore, get that matter settled first: Are you saved? If not, *salvation is at hand.* You need not wait a day or an hour, but, with a full determination to give up all your sins and all sinful connections, and make restitution, as far as possible, for the evil you have done.

### Claim Salvation by Faith!

You do not obtain any merit by giving up your sins and making restitution, but as long as you hold on to these, you have the abominable thing treasured up in your heart and God will not enter. All that is wanted just now on your part is willingness, as far as you know and understand, to give up everything that God hates. Do not try to do all this first in your own strength; you will utterly fail, and only attain to be a self-righteous Pharisee. It is willingness and the determination, at any cost, to do the right thing, God claims. That being the case—look straight to the Cross for salvation! Do not doubt the efficacy of the Blood of Jesus one moment. Then you will experience the truth of Jesus' words to Nicodemus: "For God so loved the world, that He gave His only begotten Son, that whosoever believeth in Him should not perish, but have everlasting life" (John iii. 16). You are *saved* when you believe it! The Divine Spirit does His work in the soul the very moment you accept Jesus as your Saviour. Then you get a NEW HEART—" Old things pass away and all things become new ! " " Wherefore thou art no more a servant, but a son; and if a son, then an heir of God through Christ " (Gal. iv. 7). And the Divine Spirit testifies to that fact in your heart. " For as many as are led by the Spirit of God, they are the sons of God." (Read Rom. viii. 14-17; II. Cor. v. 5).

We may therefore know definitely if we are the children of God. God Himself testifies to the work of salvation in our hearts by His blessed Holy Spirit. And with this new power, this Divine life within, you are able to do what you in your own strength never could do; to meet the old temptations and make restitution as God leads you to do.

The fault of many is that *they are trying to live as Christians* without *at heart being Christians*. And, therefore, the Christian life becomes a drudgery, and God a hard Master. Not so when you commence to love Him.

With this new life then the Holy Spirit has imparted to you, even if you do not fully realise it, the blessed fruits spoken of in Gal. v. 22 : " Love, joy, peace, longsuffering, gentleness, goodness, faith, meekness and temperance; against such there is no law." They are within you, in their germ at least, and you will feel and know that a change has taken place in your heart, and others around you will also notice it.

Now there are many who really are children of God. But their minds have been stirred up to seek greater and still more glorious revelations of His power. In reading the Scriptures, God has revealed to them the wonderful possibilities there are for all His children to develop and live a victorious life on earth, through Jesus. Having felt convinced that there is a special outpouring of the Holy Ghost to be obtained they are anxious to know how. Perhaps this is your case.

Let us, then, look thoughtfully and prayerfully at the matter as it is revealed to us in the Word of God.

### What is "The Promise of the Father?"

"The promise of the Father" *is the Baptism of the Holy Ghost with the signs following,* as on the Day of Pentecost in Jerusalem, in Cæsarea, and Ephesus, and evidently also at Samaria. It means being FILLED WITH THE HOLY GHOST. We are obliged to suppose that many have been thus filled, without the tongues, owing to ignorance or a definite resistance of this physical sign. But we believe it may attend every real infilling of the Holy Spirit.

We suppose then that you are seeking and are willing to receive this mighty outpouring, and all in connection with it that God is willing to give you, as it fell on the disciples in the "upper room" in Jerusalem. There were "about 120" there, and the Lord's promise to them was fulfilled: "THEY WERE ALL FILLED WITH THE HOLY GHOST, AND BEGAN TO SPEAK WITH OTHER TONGUES, AS THE SPIRIT GAVE THEM UTTERANCE" (Acts ii. 4).

The Apostle Peter assured the surging crowds that came together, amazed at what had taken place, that this gift of the Holy Ghost was not mercy for him and the disciples around him. "The promise," he said, "is unto *you,* and *your children,* and to *all that are afar off,* even as many as the Lord our God shall call" (Acts ii. 39).

The matter, then, is clear; what your heart is crying out for is the same "POWER" as that experienced by the first disciples. "The Promise of the Father" is a

### Baptism of "Power."

"Ye shall receive 'POWER' AFTER that the Holy Ghost is come upon you."

It was so with the disciples. "*Before* this their evangelistic efforts were feeble: *afterwards* they were dynamos. Before this they were hampered by fear, unbelief, false ambitions, and all the other hindrances which spring from a carnal nature and not yet fully conquered; *afterwards* their hearts being purified *by faith* and *filled with fire from heaven,* men 'could not resist the wisdom and the spirit' by which they spoke."\*

We notice also that in Old Testament days, *before* the mighty and more general outpouring on Pentecost, that ALL *on whom the Spirit fell* were better equipped for SERVICE. Just take a few cases.

In Numbers xi. you read of the seventy elders on whom the Spirit that was upon Moses fell, and when it "rested upon them, they PROPHESIED, and did not cease" (*v.* 25). Even the two who were still in the camp prophesied by the Spirit's power. "The Spirit rested upon them . . . and they prophesied in the camp" (*v.* 26). It seemed to be out of the proper order in the mind of Joshua, and he said, "My lord Moses, forbid them!"

But Moses knew better. The men were chosen and therefore wherever they went, in the Tabernacle or in the camp, they were merely instruments in the hands of the Holy Spirit. We must expect to be used by the Holy Spirit anywhere and at any time when fully made

---

\* "Revival Kindlings."

over to His service. Moses answered very wisely, " Would God that all the Lord's people were prophets, and that the Lord would put His Spirit upon them ! "

Something similar happened to Saul, after being anointed by Samuel (I. Sam. x.). God gave him another heart, and on coming in touch with the company of prophets, " the Spirit of God came upon him, and he PROPHESIED among them " (*v.* 10).

It caused surprise, and the people said one to another, " What is this that has come unto the son of Kish? Is Saul also among the prophets? "

On one occasion the power of the Holy Spirit fell so mightily upon him that he prophesied as he walked along the road (I. Sam. xix. 23, 24), and at last, overwhelmed by the Spirit, he threw off his outer garments *and lay down under the power " all that day and all that night."*

Here then it was POWER given in order to PROPHESY, and in this case evidently not foretelling but *forthtelling* (cf. I. Cor. xiv. 3).

When Moses was about to leave his people he laid his hands upon Joshua (Deut. xxxiv. 9), and the Holy Spirit fell upon him, filling him with wisdom—just what he wanted—in order to lead on the people after the death of Moses.

When the Midianites and the Amalekites and the children of the east gathered themselves together against the people of Israel, God selected Gideon, the " least in his father's house," and his "family poor in Manasseh," to hurl them headlong out of the country. " The Spirit of the Lord came upon Gideon, and he blew a trumpet. And at the sound of that trumpet blast thousands of his people arose in arms.

But God proved that He was not dependent on them;

with the Spirit-filled Gideon and a handful of men, merely armed with trumpets, empty pitchers and lamps, he defeated and discomfited all the hosts of the enemy.

This was power against the enemies of the Lord.

When God wanted a king to lead his people and save them from the difficulties into which they had been led by the unfaithfulness of Saul, and make them a power among the nations, He chose David, the youngest of the sons of Jesse. Samuel would have selected Eliab, but the Lord said, " Look not on his countenance, or on the height of his stature; because I have refused him: for the Lord seeth not as man seeth; for man looketh on the *outward* appearance, but *the Lord looketh on the heart* " (I. Samuel xvi. 7). It would seem that David was of little importance in the eyes of his brethren. He was not even called in by his father to pass before Samuel. But God knew him. There will be no sacrifice before he come hither, said Samuel.

As soon as Samuel had poured the oil upon him in the midst of his brethren, the " Spirit of the Lord came upon him from that day forward."

He did not immediately enter into his royal office outwardly; there were many difficulties to overcome and enemies to conquer before that would take place. But he was immediately endowed with all the qualities of a prince and a ruler. He had the Divine seal on his kingly brow, and his bearing and actions gave proof of his kingly calling.

When God wanted to send Isaiah as a prophet to a stiff-necked and hardened people, He purged him of his sins and touched his lips with a live coal from off the altar (Isaiah vi. 1-8).

This symbolised the Divine fire that would fully equip him for this difficult mission.

When Ezekiel received revelations from God he speaks of the Spirit as "lifting him up" (Ezek. iii. 14), "entering into him" (v. 24), or as the "hand of the Lord being upon him" (i. 3).

And when God prepared the "forerunner" of His Son in this world, He filled Him with the Holy Ghost, even from His mother's womb (Luke i. 15).

And Christ Himself, as the Great High Priest of His people, had to be baptised with this same Holy Spirit (Luke iii. 22), in order to perform the great work He had taken upon Himself to accomplish, and for which purpose a *"body had been prepared for Him"* (Heb. x. 5).

And the prophets who foretold His coming, and "testified beforehand the sufferings of Christ, and the glory that should follow" (I. Peter i. 11), did so by the power of the "Spirit of Christ which was in them."

There are numerous other cases that might be touched upon in the Old Testament, and in fact nothing of importance for the furtherance of God's kingdom was ever done, save by the power of the Holy Ghost. "Not by might, nor by power, but

**By My Spirit,**

saith the Lord of hosts!" (Zech. iv. 6).

This being the case under the old dispensation, it must needs be so in the new. And as the glory of the new was to excel that of the old, so that what had been glorious in that would lose its lustre, because of the surpassing glory of that which was *to remain*, then surely the Holy Ghost, producing the first, must be more effective and general in this dispensation.

And this was the promise of the Father. "In THE LAST DAYS, saith God, I will pour out of my Spirit upon

ALL FLESH: and your sons and your daughters shall prophesy, and your young men shall see visions, and your old men shall dream dreams; and on my servants and on my handmaidens I will pour out in those days of My Spirit; and they shall prophesy" (Acts ii. 17).

This promise was fulfilled on the Day of Pentecost in Jerusalem. It is an accomplished fact. The Holy Ghost is come! Just as the Atonement is an accomplished fact. *You are living in the "last days,"* the days of the gospel dispensation and the mighty opportunities that the Holy Ghost affords you.

But just as you have personally to claim the results of the Atonement by faith for salvation, so you have to open your whole being by faith and receive the Baptism of the Holy Ghost.

Some seem to find difficulty concerning the signs of the baptism compared with the method of the Holy Spirit's action on Christ and the faith-heroes of the old dispensation.

I do not think we need to mystify the matter by comparing the Baptism of Christ with that of His disciples on the Day of Pentecost.

Christ was given the Holy Spirit "without measure." No one can attain to more than that.

But the "TONGUES" were *not given to believers before the Day of Pentecost.* It was the sign Christ had especially retained for His disciples (Mark xvi. 17), and those "who should believe on Him through their word." It was, as it were, to become the peal of bells that would testify to the inauguration of the Christian Church. It had been reserved for that occasion.

All the other manifestations of the Holy Spirit, *wisdom, knowledge, faith, healing, miracles, prophecy* had been in the Church of God *before Pentecost,* but

TONGUES, also mentioned last in the catalogue of gifts in I. Cor. xii. 8-10, and the *interpretation of tongues* were first given to the people of God on the Day of Pentecost.

The fact therefore that " tongues " did not accompany mighty baptisms *before* the Day of Pentecost, does not in any way weaken their value *after* Pentecost. God Himself knows why He has reserved them for the " last days."

Still it must be remembered that " tongues " are not the chief thing. It is to be feared that some have sought " tongues " *without the power*. We do not want anything but God-produced " tongues," that is through the human agency. And in connection with the Twentieth Century Revival it seems that people are not satisfied *unless* they have received this evidence of God's Spirit within.

But the chief thing is

### Holy Ghost Power,

or the Holy Ghost dwelling within us, of the fact of which the real tongues and other manifestations are evidence.

The power cannot be separated from Him!

He is within us as a person, permeating our whole being: body, soul, and spirit. Just as blood permeates our body, as heat fills every atom of a piece of iron that has laid long enough in the fire, or as electricity fills every part of the wire in connection with the powerhouse. We cannot see Him, but His existence within is as real as the heart beat within our breast. " Know ye not that ye are the temple of God, and the Spirit of God dwelleth in you? " (I. Cor. iii. 16). In the sixth chapter of this same epistle and the 19th verse, the apostle points out clearly that the Holy Ghost does not merely intend to impart a spiritual blessing, but says that He also inhabits our bodies: "What? Know ye not that your body is the temple of the Holy Ghost which is in you, which ye have of God, and ye are not your own?" This is brought out very clearly in the next verse in which he says, "For ye are bought with a price: therefore glorify God in your body, and in your spirit, which are God's," thus defining between the body and the spirit. The whole connection from the 15th verse proves that he means the physical body.

As Christ had a "body" prepared for Him, so *our bodies* are to be prepared for the Holy Ghost, as vessels, temples, instruments, through which He may work. And our soul that is connected with the physical body is also devoted to His service, as well as the never-dying spirit. Thus the Holy Ghost having regenerated and prepared the spirit through the Blood of Jesus, takes possession of the faculties of the soul and uses them and the members of the body to the glory of the Triune God. That is, our will having been subjected to the will of God, we have opened up our whole being to His influence: and He, whilst keeping us and upholding the inner life by His power, makes us His mouthpiece or channel (surely very frail and imperfect), through which His light and love and blessing flows out to others.

The apostle says therefore, "I beseech you . . . by the mercies of God, that ye present your bodies a living sacrifice, holy, acceptable unto God, which is your reasonable service" (Rom. xii. 1); and again, "The very God of peace sanctify you wholly; and I pray God your whole spirit and soul and body be preserved blameless unto the coming of our Lord Jesus Christ " (I. Thess. v. 23; cf. also Rom. vi. 11-14, 19-23).

When therefore you receive the Baptism of the Holy Ghost, all the faculties of your being, your talents, your all, become quickened, vitalised, and energised in His service. And all the fruits of the Spirit laid down in your heart will attain a fulness and a development they never could have done without it.

Oh, what illumination of the mind! (I. John ii. 20, 27). There opens out and broadens before you *a new world of vast possibilities!* We have wondered sometimes from whence some people obtained all their information and light in the Word of God. Now we see that it was the inner illumination of the Holy Spirit on the mind, taking them down into the Bible, as through a mine, full of precious minerals.

How clearly at times one now sees God's dealings with man and His wondrous plan of salvation.

One feels somehow or other, that with all the knowledge acquired formerly, we are still as

**Babes,**

just touching the borders of God's great world of thought and light.

How the heart is touched as with a new love! (I. Cor. xiii.). But it is merely *a renewal* and *an increase* of the love we already had to God and man. Now one's heart is on fire with it. "It is the old-time religion," and it "makes us love everybody!"

You have left your little paltry stinginess, your little quibblings and austerity, your harsh criticisms and proud manners, your lukewarmness and worldliness, your struggle for honour and praise of the world, your bigotry and self-seeking—*it is gone!* And your " once divided heart " is fully possessed by the Triune God.

When the Comforter has come one feels one's own nothingness and unworthiness as never before. Some have said, that " those who receive Pentecost, lose their old selves, so that they are not as they used to be. There was some ' go ' in them before, but now they seem to be utter failures." And no one will be more willing to acknowledge it than they themselves.

They have as a fact really lost their old selves in Christ, and are *not* what they used to be. Their language now is as Paul's: " I am crucified with Christ: nevertheless I live; yet *not I,* but Christ *liveth in me*: and the life which I now live in the flesh I live by the faith of the Son of God, who loved me, and gave Himself for me " (Gal. ii. 20).

The " go " has been taken out of them, as far as it was " the works of the flesh." And how often they felt and had to acknowledge that they were " utter failures," and that it was a wonder God in any way could bless their efforts.

But now they are led by the Spirit and go the way Christ wants them to, and although, because of opposition and misunderstandings, they may seemingly not make such headway in the sight of carnal Christians (I. Cor. iii. 1), they rest in Christ, perfectly assured that their feet are on the right path and that the results are sure, and that they are well-pleasing in the sight of God.

Their eyes and ears are now opened to see God's plan and hear His voice, in small as well as great things. They " walk in the Spirit."

One thing becomes very clear to them, that Pentecost does not mean the finality of Christian experience, but *it makes possible* what was formerly an impossibility, because they are now the vessels—completely and fully

—of the almighty Spirit of God. It is the starting point of a last mighty round in the Christian race, with the breath of the Almighty upon them and His holy fire within them.

The baptism should be attained to at the commencement of our Christian life, but, sad to say, most of us have put it off until later, and have had to suffer the consequences, and others with us.

So "The Promise of the Father" means being baptised with the true, genuine and full Baptism of the Holy Ghost, giving you power with God and men, and power over the emissaries of Satan and his kingdom.

No matter if you are unimportant in the sight of men. God can, as one has said, "take a worm and thresh a mountain." It is God's way generally to "choose the foolish things of the world to confound the wise, and the weak things of the world to confound the things which are mighty; and the base things of the world, and things which are despised, hath God chosen, yea, and things which are not, to bring to nought things that are; that

**No Flesh**

should glory in His presence" (I. Cor. i. 27-29).

As we have seen, the "power" that brings forth "faith-heroes" and "overcomers" is for all, and there is no excuse for the individual, or the Church, that thrusts this blessing aside and proceeds along the old lines, wherein carnal energy is so often to the fore.

The Church of Christ has time and again been shorn of its strength and glory in the presence of the Philistines. *As long as the power of the Holy Ghost was in the Church it made progress,* in the face of all opposition, and whenever this power *has burst forth again,* up through the ages, the Church has been lifted out of its stagnation and powerlessness into a new sphere of usefulness and influence. And *now*, praise God, the *power*, and the gifts following, are being disinterred once more, and God's glory is being seen again. Zion is rising from the dust and is being clad in " fine linen" in order to prepare for the coming of the Bridegroom. Who dares to sleep now when the Master is at the door? Nearly 2,000 years have sped by since He said to John on Patmos,

### " I Come Quickly."

Surely there is no time to be idle and pamper the flesh, and give way to the wiles of sinful and careless men.

So if you, from the depths of your being, are

### Seeking the Baptism of the Holy Ghost,

we congratulate you—you have turned your face in the right direction, and God will surely meet and fill you.

### Some Words of Advice.

Now it is quite natural that, when seeking this filling, you have the experience of someone else in your mind, and, this having influenced you greatly, you are apt to desire yours in just the same way.

But that is a mistake. You must not make up your mind to have it in any exact way, save as the Word of God teaches you. You may expect the outward evidence: tongues, prophetic utterances and praises, but especially tongues (Acts ii. 4; Acts x. 46, xix. 6). But even that is not to be uppermost in your mind. Many get it, without even expecting it, when the Holy Ghost fills them.

Your chief aim must be to get

### Him.

the blessed Comforter Himself, in Pentecostal fulness. And He may come entirely different from anything you expected. Some people are boisterous and noisy, full of loud shouts and great outward manifestations; others are seraphic and celestial in their appearance and demeanour. No two people are exactly alike, and therefore the outward characteristics vary.

To us this variety of expression is profoundly interesting, and shows forth the wonderful wisdom and manifold works of God.

No two leaves, or clouds, or snow-crystals are exactly alike. There is constant variety in nature. Then surely it may be expected in the spiritual realm.

So do not look for an old experience you may have lost, or that of somebody else, *but get the Holy Ghost in your whole being,* " body, soul and spirit," and the experience He brings to your heart will more than satisfy you. Get just what He has

### For You!

Then again, we find that many seekers are influenced by prejudices and fears. This prevents them from obtaining the blessing, and they go weeks and months, even years, without getting it.

All your preconceived ideas that oppose God's perfect will, and all your prejudices must be laid aside. If you are going to tie the Almighty down to your plans and methods, what hope is there for you?

He will simply not meet you along those lines, but keep you waiting, and try you by various means until you have perfectly surrendered to

### His Will.

And what have you to fear? Are you not seeking

what God has promised you and invited you to lay hold of? Is it not the very "promise of the Father"? Has not Jesus urged you to come, and warned you against hoping to be successful without His power?

Then do you think that when you are seeking God for the very blessing He has promised you, that He will make you over to His and your enemy? Or allow the enemy to gain the upper hand?

### "Never!"

If your motives are pure in seeking, and your only object that of being conformed to the image of Christ, and honour Him by a life wholly separated unto Him and devoted to His interests, He will protect you by His Blood and power from all the onslaughts of the enemy.

One missionary, when she at last fully gave way to God, said: "If I had known that, I would have yielded before!" And then, as the holy fire went through her being, she shouted:

### "This is That!"

She had for some time felt the power influencing her body, especially when her mind was more rested; but from various accounts some would-be helpers had circulated, she supposed it was the enemy.

But the moment she realised that it was the Spirit of God working in her body, as well as in her innermost being, she gave way and relaxed in the arms of God. Immediately she was filled through and through with the Holy Ghost.

Now that may be just your difficulty. You feel the holy power of God touching your body, and instead of giving way you resist.

### "Lord, Stay Thine Hand!"

some have cried out. As if God did not know how much they could stand. And is He not able to enlarge our capacity to receive all He has for us?

Do not listen, therefore, to the voice of inexperienced and unenlightened friends, or the subtle voice of the tempter, but speak direct to God about it. Place yourself under the Blood of Jesus, trust your heavenly Father's grace and power, lift up the shield of faith against the enemy, and open all the avenues of your being to the Holy Ghost, and He will assert His presence by filling you with His glory. Your long struggle will have ended, and a paradise of joy, peace, love and righteousness in the Holy Ghost will bloom forth in your life. Thousands and thousands can testify to the truth of this in these eventful days.

This, then, brings to our consideration a matter of vital importance, that of

### Perfect Subjection

to the will of God. In other words: separation, consecration, sanctification. As we said before, it is necessary to be "the right kind of seekers." We pointed out that one *must be regenerated or saved first,* as we cannot receive sanctification without regeneration. *God cannot sanctify an unconverted and unregenerated soul!* It must have entered *into the kingdom by faith in the Blood of Jesus in order to obtain the mark of holiness.* There must be *life* if there is to be *any development* in the things of God. But it is also necessary to be cleansed before seeking the Baptism of the Holy Ghost, at least as far as we are able to see our want of it and take it by faith.

We know of cases which prove that God may fill with the Holy Ghost, even where there is little or no knowledge of sanctification. He may, as in the "drawing-room" meeting at Cæsarea, save, sanctify and baptise at the same meeting.

There was of course on the part of those present a perfect resignation, as far as they knew the will of God by the teaching of His servant, and God honoured their child-like faith and gave them *much-more,* "*far above all,*" *than they expected.* That is just like our heavenly Father! So when Peter defines their experience at the assembly in Jerusalem, he said, "God, which knoweth the heart, bare them witness, giving them the Holy Ghost, even as He did unto us; and He made *no distinction between us and them,* cleansing their hearts by faith" (Acts xv. 8, 9). Here then the apostle deliberately states, that they received both heart-cleansing and the full baptism simultaneously. God works quickly if we only give Him a chance.

We have known cases similar in our day.

What is necessary in such cases is guidance. They must be led into the Word at once. The knowledge of the heritage received must be revealed to them. They must get to know what heart-cleansing and sanctification really means. They have received "power" to do the will of God, but *that will of His* must be clearly revealed to them by instruction in His Word.

A want of this instruction has caused grief and confusion to some. They have *not understood the will of God fully* and *have not lived such perfect lives* as you would expect from Spirit-filled saints. They have trusted their feelings and wonderful experience *instead of living by the Word.*

But these cases are more rare. We generally notice that after receiving the Comforter, although there has been comparatively speaking very little preparatory work done, God has led them on in His own way by the Word, even where spiritual leaders have been wanting: He has even raised up *prophets and prophetesses* among them where it was least expected.

We would say though to those who seek the baptism:

### Get Right With God!

That is: be sure you have been cleansed in the Blood of Jesus, before praying for the Baptism of Fire.

This experience is so wonderful in itself that many have supposed it to be the Baptism of the Holy Ghost and fire. But it is not! Although there are cases as we have seen, in which they have followed close upon each other, or even simultaneously, God having fully prepared the vessels.

In our day, when the truths in the Bible, concerning the Comforter, have been misunderstood, there are numbers of Christians who have entered into the experience of sanctification and " holiness unto the Lord," who have never been baptised with the Holy Ghost and fire.

You will often be stirred by the holy and Christ-like lives they are living, and where people, lately converted, step right into the Pentecostal glory at once, you say, and hear others say, " But can it be possible that these people have received more than these older saints, who have been tried in so many a battle? "

But we ought not to draw such comparisons. Still, this being constantly done by many, the answer is this: Of course the older Christians have attained greater maturity in the life of holiness, they are more grafted in the Word of God and have more experience in the way than younger Christians. But if these have really been endued with power from on high they have suddenly been translated into an experience of Holy Ghost power for service that the older Christians have not yet attained to.

I confess it is embarrassing to many as to how it could come about, but it is nevertheless

### A Fast.

Now what is to be done? The newly-baptised souls must walk very humbly before God. They have *nothing to boast of,* but must *give all honour to God.* They need very highly the mature thought, judgment and experience of the older Christians—that is if these are sympathetic. Some older Christians even lose their balance, we find, on seeing others getting before them into this experience so abruptly, and allow *jealousy* and *prejudice* to steal into their hearts, and would not therefore be able to instruct the younger Spirit-filled Christians faithfully.

So, on the other hand, we would say to the older Christians also: *Humble yourselves before God!* Perhaps there is something in your theories, ideals, customs, lives, that have *stopped your development considerably*—yea, THERE MUST BE! Then see to it *what it is,* and enter into the Pentecostal glory with your more inexperienced brethren and sisters, who have been childlike and simple enough *to take God at His word,* and have claimed the blessing before you. In that way YOU BOTH WILL MEET IN SWEET AND MUTUAL FELLOWSHIP at the foot of the Cross of Jesus.

We so often notice at the Pentecostal meetings, that Christians who come to "have a good time" have gone away disappointed at first. Why? Because God has revealed to them as He did to us, *that they were not so far on as they thought they were.* He has humbled them DOWN INTO THE DUST! If they have been obedient to the light given they have praised Him for it. If not they have gone away with criticisms and hardness of heart.

### Let God Humble You!

There is generally *a great breaking down* before entering into the deeper and fuller experience of God's mighty grace and power.

But God wants to do more than to break down. He does that in order to get you fully into *the death of Christ*, so that *the world* may have no more power over you, but that the *cleansing, life-giving power* of the Blood of Jesus may *fully* prevail in your whole being.

In reading a book by Pastor Stockmayer, entitled *Overcomers*,. I was very much struck by some statements he cites, made by the Rev. Robert Middleton, concerning the Keswick Meetings of 1905.

Mr. Stockmayer says: " The burning question which just now is occupying such as weigh deeply these things is this: Will the Lord, before His coming, attire His Church *again with her virgin array, as at Pentecost?* Will He restore to her the gifts which she never should have lost—*healing, the raising of the dead, the gift of tongues, etc.?* The hundred and twenty had not studied foreign languages, and nevertheless all the foreigners assembled at that time in Jerusalem heard them speak, every man in his own language, the wonderful works of God (Acts ii. 6-11). It was one of the miracles at Pentecost, and I allude to it now on account of an article in the " Life of Faith," by Rev. Robert Middleton, in which he compares the ten days of the upper room in Jerusalem with the five days at Keswick, 1905, with their respective results."

Mr. Stockmayer then goes on to say: "He shows, in the first place, that at Keswick, just as in Jerusalem, there was a fixed expectation of something unusual. And what happened on the Friday evening at the end of the meetings? A great and general breaking down, with confession of sin, God's children acknowledging openly how greatly they had failed: the Holy Spirit working mightily upon them in this way. *And then?* Was not that the time to look for a FRESH ENDUEMENT from on high!

Is it enough to fall broken at the feet of Jesus, to mourn over the past without being introduced into a new world?" He then quotes Mr. Middleton again: "All return to their respective spheres *without having received the gift of tongues, or the power to work miracles,* or the gift of prophecy, or the gift of healing, or *the power to cast out devils!* The physicians who were at Keswick return to their schools of medicine and operation room; the clergy, ministers, and missionaries return to their conflict with the powers of the enemy, WITHOUT THE WITNESS OF ONE MIRACLE TO THEIR DIVINE MISSION. Missionary candidates return to pursue their tedious studies in the Eastern languages, without any better way of making themselves understood by the peoples of the lands.*

"Nothing, then," says Mr. Stockmayer, "*was actually changed* by the Keswick Convention of 1905; they closed by *a breaking down before God;* but *nothing new was definitely accomplished.*"

---

\* Concerning this statement there is a misunderstanding generally among theologians and others. It is very doubtful to my mind if God intended to supplant the study of languages by the "tongues.' The "tongues" were used in that way occasionally and are so still, and may possibly be used increasingly in that way, but they were intended for other purposes as well.

Mr. Middleton said: "My heart bleeds in thinking over this, and the question cannot but arise, What is the next step to take? Will Keswick be contented with confessions of weakness, with the partial Baptism of the Holy Ghost which has been the customary teaching for years past, and the character of which is so feeble that those who profess it have not one of the wondrous gifts which accompanied the descent of the Holy Spirit at Pentecost? I have prayed much about this, and the only answer which I receive is this: Let the conditions of the first Pentecost be fulfilled; gather together to some days of prayer the representatives of the whole Christian Church, and during these days pray without ceasing, with a true, definite expectation of an enduement from on high in the deepest sense of the word. If we thus fulfil the conditions, God, on His part, *will give the Pentecostal blessing,* and the gift which the Church as a whole has lost since the Fourth Century, *will be restored to her* by a *fuller* accomplishment of the prophecy of Joel, and a *more powerful* Pentecost than that of some two thousand years ago. It will be a Pentecost which will equip and send forth abroad a vast army of overcomers to bear witness of God in a way which will confound men: God Himself confirming the Word with signs and miracles. This is what will glorify God, and this is that which will satisfy His children; this is what will convince the world that Christ crucified is none other than Christ ascended into heaven, to whom is given all power in heaven and in earth."

No wonder, Mr. Stockmayer says: "*The article has moved me to the depths.*"

I was told that as the result of this line of thought a gathering of Christians WAS CONVENED TO PRAY FOR PENTECOST. The person who told me this was present at that gathering, and states that *one of the first things done* WAS TO CRITICISE THE REVIVAL *that had lately broken out in India,* where *fire* was also claimed as a part of the baptism. As a matter of course there was no great result of the meetings.

*How could there be?* It is very noticeable that when the Comforter is being sought in dead earnest, the individual has little time for criticising others. God has humbled him so down in the dust that he has only one thought, HOW MAY I GET THROUGH TO VICTORY?

Well, the answer to that is plain. Let Christ have His right place in your life! When God has revealed to you your shortcomings and your sins, *those that have not been forgiven and put under the Blood,* there is only one thing to do—it is *not* trying to better things yourself, no more so *now* than when you sought salvation. You have to fix the

### Eye of Faith

on Christ for full and perfect heart-cleansing and life-cleansing through His Blood.

Your trying, in your own strength, *to put off the old man* will help but little. Identify yourself with the death of Christ! " For

### Ye Are Dead,

and your life is hid with Christ in God " (Col. iii. 3).

Have you not by faith passed with Him through Gethsemane yet? Are you not as yet perfectly reconciled to the will of your heavenly Father?

If you are, you go willingly with Christ to the Cross; you " go forth unto Him

### Without the Camp

bearing His reproach " (Heb. xiii. 13). Ah, that means more than most Christians in these days seem to know!

You submit yourself by faith to *die with Him*. Yea you see now that *you* ARE *dead with Him!*

You say with Paul " God forbid that I should glory, save in the Cross of our Lord Jesus Christ, by whom the world is crucified unto me, and I unto the world " (Gal. vi. 14). You have by faith reached the place where you are cut off from sin and that which is evil, being " crucified with Christ." But in death you have LIFE! In the same Epistle of Galatians Paul says, " I am crucified with Christ; nevertheless I live; yet not I, but

### Christ Liveth in Me;

and the life which I now live in the flesh I live by *the faith of the Son of God,* who loved me and gave Himself for me " (Gal. ii. 20).

By your death with Christ you sever yourself from the adversary's power and the power of the flesh. And you are hid in the wounds of the Redeemer! There His life is poured into you. You are sanctified by His grace and have power over the evil One, the world, and the flesh, BY HIM!

Oh, what rest! indescribable peace! IN HIM! Lost in Him and His love.

I shall never forget the hour when that became perfectly real to me. When, after full consecration I could see my perfect cleansing *in His Blood* and *the Spirit witnessed that the work was done*. Not the full development of the inner man (it started then in real earnest) but the removal of the hindrances. Just as the gardener removes the impediments in the way of the growth of the fruit-tree, or as Jesus Himself expresses it: " Every branch that *beareth* fruit, He *purgeth it,* that it may bring forth *more* fruit " (John xv. 2).

As long as we keep beneath the cleansing Blood we are

safe, but the moment we leave the Cross we are on false ground. Then *being dead*, we are ALIVE! When this is a reality to you, how sweet the will of Jesus becomes!

*Now* there is nothing, as far as we can see, in the way of the

### Baptism in the Holy Ghost.

If God keeps you waiting yet a while, *there may be some lesson He still wishes to teach you before* the fire falls. And now you are willing to wait and abide His will in all things.

But remember that here, as in every step of your Christian experience hitherto,

### Without Faith It Is Impossible

to please Him (Heb. xi. 6). God has so planned it that you might " receive the promise of the Spirit by faith! " (Gal. iii. 14).

As you were justified and regenerated by faith, and sanctified by faith, so also you must receive the Baptism of the Holy Ghost and fire—the Comforter, by faith.

I know that the difficulty that may arise at this point is this: " I do not *feel* anything." But " faith is the substance of things *hoped* for, the

### Evidence

of things not seen " (Heb. xi. 1). Having received cleansing through the Blood you now cling to the " promise " by childlike faith. God will give the evidence but you leave that with Him. You have asked for and expect a similar outpouring *to that on Pentecost*.

" But," you say, " I have no great joy, no fire burning within, no ecstasy nor rapturous speaking in tongues, *how then,* can I believe the baptism is mine?" Just as you believed salvation and heart-cleansing was yours. The feelings, the evidence came after you had believed! It is just the same in this case, CHILDLIKE FAITH. You need not fear whether God will be faithful to His " promise " or not. He is always faithful and is only just waiting to see if you will trust Him.

Say " Lord, I receive *now* the blessed Holy Ghost in His fulness ! " *You take* and HE WILL UNDERTAKE.

I am supposing now that you have yielded to God at

### Every Point.

Some people believe they have, but find out that they have been mistaken. Are you really willing to become " foolish," " base," " despised," as " things which are not " (I. Cor. i. 26-29) for Christ's sake? Are you ready to be criticised and even forsaken by your nearest and dearest friends and relations for Christ's sake? (Matt. x. 16-22, 35-39).

Do not answer "Yes" carelessly! I have known many, who, when they have sought the Comforter, have been so enticed and influenced by their wives or by their men, by their old colleagues, their Mission Boards, their pastors, or other officials of the church to which they belong, that they have turned back, and as a result have become hardened and careless, not heeding the Holy Spirit's cry to press forward and obtain the power needed. It is sad—very sad! But are you fully willing to go all the way with Christ?

I trust you are, and that you have claimed a perfect, and claim a constant cleansing by faith—then claim your

### Inheritance

by faith this very moment.

It may be that when you are praying one day, perhaps *immediately,* perhaps when on the street, or when in church, or at some meeting, may be in company with some friends, or in some out of the way place, you will suddenly feel your whole being flooded with an indescribable and unspeakable glory; a thrill of celestial and Divine power will pass through you, making you worship and adore God in a new way; or you may perhaps, feel your tongue touched by the Holy Ghost, and a flow of foreign sounds, the first words or sentences of a new language (new to you) will burst over your lips, making you speak of the " wonderful things of God " in a Spirit-given tongue, as the disciples did at the beginning.

Keep on with expectant faith, as did the disciples, after seeing their Master ascend and leave them. The words were ringing in their ears:

### " Ye Shall

receive power after that the Holy Ghost is come upon you! " The same promise is yours. Do not lower the standard you have struck out for in faith. Let not your faith in God's promise falter. Continue believing and trusting! " *All things* whatsoever ye pray and ask for, *believe* that ye have received them, and

### Ye Shall Have Them! "

(Mark xi. 24, R.V.).

If anybody had left you a great fortune, and you were sure by the statements in the will that it was yours, *would you give up your claim?* Would you not *still believe* that the fortune was yours, even if others tried to provoke you to doubt it? You may not have seen the money, or as yet been able to make any practical use of it, but it is yours and you may rejoice in that fact.

So also with this glorious fortune left you by the Lord Jesus Christ. The Will is in force, because of the death of the Testator (Heb. ix. 15-18), and all you have to do is to assert your rights. The love and the grace of the Testator has opened the door for you to every blessing purchased by the Blood.

Be it far from me to prescribe any method for our Lord's work in you. But we may, according to His *own* Word, expect just as powerful a baptism now as His first disciples. So that if Peter or Paul were here they could say, that we had received the Holy Ghost EVEN AS THEY!

As to your future work, when the Holy Ghost has filled you, you need have no anxiety. You may possibly bo called to stay where you are, perhaps not. You may not be called to labour as an evangelist. Perhaps your sphere will be that of a faithful wife and mother, training your children for God. Or may be yours will be some other work in the vineyard. It may not be the one you desired, but God knows best, so *do not worry*. The Spirit will lead you aright.

When filled with the Holy Spirit, you will be willing to go to the end of the world for Jesus, if needed, or to remain by the stuff (I. Samuel xxx. 24, 25).

Only as you

**Continue**

obedient and faithful to Him will the Shekinah of His glory remain with you.

CHAPTER XI.

# A Spiritual Union of Fire-Baptised Saints

"That They All May Be One"—John xvii. 21.

THE Twentieth Century Revival establishes the fact that there is a spiritual union of believers in existence, whose numbers are increasing daily, and whose chief mark of

### Fellowship

is the Blood of Jesus (I. John i. 7), and the Baptism of the Holy Ghost. A formulation of our tenets of faith in general broad lines, may be expressed thus:

WE BELIEVE, that the Bible is the Word of God, that there is a Triune God, that Jesus Christ is the eternal Son of God, come in the flesh (I. John iv. 1-6), and we have by faith received Him as *our personal Saviour and Lord,* our All in All.

WE BELIEVE, that the Lord's decree concerning water-baptism, for all who *believe,* has *never* been recalled. The apostles and first Christians clearly practised believers' baptism, for old or young—the age is not stated, merely the necessity of *faith* (Mark xvi. 16; Acts viii. 35-40). If we would be in harmony with apostolic practice, then we must be obedient to the Lord's command also in this respect. Also as concerns the Lord's Supper or the Breaking of Bread (I. Cor. xi. 23).

WE BELIEVE, that God has not recalled His gifts of grace from His Church (Rom. xi. 29; I. Cor. xii. 1, 7-11), but that the mingling of the administrations and life of the Church with that of the world has beclouded the mind and thought of God's people, and brought unbelief into the Church, causing it to lose sight of many of the privileges it might enjoy, and many of the means of usefulness and power that would fully equip it for service.

WE BELIEVE, that the individual Christian can experience heart-cleansing, after full consecration, by faith in the Blood of Christ, and be kept pure, in the sight of God, by this same offering (Heb. x. 14, 15), and thus, by the grace of God be enabled to receive the Baptism of the Holy Ghost and fire (Matt. iii. 11), as did the disciples on the Day of Pentecost at Jerusalem (Acts ii.), and in the house of Cornelius, at Cæsarea, and at Ephesus (Acts x. and xix.). The baptism of fire comes generally as the seal of your faith in the cleansing power of the Blood of Jesus, often, as at Cæsarea—at the same moment (Acts xi. 17). In the Norwegian translation it reads: "*When* they had *believed*." Faith steps out on the finished work, and the fire consumes the dross.

We do not teach the possibility of attaining a *perfection*, from which it is impossible to fall. We may be tempted, and stand alway in danger of falling, if we do not watch and pray. But we teach the same perfection as Christ (Matt. v. 48)—which is evidently not a perfection of *degree*, but of *kind*—and Paul (Phil. iii. 15). A perfect bud may still develop and become a flower, and a babe may attain the perfection of a fully developed man. This heart-cleansing and perfection does not eliminate development, but furthers it!

All do not get the gift of "tongues," but Scripture points to the possibility of all speaking in rhapsodie utterances in *tongues* on receiving the Baptism of the Holy Ghost and fire, as in the above-mentioned cases, although many of the disciples no doubt also retained the tongues *as a constantly abiding gift*.

Many have, we expect, received the Baptism without this outward sign, as it may have been kept back through unbelief, unwillingness, ignorance, fear, distrust, or from other reasons. But it has again become the rule, during this "Latter Rain" period, to receive the baptism as did the disciples of the "Former Rain" period (Zech. x. 1), the exception proving the rule.

As a result of faulty or imperfect teaching, people have not been led to expect the Baptism of the Holy Ghost and fire at the moment of regeneration, although it appears very clear from Scripture (Acts x.) that *God may do a quick work in a short time,* if only minds and hearts are open to receive. Penitents seeking salvation *ought to be taught* to expect perfect heart-cleansing, in a biblical sense of that word, and the Baptism of the Holy Ghost, with the signs following, at *the commencement of their spiritual career.* But where this has *not* been done, it is wise to press home the necessity of full surrender, and an experience of heart-cleansing in connection with seeking the Baptism. The Holy Ghost can only reign supreme where the *ego,* the will of man has been fully subjected to the will of God. This is very important! The blood must first be applied, then the oil (Lev. xiv. 14, 17). The Holy Spirit never works, save as the result of, and in connection with, the Atonement of Jesus Christ. Even after the Baptism in the Holy Ghost, and as a result of its influence, the necessity of a still deeper consecration and heart-cleansing has become apparent to many. Accordingly the Holy Spirit has had a still fuller sway over their lives, and has made still deeper channels for the *rivers of life*.

WE BELIEVE, that the Lord has now commenced to restore to His people all His gifts of grace, and will do so extensively, in the same degree as they humble themselves before Him, and are willing to go all the way with Him.

WE BELIEVE, that those who have received the Baptism in the Holy Ghost should be filled with the love of God, as well as the other fruit of the Spirit (Gal. v. 22), and as a result love their neighbours, and seek heartily to further the evangelisation of the world, and the salvation of sinners in every land, and take a favourable position to any reform in social life, that will promote the will of God, and the interests of Christ's Kingdom. We consider it the privilege of a Spirit-filled soul to belong to the Lord fully, that is to say, that all his being, talents and influence must tend toward one object only: the furtherance of Christ's Kingdom on earth, no matter where the way may lead him, or what secular position in life he may have to fill. Any relation or position that cannot allow of this must be forsaken (II. Cor. vi. 14-18; vii. 1).

WE LABOUR that the

**Prayer of the Lord Jesus** (John xvii. 14-24)

concerning the welfare of His people, and their spiritual union in Him, may be fully realised. God is clearly raising up witnesses in all lands, to testify of His willingness to permeate all Christians, in all denominations, with the old-time Pentecostal power, and give them an influence on the world that will eclipse every previous manifestation of Divine power in the history of the Christian Church.

We pray earnestly that this movement may be accepted generally by ALL GOD'S PEOPLE. *Pentecost and its blessings, as well as Calvary, belong to* ALL! Even if all Christians do not join the Pentecostal assemblies, churches and missions, that have sprung up during the last twenty years, and are constantly increasing in number, we still pray that this glorious revival of religion may enter the churches and denominations, and clear out the debris of sin and formalism, and the false doctrines that have stopped their progress, and kindle the fire of Pentecost on their altars ! That there may be " one Lord, one faith, one baptism," and all God's people may stand prepared for the coming King, whose appearance, judging from all the signs of the times, and the prophecies of the Bible, is close at hand!

WE REJOICE in tribulation, and do not expect, or attempt, to satisfy or gratify, the opinions or desires of the world or nominal Christians.

WE RECOGNISE, that the wiles of Satan are many (Eph. vi. 10-18), and that our battles, and the persecution we have at times, arises from his influence and that of his countless demons, on the minds and imaginations of men. But we experience that our perfect refuge and strength is found in the Blood of Jesus, in whom also, by His Holy Spirit, we have power to pull down the strongholds of the adversary (II. Cor. x. 3-5).

WE EXPERIENCE that the Kingdom of God is not in word, but in " power " (I. Cor. iv. 20), not in meat and drink; but in righteousness and peace and joy in the Holy Ghost (Rom. xiv. 17). Our meetings are therefore not fixed on rigid conventional forms and methods. Although we respect order, when it is God's order, and leadership by *such as are acknowledged of Him*, methods may vary greatly, and each meeting may present new phases of the Spirit's work and influence, when we prayerfully wait on Him.

WE LOOK FORWARD to the second coming of Christ with expectant hearts and great joy (Rev. xxii. 20), and are
### One in Him.
The spirit of antichrist is at work, and numerous signs present themselves, showing clearly that great changes may be expected very soon on every hand. There are many movements at work preparing the way for antichrist, such as Liberal Theology, Theosophy, Christian Science, Spiritualism, and the growing hatred against Christ, which has even taken political forms in several countries, as well as numerous other phenomena.

But on the other hand, there are good powers and movements at work, preparing the way for Christ's second coming, and last, but not least among them, stands the Pentecostal Movement, with its hosts of fire-baptised saints in all lands. There may be some difference of opinion amongst them, as to organisation and a few phases of doctrine, but they stand, as formerly seen, for the fundamental truths of Christianity, with the one desire of saving the world from perdition, and glorifying Christ, and keeping themselves prepared for His coming. Hallelujah!

### Will Not You
*lay hold of the promises in God's Word concerning you? Time is short. Hasten to obey God! (Acts v. 32). Shake off all lethargy and dull fears. Arise out of the dust, thou child of the living God! " Awake, awake, put on thy strength O Zion, put on thy beautiful garments, O Jerusalem!" Behold the Bridegroom is at hand; prepare to meet Him!*

# When the fire fell

and

## an outline of my life

*View from Volheine.*

by
*Thomas Ball Barratt.*

Printed by
Alfons Hansen & Sønner,
Norway.

## PREFACE.

It will always be a difficult and delicate work, to write ones own life story, and the chief reason for doing so, must of course, for a christian, be the decided attempt to honour Christ.

Ever since I left College in England, I have written a Journal, and have therefore quite a number, besides the regular Journal in the "Korsets Seir". But this makes it all the more difficult to condense facts and give my readers an outline of what has really transpired during 65 years.

Most of this time has been spent in *Norway*, the "Land of the Midnight Sun," the Country I love more than any other.

I trust all will bear with me, as I attempt to relate what the good Lord has done for me during all these years! I feel I have much to thank God for, and wish to honor my Redeemer for all His Love and tender mercies towards me!

Then again, I find it necessary to give my readers the *real facts* concerning my connection with *the Pentecostal Movement,* and how it all came about. Truth will prevail against error, and I am convinced that this Movement is *the last call to all* ere Christ comes!

Oslo, 1927.

**T. B. Barratt.**

# CONTENTS.

| | | Page |
|---|---|---|
| Preface. | | |
| I. | My birthplace in Cornwall | 5 |
| II. | Varaldsøy in Hardanger | 11 |
| III. | At school in England | 22 |
| IV. | Back in Norway again | 28 |
| V. | In Christiania. Sick. At Voss | 50 |
| VI. | Appointments in Christiania | 60 |
| VII. | Christiania City Mission | 76 |
| VIII. | In America | 98 |
| X. | A mighty anointing of the Spirit | 105 |
| IX. | When the Fire Fell | 125 |
| XI. | Back again in dear old Norway | 140 |
| XII. | The tour to India. | 157 |
| XIII. | The tumults in Copenhagen | 171 |
| XIV. | Pastor Lewi Petrus | 178 |
| XV. | Divisions. Before the judgment—seat | 191 |
| XVI. | We leave Møllergt. 38. Our new hall. In America again | 210 |

# WHEN THE FIRE FELL AND AN OUTLINE OF MY LIFE.

## CHAPTER I.
### My birthplace in Cornwall.

First of all I must take you on a trip to England, where I am born. We must go right down to Devonshire and Cornwall, renowned in the religious world through the great revivals that have taken place there, and the interesting accounts by Mark Guy Pearse, of men like Billy Bray and pastor Haslem.

You may be surprised to find the general appearance of the country quite different from the extensive, flat plains in other parts of the country. The undulating and picturesque landscape before you, covered with its rich pastures, divided by innumerable hedges, and spotted here and there with mines, gives you at once an idea of the southern end of old England.

As you travel through Devonshire, you suddenly catch a glimpse of the river Tamar, and on crossing it you are in Cornwall. The first town you reach is Calstock, which is situated on the mountain side, sloping to the river below. As your train rises higher and

View at Albaston.

My birthplace.

higher, the view becomes more open and picturesque, and you see at last the finest scenery in South England.

The train stops at a little town called Gunnislake. Formerly, we took the coach from Tavistock to Gunnislake and *Albaston*. Numerous marks of mines may be seen round about Albaston. The scenery is romantic and the air fresh and invigorating.

In this little town, I was born on the 22nd of July, 1862. I visited the place in 1909 during the month of June, and it was indeed very interesting to see the spot where I first learned to walk. On the other side of the road stood the old chapel of the "Primitive Methodists". Just a few minutes walk brought me to the Wesleyan chapel.

My parents were Wesleyan Methodists. A gentleman asked me if I would not see the inside of the chapel, he remembered my parents

The Wesleyan Chapel

and grandfather very well. It was grandfather who had planned, both this and other chapels in the neighbourhood. When the foundation was to be laid my uncle said: "I'll take the first dig with the pick", and father said: "Then I will use the spade first."

Captain George Ball, my grandfather, was a well known person in that part of the country. He took part in public life in various ways. He was "Captain" at the mines, director of the dissenter's day-school, and stood at the head of the list of the Wesleyan local-preachers. He was considered by many, even outside the Wesleyan denomination, to be a most solid and thorough theologian, and a very formidable adversary in debate. Once, when the town and vicinity were being infected by unitarian ministers, the various evangelical denominations determined to have a public meeting to discuss matters with them. They selected Captain George Ball as their leader in the debate, with the result that the unitarians were defeated.

Captain George Ball.

Many great Revivals took place among the miners and the people in Albaston and the surrounding towns.

My mother was converted during her 18th year. She used to tell us how she was mightily convicted in the Wesleyan chapel, and went out into the vestry. Here she fell on her knees, and determined not to rise before she was saved.

After praying some time, grandfather came into the vestry and said to her: "Mary, shall we not go home and pray?" "No, father", she answered, "not before God has saved me!" She held out two hours; then the light broke into her heart. From that moment she was saved, and all her later life gave proof of the genuine character of the change she had experienced. Her religious training had been a great help to her, so that her views of salvation and heart-cleansing were clear from the very first. Her life's motto was: *"The Blood of Jesus Christ cleanseth from ALL sin!"*

Father was saved in Marytavy. In company with my uncle, Mr. Jackman, and two other comrades, he attended a meeting in a Methodist chapel. All four were convicted of sin, and went to a near-by house to pray. Father was then 20 years old. Each of the four men took a corner in the room they had selected, and were determined to be saved that same evening. When the work was done in their hearts, they stood in the centre of the room and grasped each others hands, and with renewed tongues they sang:

> "Praise God, from whom all blessings flow,
> Praise Him all creatures here below,
> Praise Him above, ye heavenly host,
> Praise Father, Son and Holy Ghost!"

When the tones of that old anthem died away, they all knew that they had entered into a new life.

On visiting the town in 1909, I looked up the house and room where God had met them, and standing where they had stood, I praised God for all His goodness towards me. All four where then home in heaven!

Scenes, similar to those occuring in Wesley's time, took place during the revivals in Cornwall and Devonshire. People were suddenly smitten during the singing of some hymn, or whilst the sermon was going on, and sank down to the floor, as if an unseen hand had struck them. And so it was, the Holy Ghost had touched them! In the space of twenty or thirty minutes they were on their feet again, praising God for full salvation. Of course, there were numerous cases not accompained by such demonstrations of the Spirit, but sinners were nevertheless converted. Still it was not an uncommon fact, especially when the Holy Spirit was mightily outpoured, that the scythe of the Spirit mowed the people down, even very strong men, in the dust.

Captain Kent and Captain Skewis were well known workers during these days of revival. Judging from a letter written by grandfather, which I still have, numerous souls were saved; some after six hours of mighty prayer in anguish before God. Souls convicted of the necessity of salvation, were determined, just as my parents had been, not to cease praying until salvation was attained. And oh, what joy and singing, when they broke through and caught sight of the Blood!

Father, during all his life, was connected with the Mining business. He visited Wales, America and Australia, and eventually settled down in Norway. Before leaving for America, he was engaged to *Miss Mary Ball*, but several years elapsed ere they were married, 14 years in all. It was evidently his intention to return from America as soon as he had earned some money, but the gold-fever seized him. He, therefore, sailed direct to Australia from America. There were no comfortable liners then, as in our day, and it took weeks ere they reached their destination. In later days, father used to interest us with narratives from his romantic life in Australia in that then wild and wonderful land.

Both his Mary and he himself had remained true to their decision, although months elapsed ere they could get letters from each other. So when he returned from Australia, they were married; and on the 22nd of July, 1862, I was born.

Something happened at this time that had a great influence on my life. Father might have been connected with some large copper mines in *Spain*, but shortly after a position was offered him as Manager of a mine in *Norway*. He was wonderfully led by God to decide for the latter, and as I look back on all that has happened since, I assuredly find God's guiding grace and blessing in all this.

Mother, and myself as a baby boy.

## II.

*Varaldsøy in Hardanger.*

The Hardanger Fjord is undoubtedly Norway's most beautiful Fjord. A Fjord is a long arm of the sea, that stretches far into the country, bringing the salt water of the North Sea in between mighty mountains and green pasture land.

Varaldsøy is an island, that has somewhat the appearance of a pear on the map (Conf. map, page 47). In days gone by, beacon lights were lit on its highest peaks whenever the enemy approached, and its glare could often be seen at other times of the year. It might possibly symbolize the "holy fire" that was to be lit, away up between the mountains, later on. When speaking of Varaldsøy, we would generally say "fjældet," or "the mountain," where the mines were started, and where we found our first permanent home in Norway. The Fjord made its way like a broad, shining band of silver round the island, and proceeded on its way past Bakke and Strandebarm, beyond Jondal, until it stopped its course at Odda, where the "Folgefond" glacier and its eternal ice beamed forth overhead. A part of Folgefond could also be seen from various places in Varaldsøy.

On the North-western part of the island, a little village may be seen. In this village, a peasant girl, *Herborg*, lived. It was her duty to attend the cattle on the mountains. This woman had a remarkable dream. She saw in her dream, numerous houses standing on the spot where she generally allowed her cattle to feed. There was one house especially, that attracted her notice. It was better and of more importance than the others, she thought. At last she went to this house and asked the good lady there,

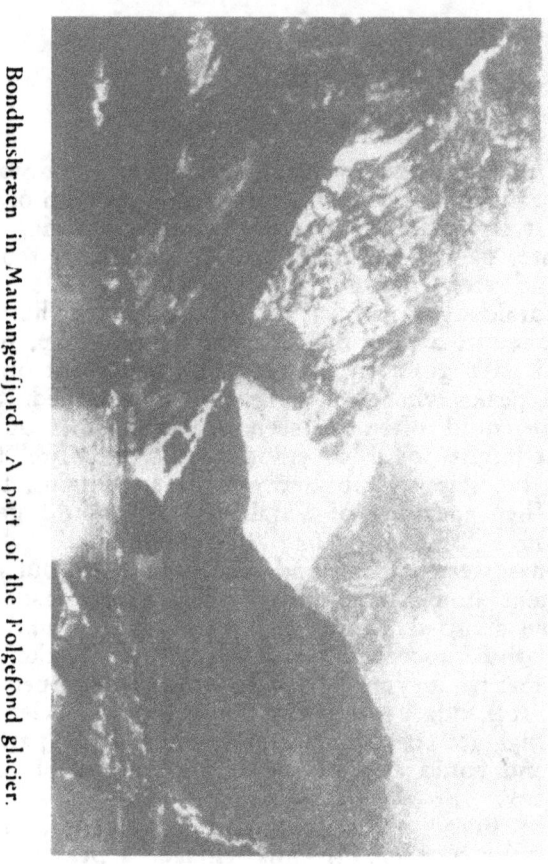

Bondhusbræen in Maurangerfjord. A part of the Folgefond glacier.

if she might become a servant in the home, and she was accepted as such.

She continued to dream, and saw a large company of people assembled in this home to hear a Missionary preach. To her surprise, she saw the good lady of the house fall on her knees during prayer, something very unusual amongst the Luther-

Tvinde Waterfall in the Hardangerfjord.

ans in those days. Then she awoke, and exclaimed "Surely this can never take place!" But she fell asleep again and dreamt the same dream a second time, and a third time.

She at last forgot it. But on the other side of

the Fjord, at *Gravdal*, someone found some stones of sulpher ore, and a mine was started there. One day an old woman found a stone of bright crystalised sulpher in between some shrubbery, away up on the "mountain," on Varaldsøy, and thought that it must be gold. That was not the case however; the ground was searched, and large veins of sulpher ore were found there, and immediately a Swede, *Mr. Berg*, started mining. The first thunders of the work of blasting began to roll between the mountain peaks. A company was formed, composed of English and Norwegian shareholders, and the question arose: Who is to take charge of the work? As we have already seen, the lot fell on father.

He started for Norway alone.

Of course, he was quite unacquainted with the language, and the manners, and customs of the people there. He had seen much of life elsewhere, but far away in the heart of Norway, he met with a people he had never been in touch with — a people both he and his family would learn to love and respect — a country that was to become his future home.

Many amusing episodes might be related from his first attempts to master the language. In those days too, the miners were much given to strong drinks, with the result that many a wild scene was witnessed amongst them. There was no police there on the mountain, and it was a long way to the "lensmand" (bailiff) in Strandebarm, but father's firm and resolute grip on the men, his christian spirit, conquered the difficulties that arose.

It caused quite a stir in *Albaston* when word came, that father would continue in Norway, and that mother had better come with her two children, Tom and Mary (Polly). Mother had been one of the strongest workers within the church, and her labors for the salvation of souls were known throughout the district. All felt it would be a great loss to the Church in Albaston should she leave for Norway, but God had, nevertheless, planned it thus.

I was then about five years old. According to several notices in the Journals, made later on, I had, even at that age, a few adventures that might have cost me my life, if Providence had not intervened.

It may also sound strange to some, but mother once said that an old catholic priest, during their trip in Scotland, when I was about one year old, had shown a more than usual liberal spirit, knowing that I was the child of a Protestant. — He dared to bless a Methodist child! When the time came for her to leave her many friends in Albaston, Calstock, Gunnislake, Mary-Tavy, Tavistock and the districts around Albaston, who thanked God for her holy influence, they wept. Just then the pastor of the church at Albaston, laid his hand on my head, and said to mother: "Don't weep, Mary, perhaps this little boy may become a Methodist preacher in Norway some day!" The prophecy was eventually fulfilled.

Time and again I have been touched with the fact, that *God* Himself has guided our steps, and that it was He, who in His wisdom, led father to choose Norway instead of Spain. How changed everything would have been, had he gone to Spain!

On our way to Hull, I was very nigh meeting with an accident. A passenger seemed to be very interested in me, gave me sweets, etc. Suddenly the train stopped and he slipped off, although it was outside the station: he was a railway man. I stepped off the train as well, but he didn't see me, and immediately the train began to move. There I stood, all alone. Mother just happened to see me through the window, and great was her consternation to see her only boy standing on the rails, just where the express was expected to come in a little while. At last another railway-man saw me, and took me to the station; and there was some rejoicing when mother saw me unhurt!

We crossed the North Sea on the "Scandinavia," one of the Wilson boats. We met an awful storm, but at last land was sighted. As we approached the coast and some of the great mountains appeared in sight, I said to Mr. De Bussy, a french engineer, who was to go with us to the mines, "If I only had a little ladder on the top of those mountains, I might climb right into heaven." That was my first impression of the Norwegian mountains!

On arriving at *Bergen* we proceeded to the Hardanger Fjord, stopping at *Varaldsøy*, where we were to make our future home for several years at any rate.

*Øierhavn* became the harbor, where the ships took their cargoes of sulpher-ore. A road, built by the Company, but now quite abandoned, wound its way up from the Fjord to V o l h e i n e on the "Mountain." Houses were built for the miners on Volheine, and it was found necessary to erect one also for the Manager and his family.

This spot, between mighty and towering mountains, about 800 feet above the sea, where the air was sweet and fresh, and the scenery wild and majestic, was to become the centre of life for quite a number of men and families — the place where I was to have my start in the Lord's vineyard.

In company with my wife and other relatives, I have visited *Volheine* a few times of late years. All that can be seen up there now are the ruins of the houses that formerly stood there, and a house erected by a new Company, that started mining several years after father's death. However, this Company has also finished its work there. An intense feeling of loneliness crept over me, as I visited all the old spots, so well known from my childhood and early youth. But let me continue my story.

Not long after our home had been erected at Varaldsøy, Miss Herborg came and asked if she

Ruins of chapel. Photo taken in 1926. The writer standing on the ruins. The birch-tree mother planted years ago. Vivian's Fjeld is seen to the right.

might be a servant in our home. Yes, mother received her as such.

Her dream was already in part fulfilled. The houses for the miners were there, and the Manager's home, and she had become a servant in that home.

The life among the miners was far from sober. They used to drink, fight and cause much disturbance. It was, of course, very difficult for my parents to control them: they had need of all the religion they had received in Old England.

One day a missionship anchored up in our harbor at Øierhavn. The Captain was an earnest christian. No Chapel had been erected as yet, but my parents arranged a meeting in our home for the miners and peasants. When prayers were held mother fell on her knees, and immediately Herborg remembered her dream. Now it was perfectly fulfilled!

As soon as it was possible for mother to acquire the language somewhat, she commenced with a Bibleschool for the young men at the Mines, and told them the old story of salvation. It evidently had a good and blessed influence on several of them. Still the drunken brawls amongst the miners were, at times, a great source of distress to both father and mother. But mother went in amongst them all as an angel of peace and quieted them during their fights and quarrels, whilst father exerted a rigid, firm, but christian discipline amongst them. Several scenes might be related from those days of almost a sensational character.

The Lutheran priest, Mr. Lampe, had, as usual (in Norway, the country has a Lutheran Statereligion), his regular services in the churches that belonged to his parish. One church was at the South end of Varaldsøy, the other in Strandebarm, and the third in Jondal. Three weeks passed ere he came round to the churches. The miners on Volheine were mainly composed of strangers, who had come to the mines from various parts of the country, yes, even from Sweden. One of the buildings for the miners was called "Svenskebrakken" (The Swedish barrack). They had little or no interest in the services in the churches. In those days there were very few "Emissaries" (evangelists) travelling in connection with the Lutheran church, visiting the villages. However when they did appear, they were not generally received with any real joy by the Lutheran priests; they even had to go through a good bit of persecution in various parishes.

It may safely be said, therefore, that the evangelistic work my parents started on the Mines was something quite new in that part of the country; but their home and their hearts were open for all, that they might bring the miners and their families the Gospel.

It was a long way to church. First came the walk, or drive, down to the harbor at Øierhavn;

then the long water- tour to the Southern part of the Island, with generally six rowers. However if the weather was fair, the tour was like a splendid picnic. The scenery on the Fjord was such, that go where you will in the world, you will find nothing that can surpass it.

In those days, the priest had great power. When his boat came in sight (his residence was in Strandebarm) there was a general stir; and when he was seen close by the church, they commenced to ring the Church bell, and the men lifted their hats.

Had there been place for a detailed account of the church services in those days, in the old fashioned Church, that at that time was in use, it would no doubt interest many. But I will be obliged to pass by many a scene of real interest, in order to press my "life" story into as short a space as possible.

Some of the Lutheran emissaries were very evangelical, and mother asked them to *press home* the importance of a momentous and present salvation, when they preached to the people, and the results were soon seen amongst some of the men.

Grandfather, Captain George Ball, came to Norway, as well as other relatives. We made quite a respectable choir, when all started singing. Father was an excellent tenor; grandfather had a deep good bass voice; others sang soprano and some alto. Many an enjoyable hour was spent away up on Volheine with good singing and music. The men were also delighted to hear it.

Down at the harbor, the steamers came from Hull to take away the sulpher—ore, that was driven down to the harbor. At times, some of the passengers aboard would come up to the mines to visit us and catch a glimpse of the beautiful scenery from the mountains that surrounded the Colony, especially from "Viviansfjeld." This mountain peak derived its name from the fact that one of the engineers, Mr. Vivian, had his home close by.

Mrs. Barratt sitting on the top of Viviansfjeldet in 1926.
A faint outline of the road may be seen.

One of the passengers who visited us one day, was the world famed violinist, *Ole Bull*. I can still remember his stately and powerful form. Father asked him to play on an old violin we had at hand, but it was too poor to play on. He generally used to "smash violins of that caliber and reconstruct them," he said, "in order to get the right tone out of them." But he invited us to visit him at his home at Lysøen, and then he would play all we desired. We never visited him there while he was still living, but went there when he was dead, with the crowds that went out to see him for the last time.

I nevertheless heard him play once in Bergen. I was still a boy, but I remember his appearance — how his long hair fell at times across the violin, as he drew forth the sweet strains of "Sætergjentens søndag" on the instrument.

As I grew up, I was evidently a daring young fellow. I used to climb the mountains, and passed through many an adventurous scene, and at times not always so good as I ought to have been. I remember one scene from my home life. I was afraid to tell lies, but I had several times tried to evade the truth. Grandfather would stand it no longer, so mother took me up in his room and gave me a thrashing. I tried to get out of the way, but to no avail. Mother gave no pardon, and it was well for me that she would not spare me. But after that, she went into a little room close by; threw herself on the bed there, and wept. That scene, I can never forget

No parents have prayed more for their children than ours. We were four of us—Polly, Louisa, Alexander, and myself. Alexander was a wonderful little boy. He won the hearts of all. When he died, I sat in the room where his body lay and wept as if my heart would break. He was buried near the old church at Varaldsøy.

The first deeper drawings of the Spirit on my heart, I felt when nine years old. I had often been touched by one thing and another, but this was a definite influence of a higher power. I was sitting upstairs in grandfather's room reading my lessons— grandfather was my teacher. Suddenly I felt a warm, good influence creep over my heart and draw me down on my knees. I folded my hands and lay on my knees under the table, praying. When I had prayed a while, I heard grandfather's powerful voice cry out from the room underneath: "Tom, do you know your lessons?" I was so bashful, that I did not want anybody to know anything about my inner feelings and prayer. I therefore sprang up and resumed reading my lessons. Had I only told mother about it, or even grandfather, nothing would have gladdened their hearts more than that.

## III.

*At school in England.*

My parents decided that I was to attend school in England. Mother took me across the North Sea once more: this time back to Old England. I commenced at the Junior School of the Wesleyan college, at Taunton, Sommersetshire. Mr. Hancock was Master of the School. It was quite natural, that my parents wished to give me, and later on my two sisters, the very best education possible, under Methodist influence. My sisters attended Flook House, of which Mrs. Sibly was in charge, wife of the headmaster of our college. Mr. Sibly himself, and the Rector of our College, Mr. Slater, were no doubt warmhearted christians, but the old time Methodist influence, throughout the school, was wanting. The college has since then changed its name, and is now known as Queens College.

I was full of life, and had imbibed a good bit of Viking blood during the few years I had been in Norway. I used to jump and climb the mountains and took no doubt the breath from good Mr. Hancock, when I one day jumped from the second story window to the ground. The result was that he ordered me to remain indoors all day. When I was in Norway, the boys called me the "Englishman"; but at the junior school and at the college, they called me the "Norwegian". I loved sport, and there was ample room for it, both at the junior school and at the college. I am afraid that I did not give heed to my lessons as I ought to have done. However at the junior school a remarkable revival broke out. I cannot remember the source of it now, save that my loved ones in Norway were constantly praying for me, and, evidently, for the school. All the children were suddenly driven by some unseen power to pray to God. The teachers could not understand it, but did not oppose it. Use of the large dining hall was granted to us, where we had *Prayer meetings.* If only some one had been able to lead and direct us! I remember, that several of the boys scarcely dared to pray aloud, but I wrote prayers for them on a slip of paper, and sent it round through the praying rows of boys, and they read it aloud on their knees.

When at school, I spent my Christmas holidays in Cornwall and Devonshire with my relatives: my summer holidays were spent at home in Hardanger. Just before leaving the junior school for the summer holidays, I became very ill. On arriving at London I, as usual, stayed at my Aunt's home, Mrs. Raven. The doctor said, that if my folks would see me alive, they had better come at once: it was scarlet fever. Mother was telegraphed. When she arrived, the fever had reached its highest stage. I opened my eyes the very moment she stepped into the room. I saw her, and the joy of seeing her brought about a change. I fell into a deep sleep, and rallied from that hour. My stay at home was prolonged in order to rest sufficiently, but the day I left home, I met with a severe misfortune. The driver, on our way down from Volheine, drove too near the roadside, and rushed against a large stone. I was seated by his side, and was thrown with great violence to the ground, dislocating my elbow, breaking it in some parts. That was a hard trial for me.

Grandfather was sick those days, and had warned them against my staying at home longer than my holidays. When he saw them carrying me in, he said: "That's just what I said!" That is the last scene I can remember from grandfather's life.

On returning to Taunton, I was removed to the college.

A very rigid discipline was in force there, and several of the teachers, I remember, were very severe

The Wesleyan College, now Queen's College.

in their exercise of the college rules. Possibly, that was beneficial to me. I was not evil minded, but full of life and frolic, and had to suffer for my breaking the rules many a time.

I loved football and cricket. I might write a book filled with experiences from my College days. Several of my old chums, I remember very distinctly. One of the students became the means of my conversion — *Thomas D. Barnes. G. Whelpton*, another student, was a great help to me. However Barnes was evidently a revivalist in spirit; his greatest interest was to get the young men and boys at the college converted. I have still the letter he wrote home to my parents, after my conversion (it is dated Nov. 22nd., 1874), as well as the letter I wrote home the day before. My letter reads in part thus:

"My dear parents, I hope you received my letter No 6, this is No. 7. On Sundays we have three Prayermeetings. The boys all join together, those who want to. You could not have found a much better school for me. There are several of the boys converted here. A few days ago one of the boys called Michell, and then a little while after that Budgett was converted, and on Tuesday last Noel II was converted, and *on Wednesday after tea I was converted*, which I know you will all be glad to know. I have been spoken to lots of times by G. Whelpton and Barnes I. I was very much affected by their words and others On Wednesday Barnes took me up to the top class room, and there I sought the Lord who died to wash away my sins and the sins of others. I hope that there will be a great many more soon . . . Now you must ask Polly (my eldest sister) to be converted as well. She will be a good deal the better for it. Tell her that Jesus is ready to receive if she will only come and believe."

The change was seen at once. I was more attentive and studied my lessons more intensely. I remember well, that a senior student came to me one day and asked me how I felt, and how it all came about.

Then Barnes left the college, and I became lukewarm. Shortly a great revival broke out in Taunton in 1875, in which, as far as I can remember, about 200 students at the various colleges, were converted, besides a great number of the people in the town itself. *Mr. Robinson Watson,* was the evangelist God used. He seemed to know the bible by heart and held *aftermeetings.* As a rule we marched down to the chapel to the ordinary services, and now we had liberty to march down to the revival services. At one of the meetings, when he desired all, who were willing to own and follow Christ, to step into the schoolroom by the side of the chapel, I immediately arose and walked in, in the midst of my comrades. That step helped me, others followed, and I became greatly renewed in spirit again.

College life however, was not a means of promoting my spiritual growth. I became lukewarm again. I was in fact but a boy, being saved when only 12 years old. But in 1876 I visited, during my Christmas holidays, the home of Allen, one of my comrades at Liskeard. His parents were warmhearted Methodists. It was at the watch-night service of this year, that I renewed my vows again and was greatly blest.

The leading men at the college found it necessary to start "*classes*" for the boys who desired to take part. These were the ordinary "classes," customary amongst the methodists. I was placed on *Mr. W. P. Slater's,* the rector's, class. I have still my "Quarterly Ticket for June, 1877," with his signature.

I left college on the 15th of June, in 1878. I dare not boast of any great attainments in my studies, with the exception of drawing and music. I took several first prizes on those lines, and have still some of the drawings hanging on the walls in my home.

The stern methods of some of the teachers rather embittered the spirit of several of the boys. We determined to avenge ourselves in some way or other, but when the time came for my departure from college, I found that the revengeful spirit did not have much hold on me. I went to all the teachers and begged them to forgive me for anything said or done that was not right. As I left a few days before the other comrades broke up for their holidays, I passed through the great dormotories, on the morning of my departure, and bade them all farewell. They wept and would not let me go: we really loved each other and did not care to part.

Five years of my life had passed by, and I felt assured that the experiences I had made during this time were of lasting benefit to me in many ways.

On leaving College.

Shugg left College with the same train, and we parted at Bristol. When I visited America in 1906, I met him again. He is the only College boy I have met since I left Taunton. I met him close by Des Moines. He was then a methodist preacher, and I spoke in his church. We had not seen each other for 28 years, but I knew him at once.

## IV.

*Back in Norway again, and my Call to the Ministry.*

My mother and Polly met me at *Stavanger*. We spent two bright, never to be forgotten weeks there. It was here I heard *Pastor Ole Olsen*, of the Methodist Church, for the first time in my life. He was evidently one of the greatest preachers of Methodism in Norway. His mode of preaching took hold of me at once. I wept right through the first meeting, and received a mighty impulse to live wholly for God. There was fire and a mighty stir in connection with Methodism in Norway during those days.

Methodism had to pass through the fires of persecution then, as the Pentecostal Movement has

Pastor Ole Olsen.

in these days. But the freshness of the preaching "the great outpouring of the Spirit" at the meetings, carried them through to victory. I was also influenced to join *the Temperance Movement* when in Stavanger, and have still my card of membership, signed by *Peder Sunde*.

When I arrived home in Hardanger, I immediately commenced a *Sunday school* amongst the children of the miners, and by the aid of Mr. Larsen, from Stavanger, we also started work for the Temperance cauce amongst the miners and pe ple on the Island. Pastor Olsen visited us from Stavanger. There was no Methodist work as yet in Bergen. His visit was a great blessing to the miners.

A "bedehus" (chapel) was erected. Here I held our Sunday school, and here all the services and revival meetings took place, when the Lutheran emissaries came round. We arranged also for a regular Sunday forenoon service. Mother could not preach, nor father; but we got the chief "formand", *Mr. Claus Pedersen*, at the Mines, to read a regular sermon from an *"huspostile"* (collection of sermons), in connection with singing and prayers. It was rather a dry service, but better than nothing.

On the 2nd of Dec., 1878, *pastor Ole Olsen* visited us again. I played the harmonium and led the singing at the meetings, and his sermons had a striking influence on the people. He remained with us several days.

At Christmas we had a delightful festival for the children of the Sunday school and their parents. The chapel was beautifully decorated, and the Christmas tree was very attractive. We continued this annually.

I have not space to dwell on everything of interest at the Mines and all my experiences there. I might relate several incidents in connection with my comrades, Bob Sparre, Frederic Holst, the sons of Dr. Kinck, and others, but there is no room for it in

My first Sundayschool. Back row (from left to right) K. Klemmetsen, Gustav Olsen, Claus Pedersen (The foreman at the mines) The writer, mother, my sister Mary (Polly).

this condensed story of my life. I especially wish to dwell on scenes of *religious* interest.

On the 16th of January, 1879, we were visited by *pastor Lars Pettersen*. He was sent to

Volheine by pastor Ole Olsen, and was on his way to Bergen to start the Methodist work there. Our little chapel was crowded to the doors, and a wonderful spiritual power was present at the meetings. Souls were saved. He preached also at Øierhavn and in *Strandebarm*, and continued his journey from there to Bergen.

The result of his visit was a revival among the miners, and we started with prayer meetings in

Pastor L. Pettersen

real earnest. At these prayer meetings, I commenced for the first time to pray aloud in the Norwegian language. The thought then struck me, that I might commence to read sermons, just as the "formand," but instead of the oldfashioned Lutheran sermons he read, I started reading Dwight *L. Moody's* sermons, of which we had a translation. I had never attempted as yet to speak or preach, but on the 26th of January, 1879, mother had a "Kvindeforeningsmøte" (Womens meeting), and at that *I read a sermon and prayed aloud*, and as a result souls were saved that very day.

I continued reading Moody's sermons, and acquired considerable freedom in the spirit, and knew them almost by heart at last. The practical and spiritual method of presenting Gospel truths that made Mr. Moody so well known, had a wonderful influence on the hearts of the people. They were not used to hear that kind of preaching. I closed the meetings with an after-meeting and prayed with souls.

In March, we had a renewed visit by Pastor Pettersen. There was much rejoicing when we saw him again. The revival had broken out in Bergen, and the Lutheran priests had commenced their opposition to this work of God — but God was with him! He visited Strandebarm again and some souls were saved there. The priest there made no opposition.

I started a choir amongst the miners: it was a good help in the meetings. On the 6th of April, I held my *first extemporaneous speech* in connection with the reading of Moody's sermons it was really a glorious evening service. At the close, I prayed with seekers for salvation.

On the 11th of April, 1879, I commenced to hold meetings outside our own chapel. The first was held at Øierhavn, down by the harbour. One of the most well known persons in connection with the mines, was Mr. Olsen, our stablemaster. He took charge of the horses used at the mines. We always dropped in and had a chat with him and his wife, when we went down to the harbour. Last summer I met him again—the summer of 1926, at Varaldsøy. He was still alive, and we had a long chat about by—gone days.

I was always a joy to me, when I returned home from the harbour, to be able to ride on one of the horses from the stables—I loved riding. The free and invigorating life on the mountains was delightful, so in between my work at the mines (I became my fathers assistant) and the meetings, I often fished in the lakes close by, or down on the Fjord; sometimes I threw my gun on my shoulders and went off on the mountains in search of game. I started in with various kinds of study, but *my line of life was still unsettled*

The old Lutheran priest, *Mr. Lampe*, left his parish for good during those days. I remember his last visit at Volheine. He expressed the hope, that his long pastorate had not been in vain. The new priest was *Mr. H. Stub*. Our connection with the personage in Strandebarm was kept up, although he knew we were Methodists. Occasionally, I still meet with some of the family.

On a visit to Bergen I met pastor *C. H. Johnson*, one of the most earnest preachers amongst the Norwegian Methodists in Amerika. He had a fascinating and vivid way of presenting Gospel truth. Crowds attended his services. I very often visited Bergen in company with my father, who went there on business. This brought me in connection with the Methodists there. All within our family were still members of the *Wesleyan Methodist Church*, and had not joined "*The Methodist Episcopal Church*". It was the last named church that had commenced the Methodist work in Norway. In July, 1879, Bishop Wiley held the Annual Conference in Bergen. This was the first conference held in that town, and the first I had ever attended. Here I also had the opportunity of hearing pastor *M. Hansen*, one of the founders of Methodism in Norway. The Conference was a marvellous success for Methodism in that town.

*Pastor A. Olsen* (Presiding Elder), and *pastor C. H. Johnson* accompained us to Hardanger after the Conference, and held several glorious meetings among the miners and people there. *Pastor Pettersen* visited us whilst they were there. This gave the meetings even more impetus. In between, we took several delightful picnics to various parts of the isle and elsewhere.

In my Journal, on the 9th of August, 1879, I wrote as follows: "I spent the day in quiet study and constant prayer, with religious music. *Prepared my first sermon*; went up on the top of a high mountain and preached it to the winds." The next day I wrote: "I preached to the children, or rather gave an exposition on Eccleciastics 12." These sermons were no doubt *written*, and read publicly, in between sermons by Moody and John Wesley.

I was on the start, it will be seen, not knowing as yet what line of life work the good Lord had prepared for me.

When I visited Bergen in September, I met whith *Mrs. Fredrikke Nielsen*, who was famed as an *actress* at the Theater there, but had been converted at pastor Pettersens meetings. It was in those days the Methodist church in Bergen was organized. Wonderful days of blessing!

In 1880 I organized a *Temperance Society for children*, and soon commenced to work for the Temperance cause amongst the miners and elsewhere. On the 12th of November we commenced with „*Thanks giving meetings*", in order to thank the good Lord for all His goodness towards us as a people, away up on the mountains. The meeting held on the 2nd of February, was wonderfully blest. "A special spiritual atmosphere came over us all." On the 5th, I note that I have "won some stars in my crown in heaven—some precious souls." On the 7th of March I write: "*The Holy Spirit worked truly with power in our midst*, so that souls were saved and *his* name glorified, Hallelujah to God in the highest!" I proceeded with a *still more definite revival work*, and souls were saved.

This led to revival meetings outside the Mines. On the 13th of March, I visited *Mundheim* and had two meetings there. I wrote: "The place was full of people and the Holy Spirit was with us. I feel that the seed sown will bear fruit." On a visit to Bergen in March I held a meeting in the chapel there, and remark in the Journal: "The Holy Spirit was with us." *I still read Moody's sermons* and spoke in connection with them

Mrs. Fredrikke Nielsen had by this time left the Theater. She accompained us home to Hardanger. On the steamer, I arranged a meeting and got her to read one of Wesley's sermons — "We shall all stand before the Judgement seat of Christ". Several "young people laughed," but we "did not care about that, as we knew that God was able to save to the uttermost." *)

This method of work was especially suited for Mrs. Nielsen. As an actress she had attained great proficiency in elocution, and she commenced to labour for the Lord in this way, until she, little by little, as myself, was led to speak directly to the people.

It is of interest to notice how often I state in my Journals: *"The Lord filled me with the Holy Spirit,"* or *"The Holy Spirit filled the place."* My knowledge of this subject was, of course, at this time not clear, although my longing was intense at times. I therefore mistook *strong unctions of the Spirit for the Baptism of the Holy Spirit itself.* But I was often too weak spiritually in between these greater uplifts in the Spirit, although I was wlling to be led and guided aright.

The Temperance Society among the miners counted 80 members in March, 1880. I was the leader, and Mr. Claus Pedersen the Vice President. This work met with considerable opposition, but I "went into it with all my soul." This led to the visits of men like Hogarth and Ole Kalem.

I commenced *some literary work.* I translated the book, "*Pioneer Methodism in America.*" (*Banebryter Metodismen i Amerika*). This work influenced my young mind greatly. It was just that kind of selfsacrificing, adventurous and interesting life, that solicited my full sympathy.

---
*) When remarks are quoted, they are as a rule taken from one or other of my journals.

Skjæggedals Waterfall in Hardanger.

About this time there was a priest within the Lutheran circles, especially the *Inner—Mission*, who wielded great influence on the west coast — *Sogneprest Lars Oftedal*. I 1880, in the month of June, he visited Strandebarm, and about 7000 attended the openair meetings there. Some say there were 12000 people present from various parts of the Fjord and the west coast. The services were very interesting. Later on this lion among preachers fell a prey to the devils temptations, and brought disgrace on the work of Christ.

We had considerable connection with the "*Inner Mission*", as our home was open to receive preachers from any denomination. We even received *pastor Hellebostad* of the *Baptist Church*, although our views of Baptism in those days were far from those of the Baptists.

I was now *18 years old*. I often visited Bergen. The Hall there had by some accident or other been burnt down, and the most fanatical Lutherans said: "There then you have proof of the fact that God is not with them." But a new chapel was built.

It's strange to think how blinded some people are! But truth will conquer in the long run.

I still read sermons. Once when reading the sermon by Charles Wesley: "Awake, thou that sleepest, that Christ may be thy light!" I happened to strike the lamp close by, which fell to the floor and was smashed to bits. Fortunately, the oil did not ignite. It happened just as I pronounced the words "*and Christ shall be thy light.*" I labored for the salvation of souls at the meetings and elsewhere, *but I had no definite plan of becoming a preacher*. I had commenced to take lessons in picture painting at Bergen with the artist, *Mr. O. Dahl*, and lessons in harmonics with *Edvard Grieg*. At college I had shown considerable ability in drawing and music, and felt that I should like to develope on those lines. I note in my Journal, that I was now able to "speak almost as readily in Norwegian as in English."

The Temperance work interested me greatly, and I held "lectures" at the mines and elsewhere, in order to oppose the the drinking customs amongst the people.

On the 4th of December I read the *"War Cry" of the "Salvation Army"* for the first time. On the 5th I preached on the words *"Prepare, O Israel, to meet thy God"*, and write: "God blest us greatly, all glory to His name!" This was evidently my *first extemperaneous sermon.* This took place in 1880. I was then 18 years old. I continued the *"Thanksgiving Meetings."* They were of a more free nature than the meetings in general. On the 8th, I preached again. "God blest us, praised be His Holy Name!"

I had now commenced to touch on the line of work, that God had called me to follow. The Day Journal is full of notices about the various meetings which were held among the miners and at the surrounding farms. The people began to know that Barratt's son, Tom, had commenced to preach, and that souls were being saved at the meetings.

In February, I was attacked by Influenza. Several of the miners suffered also from this epidemy. As I went out too early, I caught bronchitis. This was the commencement of several similar attacks in coming years, but I was always of good courage, and by God's grace I recovered from every attack.

Word came from the farms round about, asking me to come and hold meetings. There was a good deal of political talk in those days among the peasants and miners. Personally, I held to the more liberal view. Great battles raged here and there, but I never entered into political life to any extent. When I met with the Lutheran priest, *pastor Stub*, we were the best of friends, although he was a strong Lutheran and had very conservative views in politics. He preached a sermon on holiness at the mines once, which I could not of course accept. I notice in my Day Journal, that I even then considered it very necessary to be *"filled with the Spirit,* otherwise our work for the salvation of souls would be in vain."

On the 9th of March I wrote: "At the meeting in the evening, *the Holy Spirit filled me* so that I spoke with great influence." Of course I did not then know the whole truth concerning the Baptism of the Holy Spirit, but I had evidently again received an annointing of the Spirit.

On the 15th of March, I took part in a funeral amongst the peasants. It was attended by the old customs prevelant in the Fjord. I determined to practice 1. Cor. 9, 22. My presence influenced many, so that the ale jug passed by them untouched. I went aside to speak with God, and when I returned He gave me grace to hold a meeting amongst the people present, and "I have never before spoken with such boldness and ease. *The Holy Spirit filled me greatly,* and the tears rolled down the cheeks of the people. Old and young were strongly influenced by the Holy Spirit. The women were quite broken down. The Lord was indeed present amongst us."

Thus the account runs. There are several interesting notices in the Journals of the meetings I held in the villages. At the "atter—meetings," I spoke with the people personally and prayed with seekers. In between, I also held temperance meetings, lecturing on temperance and enlisting new members in the Society.

*Mrs. Nielsen*, the converted actress, visited us, and we had revival meetings together. We continued the meetings after her departure, and witnessed many *"revival scenes"* every now and then.

I visited Bergen on the 6th of June, 1882, and

Springtime in Hardanger. Photo taken at Odda, showing the blossoming fruittrees down by the Fjord, and the Folgefond glacier on the mountain top.

Deep winter in the Norwegian woods.

passed my examination at the Quarterly conference as *Local—preacher.*

In 1883 I wrote *sermons* to the religious papers, and an article against *Pastor L. Skavlan's* (Lutheran) lecture and tract about the so—called "*Errors of Methodism.*" This answer was published in tract form, and spread far and wide.

On a visit to Bergen in 1883, I heard the well-known *Evangelist Franson* speak on various occassions. On the 27th of April that year, I gave *a report to the Quarterly Conference* in Bergen. *Bro. Doublough* was pastor. *This report, no doubt the first of its kind I ever gave,* comprised the work done at Varaldsøy and elsewhere.

It is easy to see, that the Lord was leading me on to something definite, step by step. I continued helping father with office work and attended the work at the Mines. In between I practiced sport, both summer and winter, as I found that healthy exercise strengthened me physically, and was necessary during all the work I had on hand. My correspondance increased continually.

The 22nd of July 1883, was the day of my "*coming of age.*" I was 21 years old. "I held service before and after dinner. God blest us greatly all through the day." But the day was commemorated on the 24th with a great festival. We thus kept up the old custom, away up there on the mountain.

On a visit to Bergen in August I met again the *Rev. Ole Olsen,* and describe in my Journal the mighty influence he exerted, both as a preacher and as pastor of the Church at Bergen.

During those days my sister *Louisa,* now Mrs. Abrahamsen, left for England with mother, in order to attend school at Flook House, Taunton, the same school where my sister Mary received her education.

On the 31st of January, I wrote: "I preached to the people on the 18th from Joshua 24,15: "Choose ye this day whom ye will serve." *God was there!*

— it was a wonderful meeting. Since that evening, the *revival* commenced in real earnest. We have held meetings every evening since then, with the exception of Saturday. Many are converted. I have preached both up here at the mines and down by the sea at Øierhavn. A general revival has com menced. All glory to the living God. Mockers have been slain by the power of the Spirit and have been converted. Old and young men and women have sought and found the Saviour, and God be praised, many are still seeking. God grant that the beacon light on this mountain top may blaze with great brightness, so as to be seen far and near. It's the Lord's work, the Lord alone is to be praised!"

In 1884, I commenced with "*Samtalemøter*" (Conversation meetings.) On the 8th of March, 1884, I left for Strandebarm, and held a temperance lecture in the evening, after which we had a "samtale—møte." The meeting place was filled with old and young, and it took a good while to write all the names of those who signed the pledge that evening. I held a short sermon at 9 o'clock Sunday morning, and a greatly blest prayermeeting followed. At 11 o'clock the Lutheran *Emissary Ekeland* preached at *Berge*. I played the harmonium. God blest us. E. preached very well. At 3 o'clock I preached at *Borsheim*. The room was so full of people, that I could scarcely get to the place where I intended taking my stand. The Spirit of the Lord was there, and worked with wonderful power. After the meeting the people would not go, so we stayed on, praying, singing. etc. until 6 o'clock. At 6 the "samtalemøte" commenced in Borsheims school-house. I had chosen as a subject for discussion: "*The duties of a christian.*" We divided the subject thus: 1) A christian's duties towards God. 2) towards his fellow men (both christians, neighbours and enemies), especially turning the subject towards the question prevalent at the time being: A **christian's** duty towards brethren or christians belonging to other denominations. 3) Towards a *revival*, for example the one that now took place in our midst. This last point I devided again into two extra points: 1) *Truth* and 2) *Tolerance*.

The meeting was most excellent. It was one of the most greatly blest and interesting meetings of the kind I have ever attended."

I notice that I had commenced *to write poems* now and then.

In connection with a renewed attack of inflamation of the bowels, I make a remark about mother, who attended my every want: "God be blest for giving me a loving and holy christian mother!" It was no doubt her *prayers* and holy influence that pervaded my life more than any other influence apart from God. Not long after this, I was laid very low with bronchitis and a slight touch of inflammation of the lungs. The healthy mode of life I had been used to helped me much, "but the hundreds of prayers that were sent up for me, were no doubt of still more avail. I felt prepared, because the Lord of Hosts was whit me and did not forsake me." He wanted me to continue the work I had commenced in His vineyard.

Later: "I am still weak and not able to preach. Lord, if it be Thy will, then strengthen my body, soul and spirit. Fill me with power from on high! Let my heart be a temple for Thee, Thou Holy One of Israel! Come! Come! Glory to God Eternal, Son and Holy Ghost! Praise and power be to Thee, Omnipresent and Everlasting Three in One!" Not long after this I was at work again for the Master. Still it must be remembered, that I had not as yet severed myself from the business at the mines, but the good Lord was preparing me for future days.

On the 29th of Aug., 1884 I left home for Bergen. *The Rev. Ole Olsen* had "given me charge of the Church in Bergen during his absence. He was appointed as delegate to the Evangelical Alliance

meetings at Copenhagen. That Sunday was eventful."
Aug. 31: Prayermeeting at 9:15. Preaching at 10. Sundayschool at 12. Preaching at 5, and aftermeeting at 7. The day was full of blessing. God laid bare His arm all through the day and strengthened both my body and soul. At the aftermeeting the communion rails were encircled by penitent sinners. In fact, all over the chapel we could feel the presence of Almighty God. Glory be to His name! Many professed that they had found their Saviour that evening." At the Wednesday meeting "the Spirit of the Lord worked greatly upon the hearts of the people, as the aftermeeting especially proved."

The Thursday following I was obliged to leave for Osterøen, in order to pay our workmen there (The company had mines there also), and held at the same time revival services, with real revival results. Hallelujah!

In October, 1884, I restate in my Day Journal some facts concerning the commencement of things that had transpired in my life so far. I state that I commenced my first Sunday school on the 13th of October, 1878. My first temperance lecture was held New Year's Day, 1880. I commenced religious meetings for grown up persons on the 26th of January, 1879, by reading one of Moodys sermons. The first Prayer meeting for children was held on a Friday, Febr. 6th. 1880. The first extemporaneous sermon was delivered on Dec. 5th., 1880. "I little thought then, that I should in so short a time after this be enabled to preach several times a week to eager throngs. But I waited on the Lord, and He blest me! It seems wonderful that he has chosen so weak a vessel to expound and preach the Gospel, but He continues to bless my humble efforts. Strengthen me, O Lord! Keep my feet from falling, and in Thy Name I will meet every foe and conquer! By Thy grace and the sword of fire, I will bring sinners to the foot of the cross and point them to Thee, the Saviour of the World!"

This then was the Spirit in which the good Lord led me on, right at the commencement of my work for Him. Doors were constantly being opened. It must be remembered that I was a methodist, and the prevailing prejudices against methodism could be felt every now and then, but as my work was merely evangelical, and no attempt was made in the Fjord to start a new Methodist church, the steps taken to prevent my efforts were of no avail. The people came from far and near to the meetings, and revival scenes were constantly attending them. A book could easily be written, with accounts from these glorious days. I often visited Bergen and took part in the meetings there, and became in this way more and more vitally connected with the Methodist Episcopal Church. My parents were, as formerly stated, Wesleyans.

At last a letter from *the Rev. Lars Pettersen*, dated 2nd of Sept. 1885, was sent to my parents, from Christiania. He states that they were in want of a preacher in 2nd Church there. If they were willing to give me up to this service for the Lord, and I was willing to go, he felt I ought to come. I decided, in the Name of the Lord, to go.

*Farewell meetings* were held several places in Hardanger. The Lutheran minister, *Mr. Stub*, announced them himself in the Church, and "made some very friendly, touching remarks about my labors in his three parishes and elsewhere. He was so affected himself, that he at times spoke with difficulty. I feel thankful to the Lord, that He has used me, the most unworthy of all His servants to glorify His holy name."

The account of *my farewell meetings* appeared in the "Kristelig Tidende", the Methodist Episcopal Church paper, and the next entry in the Journal was made in Christiania, 1885. A chart of *Hardanger*

A map of Hardanger Fjord, which I have kept and on which I marked the places where I held meetings, before leaving for Christiania (Oslo).

*Fjord*, that I have kept since those days, showing the places where I held meetings before I left for Christiania (Oslo).

I received a word of greeting from *Mr. Edvard Grieg*, after my decision to become a minister of the Gospel, that will interest many.

"Troldhaugen, 12. Sept. 85.

Bedste Hr. Barratt, (My best Mr. Barratt).

In answer to your letter, allow me to send you my varmest wishes for your future. May the position you now have chosen, be the means of making you and others happy!

With friendly greetings,
Yours respectfully
Edvard Grieg."

I received also a very flattering recommendation from the Director of the Varaldsøy Mining Co., Limited, on leaving my position at the mines. It is dated August 14th, 1885; 8 Old Jewry, London. E. C., and read as follows: "I have much pleasure in certifying that I have known from boyhood *Thomas Barratt*, the son of Captain A. Barratt, long resident at Varaldsøy Mine, Hardanger, Norway, and who has, since he left school, been assisting his father in the office and in the practical management of the mine.

In my judgement, Thomas Barratt has proved himself to be a good son, and I consider him of a hard—working and industrious disposition, quite reliable, and of an honorable mind.

G. Barry.

But one of the most interesting letters was a letter written to me later on by mother, concerning *my calling to the Ministry*:

"You will remember that you and I were at

home alone, and that we were having the stairs painted; so you slept in the office and I in the parlour. First, a telegram was sent by the *Rev. Ole Olsen*, stating that you were appointed to help him in Bergen; and a day or two before you were ready to go there, the letter came for you to go to Christiania.

Now, I had always prayed and hoped, that God would use you in His vineyard; *I had dedicated you to God from your infancy, Yes, even before you were born*; I hoped, that if God should give me a son, that *he might be a preacher of the Gospel;* but now that the time had come for you to go out in the vineyard, to really leave your home, I felt sad for a time, and asked myself if I had been sincere when I offered you to the Lord. Yes, I knew I had been; still I felt a sort of trembling, and said to myself I would see what the Bible say to me, and I opened at Matt. X, 37. I need scarcely say, that I prayed and wept, and offered you afresh to the Great Master.

When I told you this the next morning, you turned quite pale, and said: "Was that your text mother, why, it was mine also; I was feeling how hard it would be to leve my home, and I opened my Norwegian Bible at the very same passage."

Your loving mother!

## CHAPTER V.

*In Christiania. Sick. At Voss. Married.
In Christiania again.*

On the way to Christiania the steamer remained some hours, both at Stavanger and Christiansand. "I had therefore the opportunity of preaching in the Methodist churches at both of these places." Before the call to Christiania, now Oslo, I had received a call to "be Bro. Ole Olsens helper in Bergen, but an alteration of affairs in Christiania made it necessary for me to come there." In company with the *Rev. H. Ristvedt*, I was to take charge of the Church at Kampen," in the Northern part of the city, among the working population.

Concerning my departure from home, "I felt it hard to part with my dear old home (Ah, what a home! Such love! Such harmony! God bless my dear, precious parents and sisters!), but I was willing to go and do as my Heavenly Father bade me!"

In addition to my evangelistic labors, I continued my literary work. Of course it was all in the bud, so to speak. I commenced a book entitled "The Faithful Sons of Methodism." Not long after my start in Christiania, I wrote: "Souls are being saved and God's cause is prospering. Last Wednesday I lectured on "Utholdenhet" (Endurance) at the bazar in Grunerløkken (Ist Church)."

"I evidently overtaxed my strength, at the commencement of things in Christiania. My health failed me, and I was obliged to leave the City. A whole year passed by ere the next entry in the journal. On the 10th of Nov. 1886, I wrote: "I have been down at death's door, but was not allowed to pass through. However, the lessons taught me during my illness, will prove useful to me in after life; lessons that, had I remained well and healthy, I would perhaps not have had the chance of learning."

"I labored on a little while after the last entry with success, but the constant strain on my system, brought me down at last. I became very ill. After some suffering, I revived and obtained my physicians permission to commence preaching again. But had I rested then a few months, I might have been fully restored. The same illness returned with double force, and prevented me from working a whole year."

"My sister, Mary, came to Christiania to fetch me home. The Lord has now in answer to prayer strengthened and blest me most wonderfully. Little by little, I began to shake off that awful weak state. Jesus laid His blessed hands on me and revived my spirit. I commenced laboring again as my strength revived, and souls were saved.

On the 18th of Sept. I became engaged to *Miss Laura Jakobsen*. In the journal I remark: «God bless her! and make us both very happy!» That prayer has been fully heard!

After this I left for *Voss*. This was to be "my new battlefield." I stayed there about a month, and the results far exceeded my expectations. Besides preaching the Gospel I lectured on temperance, and on leaving the Temperance Society held a farewell treat for me, favourable accounts of which appeared in the papers. "The word of God had a powerful influence over the crowded congregations. Some professed to have found the Saviour, great numbers became convinced of their sins and the necessity of seeking salvation. One remarkable feature of the tour, was the enthusiasm with which the Lutheran friends received me. Even the "Provst" (Dean), *Mr. Hansteen*, and the chaplain and their friends." But I remark: "I don't suppose that will be the case though, if a Methodist church should spring up there, as a fruit of our labors. May the Lord enable me, both in storm as well as sunshine, to do *His* will and honor *His* name."

Mrs. Mary Barratt.

My conjectures proved only to be too true.
After leaving Voss I preached both in Bergen and Hardanger. I issued also a small hymnbook during those days, containing my own songs and hymns. Revival success attended my labors, praised

be God! At one meeting "sinners cried aloud for mercy, and it is to be hoped, that several found peace through believing."

The Methodist church sent me back to *Voss*.

Captain Alexander Barratt.

This time I came, therefore, as *their* representative, and if it was the will of God, I was to start a Methodist church there.

On the 19th of Jan., 1887, I wrote: "The current has turned. I've wind and current against me, *but the*

*Lord is with me!* When in Bergen I received a letter from the provst, in which he said, that he had reason to believe, that I intended coming to Voss to found a Methodist church there, and that he and his friends would do all they could to hinder me in my labors. On reaching Voss, I had a long conversation with the provst. He could not understand why I came there to break the peace of centuries. I thought it time to break the peace of so long standing. My first text was Acts XIV, 22. Of course all the public halls were closed against me, and the provst held public meetings «for Lutheran friends» in order to decide what to do, to prevent the planting of Methodism at Voss.

However an unconverted Hotel manager opened his hotel for my meetings. The large saloon became the centre for meetings for some time. It is a remarkable fact too, that the son of this man is to day the pastor of the Pentecostal Assembly at Voss.

The provst of course managed to close the hearts and the homes, especially of the better class people against me, but a storm of indignation and reproach met him from the people generally, and the hotel "was crammed full of people, and a blessed influence prevailed". Lectures were held against Methodism, but the people flocked to our meetings.

On the 12th of Febr. 1887, the ministers got the Lutheran Emissary, *Mr. Lavik,* to visit Voss, but he would not speak against me. Still they hoped that, by getting the people to attend Church, they would not attend my meetings. He preached Saturday evening in the gymnasium. Sunday morning at 9 : 30 I preached at the hotel and he at the gymnasium. Then there was church service at 10 : 30 o'clock. Lavik preached in the church at 3 : 30 P. M. *This was quite a new thing for Voss,* as no lay-man was allowed to preach in the churches in those days, but it was of course allowed in order to draw the people away from our meetings. "But blessed be God, the people

came all the same. I preached at 5 o'clock, so the people went straight from the church to our meeting."
God was with us!

«Laura visited me from Bergen, as well as Mrs. Nielsen, the converted actress. A Lutheran preacher, Mr. Eriksen, visited Voss, and took lodgings with me, and preached in our Hall. This had a good effect on the people. It was an object lesson in brotherly love. The *Rev. I. H. Johnson* and the *Rev. A. Olsen* of the Methodist Church visited me, and others, and were of "especial blessing to many."

We commenced building a chapel at Voss. In the meantime several public halls were opened for me, and I held meetings on the farms round about Voss. The Lutherans had not been able to erect their "bedehus," but as soon as we erected our chapel, they got up their "Nain."

I became very sick once at Voss, and "Mrs. Hansteen, the provst's wife, showed me not a little kindness."

When the bitter strife was ended, several of those who had attacked me most, began to show a more fraternal spirit.

On Tuesday, *the 10th of* May, 1887, *I married Miss Laura Jacobsen.* The marriage took place in *Bergen.* In my diary I write concerning this great event of my life: "God be blessed for this great gift, may I ever prize it and cherish it, and may our married life prove a blessing, not only to ourselves, but to all we come in contact with."

On the 12th of may, we both started for Christiania, in order to take part in the *Conference* at Porsgrund, presided by *bishop Ninde.* I visited the Church at Kampen, and all were delighted to see me back, and hear me deliver my testimony once more. The doctors had said, that at least 3 or 4 years would elapse ere I could preach again, "but ere the year was fully past," I was at work again. All thanks to God!

Mrs. Laura Barratt.

On our return to Voss, we dedicated our new chapel "Zion". "The chapel is most beautifully situated. The white flag, with the red borders, and the word "Zion" printed in blue letters in its centre, floating from a very high pole close by, attracted attention, and was hoisted some time before each meeting, so as to announce the services." This chapel has since then been burnt down, but a new one has been erected in its place.

On the 22nd of July, 1887, my wife end I were on a visit to Hardanger. It was my birthday, and I wrote in my journal: "I'm now 25. A quarter of a century is passed, may the second quarter be spent better than the first." I meant of course: be better in spiritual results than the first.

My new songbook "Evangeliske Sange" (Evangelical Songs), was ready for sale in October, 1887. My time was devoted to lecturing on various subjects, especially in favour of the Temperance Cause. Several lectures on "Pilgrim's Progress" had a wonderful deep influence on the people. I did what I could to cultivate good singing at our meetings. A choir was started, and religious concerts were held in between. But my chief delight was in the Evangelical work, and souls were saved at the meetings and elsewhere, Glory to God! In Journal, No. 2, there are numerous clippings from the "Kristelig Tidende" and other papers, containing articles, sermons, letters and descriptions of my labors and work in those days, that may interest someone perhaps to read when I am gone. This little book has no room for them; but they may possibly give some historical light on the condition of things in those days, and the kind of work then done by the Methodist preachers.

The 3rd Journal commences with the year 1888, and has as its headline the words of the Psalmist (119,9) "Wherewithal shall a young man cleanse his way? By thaking heed thereto according to Thy word".

"Up to the present day, I have held 570 sermons and 83 lectures on various topics, besides numerous short speeches and addresses at meetings, etc. The Temperance Cause has been pushed forward with great success in several places. Hundreds have joined its banners. Hundreds have also been awakened to see their sins and long for salvation. How many have been saved, the Judgement Day will tell: but I feel happy to know that many have been brought from darkness into light, and in an especial degree has this been the case during my stay at Voss, Hallelujah! I feel I am unworthy of so high a calling, and give Thee, *everlasting King, all the glory!* — — Strengthen me, sustain me, and give more wisdom, grace, light, and influence, in the days that may come. Increase my faith! *Baptize* me and my dear wife with the *Holy Spirit!* We consecrate ourselves afresh to Thee. Sanctify us wholly! Take our lives and let them be, consecrated Lord, to Thee! *Amen!*"

The Journal tells of continuous meetings at Voss and elsewhere.

On the 9th of April, 1888, our first child was born, *Mary*. Just after this notice comes the statement: "*The mine is stopped!* After more than 20 years, the workings are stopped and the experiences of so long a period are brought to an end". I went straight to Hardanger to have some *fare-well* meetings with the people there. "I cannot describe my feelings when I remember that it is the home of my boyhood that is to be torn down, and the place I love is to be left entirely to the winds and birds of prey; but the scenes of love and paternal advice will ring in my ears whereever I go, and fill my mind and heart with pleasant recollections." On the 11th of July, I state: "*My parents have left the dear old home at Varaldsøy for good.*" They settled down a while at *Østerøen*.

On the 4th of Sept. 1888 the "*first Quarterly Conference* was held at Voss. Interesting!"

At the various services "souls were saved. Hallelujah!" I cry out: "Lord, I praise Thee for Thy boundless grace. Fill me with a greater measure of Thy tender love. Give me physical and above all spiritual strength to carry on the grand work of saving souls. Seal my efforts with Thy own glory. *Baptize me fully with the Holy Ghost and Fire!* O Lord, give me *"holiness on fire!"* Enable me to bring thousands to the Cross of Jesus and to Heaven! Amen".

Jan. 31st, 1889: "Dear *Bro. Lars Pettersen* (the minister who first invited me to Christiania) *died Wednesday at 9 o' clock*. A triumphant death after much suffering. His life was holy and full of love. He was one of my very best friends, and my brother-in-law".

On the way to the *Conference* at Kongsberg in 1889, I preached in various places, as well as at *Kongsberg*. "In company with 5 other ministers, I was ordained to deacon's orders by *Bishop Fowler* — A splendid man! I had to act as interpreter instead of *pastor M. Hansen*, at one of the conference sessions". This was, I suppose the start in that kind of work. In later years I was the constant interpreter of the bishops, that visited Norway, at the Conferences and elsewhere.

"When the appointments were read at that Conference, I found that my place was assigned to Christiania 3rd Church, and Bro. Aas was to take my place at Voss". My last services were held at Voss on the 11th of August, 1889. "The chapel was crowded in the forenoon, and I was enabled to preach with a power and influence, such as I have seldom felt. The whole congregation wept. My text was Rev. III, 21. God blest the Word; friends and enemies alike were moved by the Holy Spirit, and much good was done, Hallelujah!"

*My wife* had been a constant help to me in the work, often conducting meetings during my absence, and at the last services she also spoke to the people with great fervour and effect.

## CHAPTER VI.

*Appointments in Christiania, from 1891—1906, 15 years.*

On our way to Christiania, we visited Osterøen. My wife's parents came also to Osterøen while we where there, so *that we were assembled once more ere we left for the city.* I preached to the people and God gave us some blessed days there.

"*I held my inaugural sermon on Sunday, the 25th of August, 1889, in 3rd Church, Christiania. The Spirit of the Lord was indeed present amongst us*".

Since that time my home has been in the city; and, from that hour, the regular work of a *Methodist Minister*, in the central church of the Norwegian capital, occupied my time and strength and prayers for years.

On the 6th of Sept., "I commenced a society for young people" — "Unge folks kristelige forening" (Young people's Christian Society). To this special work for *young people*, I offered much of my time and prayers, and it led up to the work of "*The Epworth League*", in Norway.

During this year, I also met with "Farbror *Bolzius*". I was thus brought in touch with a man, who fully believed in and practiced *faithhealing*. This had considerable influence on my mind. However it did not save me from a very hard attack again of influenza at the close of the year, but possibly led me to confide *more fully in the Lord for health and strength*. At the commencement of the year I was able to resume my work, little by little, and was *thirsting to* "*save souls for heaven.*"

Father had recently been very ill. On the way to Chapel on the 21st of Jan., 1890, I met pastor Torjursen with a telegram from my sister Polly (Mary): *"Prepare Barratt carefully. Dear father slept quietly away to-day quite unexpectedly. Dr. had said worse was over. Come home."*

This was a hard blow, but I "felt the love of Jesus sustain me in this extreme grief. Twenty second of Jan.: "A deep and lasting love ever existed between father and me, but now he is safe beyond all grief, pain, sickness and death. He has conquered and gained the victory through the Blood of the Lamb. Praised be the Lord!",

I immediately left for Osterøen and attended father's funeral. "Remarkable were the effects of the very impressive services attending it, leaving on all our minds a feeling of *"peace"*. A full description of the services, with a short account of father's life, was inserted in the "Kristelig Tidende".

After the funeral, I took mother along with me on a short visit to Voss. We had a splendid time there. Then I returned back to the constant and hard work of a Minister in the City.

I stood on a good footing with the *Salvation Army*, and took part in several of their meetings. On Wednesday, 30th of April, 1890, I called together the *"first meeting of ministers of various denominations* at 12 o'clock, in our Meeting-Hall". We made some arrangements for *special meetings*. These meetings were made a great blessing to many.

June, 20th, 1890: "Heard *lektor Waldenstrøm* preach, at 1 o'clock".

"The Methodist Conference of 1890 was held at Skien, in July. *Bishop Henry W. Warren* presiding". "Aug. 22nd: Much writing for the *Epworth League*, having been elected *Secretary for Norway*".

In 1890, I went to *England* to raise funds for a church in Christiania. I left on the 19th Sept. with the "Angelo". At Hull, I heard *Gipsy Smith* lecture. His subject was "*From Gipsy tent to platform*". I preached in "Strangers Rest" the following Wednesday, and it is a remarkable fact, that my first sermon ever preached in England, was preached in the *Norwegian* language".

*Bishop John J. Hurst* gave me a very cordial recommendation to the methodists and the christians generally in England. He "commended the enterprise to all true friends of the Gospel".

The tour did not meet with any special success financially. I lectured in several towns on "*The land of the midnight sun*", and illustrated the lectures with splendid lantern slides, "dissolving views of exceptional brightness and beauty." ("Western Daily Mercury"), and I preached in between. I visited Cardiff, Bristol, Bath, and other towns, also several towns already mentioned from the days of my childhood: Gunnislake, Albaston, Callington, Calstock, Petertavy, etc. I have still clippings from the various papers, giving an interesting description of the lecture and my slides in the "Bristol Times and Mirror", "Western Daily Press", "Methodist Times", and several others. At the lecture, "several phases of Norwegian life were represented by ladies clad in national costumes, and Norwegian songs were song. ("Bath Herald"). The critics were very favourably impressed, but the expenses were too great for me to be able to realize any profits toward the cause for which I was working.

However, I was brought in connection with the religious life of England in a very direct way. At Callington, I also took part in a "Rechabite" (Temperance) meeting. One of the most interesting visits I made was a visit to *Taunton*, to the colleges there, especially to my old College, now Queens College, that I had not seen for several years. After my lecture there, the Headmaster, *Mr. Darlington*, gave me the following recommendation to the Headmaster of the Kingswood School:

"My dear Workman!

This is to introduce to you the Rev. T. B. Barratt, a Norwegian speaking Englishman and now pastor of the Methodist Episcopal Church in Christiania. He is an old boy of this college and last night lectured to our boys on Norway. They — we, rather — were delighted and I am quite sure you and your boys would enjoy it equally, if you could see your way to give him an invitation to Kingswood.

With kind regards,

Yours faithfully

Thw. Darlington."

I also received letters of recommendation from the Principal of the Independent College at Taunton, *Mr. F. W. Aveling*, stating that "the lecture at the college there was very instructive, and the views of Norway superb."

When in England I received a letter from mother stating, that friends in Norway were desirous for me to become *Sunday-school agent* for Norway. I also received letters from S. S. Union officials whilst in London to that effect. In regard to this I have noted in my Journal that *"God* must decide that for me, or rather help me to decide what step to take. It's a very difficult question." Time has proved that I did not feel called to that position.

Whilst at Bath, and in the Railway carriage between Bath and Liverpool, I wrote the following lines, to the old tune "My Jesus I love Thee, etc."

O blessed Redeemer, my hope and my joy,
To Thee all the days of my life I'll employ;
To rest on Thine arm and to speak of Thy love,
T'is joy everlasting — ti's heaven to prove!

Ah, nought as the joy of a sanctified heart,
Can brighten my life and such beauty impart,
It leaps at the touch of Thy finger within,
And leaves in the fountain the stains of its sin.

I rise from the debris of sin at Thy call,
And give Thee to reign in the depths of my soul;
Take loved ones and life — *all* now lies at Thy feet.
With Thee in my heart I have fellowship sweet.

*Thee only* to know and right faithfully own,
*Thee only* to serve — if left standing alone;
This purpose inspires all the powers of my will.
Then keep me, dear Saviour, Thy promise fulfill.

I'm conquered by love and constrained by Thy grace,
With faith I the horns of the altar embrace;
The *fire* in my heart shall burn bright as the day,
*The temple is cleansed* — and my sins washed away!

At the close of this song I remark: "My happy experience, Hallelujah!"

I evidently sought and experienced many rich blessings of God during those days, and then, as generally is the case, when greatly blest of God, my feelings burst forth in poetry and song. The above song stood, I believe, in "The Wesleyan Methodist Magazine."

Here is another, written in Providence House at Liverpool, on the 16th of March, 1891.

### *Ezekiel XLVII.*

Ye friends of Christ, draw near.
Behold the living stream,
That bursts from 'neath the temple door,
With beauteous, radiant gleam.

It deepens as it rolls
Down through this vale of strife,
The «dead sea» brightens at its touch,
And quickens into life.

It seems but small at first,
But *on* the waters ride!
Now haste thee, swimmer, wade no more,
But plunge beneath the tide!

> Ah, would you know the name
> Of that deep shining flood — ?
> Tis love, tis love — tis wondrous love!
> Tis Jesus' cleansing blood!
>
> Then haste thee, brother, now,
> Stand trembling there no more,
> Spread forth thine arms, a swimmer bold,
> And strike for yonder shore!

I came in touch with several able and greatly used ministers of the Gospel, during that trip to England. On the 6th of May, 1891, I returned to Christiania. Just after this I received a renewed attack of influenza, but already on the 26th I was "restored so far to health, that I was able to continue my work for the Master."

On the 4th of Sept. 1891, I mention my plans in the journal concerning a "*Central Mission*" in Christiania. I laid it before *bishop M. Walden*, and "it met to a certain extent with his approval. In fact he would endorse the scheme, provided the means were forthcoming."

During my visit to England in 1891, I wrote the following poem on Easter Sunday, at Ealing Dean:

### *Our hope is in Thee!*

> Great God, from whom each ray of love,
> Beams on the sons of men,
> Thy presence fills the earth and sky,
> The mountain and the glen.
>
> The creatures, Thine own hands have made,
> Depend on Thee each day,
> *Thou* art the hope of earth and heaven,
> The life, the truth, the way!

If Thou one moment didst withdraw
Thy hand of tender care,
The sun would plunge in deepest night,
And earth its darkness share.

Death's treacherous grasp would chill the heart
Of each bright flower of life;
The sons of light would waste and sink
In dens of hopeless strife!

Eén now, midst showers of heavenly rain,
The wicked curse Thy name,
And those, who say they know Thee best,
Have oft caused grief and shame.

• • •

*Forgive the past!* — o, mighty King,
With all it's thoughtless guile,
Shower now upon us as we pray
The blessings of Thy smile.

Shut out from every heart this day,
*All* — save Thy presence sweet,
That love and peace may dwell therein,
And truth and mercy meet.

• • •

*Now* Lord, Thy fire consumes the dross,
And purifies the gold,
Thy bloodwashed army hurries on,
To tell that tale of old!

The barren waste bursts forth in song,
The chains of darkness break,
And struggling masses gather hope,
Thy great *salvation* seek.

The angels hear their joyful shout,
Whilst crouching devils flee,
Our anthems blend with those above,
To worship *only Thee!*

I was ordained *an elder* of the Methodist Episcopal Church at the Annual Conference at Bergen, by bishop M. Walden, in 1891.

On the 26th of Aug. 1891 I wrote: "Much business in connection with our "Methodist Central Mission." Under this new name, which I gave our work in the centre of the city, I hoped for great things. Besides revival work, I also made considerable use of a large magic lantern, the one I used in England, and held *"Magic lantern evangelistic services."* They proved to be a great attraction, and several were led to Christ.

In Sept. I write: "My sister, *Mary B. Barratt,* has been appointed governess of the childrens home, and intends to visit Stephenson's homes in England, in order to see the style of work there." The *"Emmas barnehjem"*, of which she took such care for some time, has now developed to be quite a solid institution. My sister left it eventually, and has been living in New York for several years.

My sister *Louisa* was later married to *Mr. Arnt Abrahamsen,* and has settled down in Bergen.

My life was now fully devoted to the cause of the Methodist Church, and in a country like Norway, where *the State Church* (Lutheran) prevails there was much to be done, but I always tried to show a fraternal spirit towards the other denominations, although I worked hard to *make Methodism a power in the country.*

I heard *general Booth* for the first time in June, 1892, at 3 o'clock, in the Salvation Army Temple. Just after this, we had a meeting in our Hall which went on till 11:30 o'clock at night. I wrote: "Souls saved to the very last. *Hallelujah!* O Lord, I do praise thee for thy sanctifying and cleansing power. I've never been more happy than of late. The cleansing power of Jesus blood is a reality. Praise God!"

Aug. 23rd. 1892: "I have been on a tour in *Sweden* with bishop I. W. Joyce, D. D.; L. L. D. He presided at the annual conference in Drammen. Great changes took place in regard to our work. Amongst these was one very startling for me. *Bishop Joyce* appointed me *presiding Elder of Christiania district."*

We were in want of means to carry on the work of the Central Mission effectually, but the bishop endorsed my plan and I still hoped to be able to realize my ideas concerning it. I had to leave my position as pastor of Third Church, and take over the still more responsible position as *presiding Elder of the whole* Christiania district. My heart became filled with a burning desire *to kindle revival fires throughout the whole district*, and not merely perform the duties devolving on my new position within the Churches. I therefore remained longer than usual at each church, that was prepared to hold extra revival services in connection with the quarterly visits of the Presiding Elder.

The annual conference of 1893 was presided over by *bishop John H. Vincent*, L. L. D., one of the most interesting bishops I ever met, who always, later on, showed me the greatest kindness and brotherly love.

In my private statistics concerning the meetings held, I also note that *my wife* had held several, but as the family grew in numbers, she had more than enough to do to take care of them all.

Bishop John H. Vincent.

However at the same time, she was always willing to give her testimony and honour Christ! At the age of 31, the 22nd of July, 1893, I had held about 1520 sermons, 340 lectures, and about 600 various kinds of meetings — in all about 2460 meetings.

The visit of *bishop John P. Newman*, in 1894, was a great blessing to us. He stayed at our home, and my wife took a trip to the North with *Mrs. Newman*. I made at that time the following note in my Journal: "Quite unexpectedly, but without the slightest hint from me or my friends, the bishop stated at the annual conference: *"The presiding Elder has throughout shown an impartial and brotherly spirit, and a wise administration."* I also became editor of the "Varilden", the Epworth League paper.

In 1894, I broke down under several violent attacks of cold. I tried to hold out as long as possible, but *bronchitis and asthma* came on, and I was ordered to take a rest for two months at least. But I wasn't quite idle, and rejoiced in the fact that *"the Lord was my hope and joy!"*

Some great battles for *the temperance cause* were waged for several years, in which I took part, and was elected nember of the Municipal Board on the list of the temperance party. We held large *"Demonstration meetings"* in the openair, as well as in the largest halls. I was called upon to write songs, and to lecture quite often. I felt it a joy to be able to do something for the furtherance of temperance and strike a blow at the drinking habit, and all the devilry that existed amongst a great number of the people. God be praised because he gave strength and helped us in these great struggles. The temperance people showed their appreciation of the work done on several occasions, by publicly giving me words of approval and several valuable presents. This was not the object of my exertions, but an intense desire to do good and bring some blessing to the people. Words of appreciation and thanks are good stimulants when you are right on the firing line.

Oct. 15th. 1895: *"The subject of Holiness* has been impressed upon my congregations more than ever, and has been developed in speech with more clearness than I have ever been able to do before.

O. P. Pettersen

I thank God because I am able to rest in His precious promises. The meetings in various towns, have been wonderfully blest. *Many are now seeking the blessing of perfect love,* many who have for some time been very indolent and lukewarm."

June 23rd, 1896: "Met *Rev. O. P. Pettersen,* the *father of Methodism in Norway,* on the pier, coming that evening from America, in company with the Rev. A. Olsen." On the way to Fredrikshald, I wrote a song of welcome on the train for this hero of Methodism in Norway. It was sung at the reception.

I have often to write such songs, as well as poems, and hymns, and temperance songs. They seem to come along under the influence of some good power.

The *Deaconess work* was started in 1896, and itt fell to my lot to start it. It has developed of late years very rapidly, and is now quite a great institution within the Methodist Church.

April 7th 1897: «I've prepared and sent to the printers a "*Constitution for the Bygdemission*". (Country Mission). In company with pastor E. Halvorsen and pastor Ole Olsen, I have prepared statutes for «*The Norwegian Methodist Temperance Society*". We have prepared "Statutes for our *Deaconesses*" at our last Committee meeting, and I have just now taken upon me the work of translating the "*Constitution of the Epworth League*".

Much preparatory work along these lines was done during those days. My correspondance in the "*Kristelig Tidende*" gives a pretty clear description of the evangelical work done, and the various phases of the spiritual life as it appeared within the Methodist church.

"*Bishop Goodsell and wife* stayed with us whilst in Christiania." This was before the Annual Conference at Trondhjem in 1897. "I was asked to continue as presiding elder of the District."

Febr. 3rd 1898: "I returned home to—day after bening absent about five weeks. In each town God has blest my efforts and numbers of souls have been saved. This was especially the case at Horten, where a glorious revival broke out. Hundreds have been awakened and numbers saved. The aftermeetings have at times lasted for hours together."

Now and then at the *political* elections, I wrote articles in favour of the Dissenters. All, who belong to denominations outside the Lutheran State Church, are "dissenters", and there have been rights to fight for in various ways.

Aug. 3rd 1898: "Conference is past. It was indeed a season of hard work, but also of refreshing. Notable changes took place. Pastor A. Olsen was appointed presiding elder in my place. I gave my own personal vote for that. It was proposed to make me presiding elder of Bergen District, but I felt that pastoral work would be a good change, and that it was not wise for so young a man as myself to keep away from it. I was therefore appointed *pastor of 1st Church*, and *Superintendent of the Deaconss work.*» *Bishop Walden* presided, and stayed at our home on his way to Stockholm after the conference.

In September I received a letter of thanks from the Secretary of "Norske kvinders totalavholdsselskap" (The Temperance Society of the women of Norway), for acting as interpreter for *Miss Slack*, during her stay here, and "for other favours shown them."

Sept. 12th: "Have had a good time in 1st. Church so far."

I was poorly again in February of 1899 with the "La Grippe", but God helped me through it.

Besides the general work of the Church, I arranged "Religious Concerts" and held lectures to reach the people and elevate their minds and hearts. Large gatherings for ministers from various denomiations were arranged for, in order to awaken *Brotherly sympathy and love between the various groups.*

During the special services in 1st Church, I issued a small paper suited for the work there: "*Gløder fra alteret*" (Coals from the Altar), with songs to be sung at the meetings, on the last page.

A letter from the Secretary of the *Lutheran Home Mission* will interest many. It refers to my defence of the Lutheran Inner Mission (Home Mission), during a debate in the Municipal Board, and is dated 15th of April, 1899:

Hr. Pastor T. B. Barratt!

In the report of the discussion at the M. Board in "Morgenbladet", I see that you defended Christiania Inner Mission against Dr. Nissen's attack. It caused us much joy, and I wish through these lines to extend our heartfelt thanks. Yes, we thank you for the Brotherly hand, and may the Lord bless you in return.

Respectfully and heartily yours,
A. Mortensen.

At the same time, I publicly attacked the Lutheran Bishops and others of the Lutheran clergy, in an article on "*The Bishops and the Temperance cause*", for their opposition to this great cause.

### Openair services.

May 10th: "We have started openair services of late. I have, in company with *Mr. Buck* and Mr. Aall (Mr. Buck was the soul in the matter), applied to the authorities about it time and again, getting up petitions to the Government, etc., and now at last it seems as if we are about to gain a perfect victory after all our trouble." The newspapers wrote later on: "Permission has been definitely given, and as a result we have seen the Salvation Army unfold its banners on the market places. The Methodists are not behind. Last Sunday afternoon, a well attended open air service was held in Birkelunden, at which pastor Barratt spoke."

This then was the commencement of the openair services that now are conducted at the Market places and public grounds quite regularly during the summer months.

I worked considerably, at that time, for the "*Unity of the people of God.*" In a letter, dated 29th of June, 1899, from the editor of "*Missionæren*", he thanks me for an article, which was in fact an answer to their question about the subject, and promises to send me a copy of the paper regularly as a reward for the article. This rather amuses me now, although I appreciate the fraternal spirit it evinced.

Sept. 30th: "I commenced the translation of *"The Miracle at Markham"*, by C. Sheldon. I started also on my new book: "Eric Arnesen".

June 22nd: "*My wife* has left for Scotland, as a delegate for Norway to the "*White Ribbon Army*" convention, then in session in Edinburg".

"*Five thousand Meetings.* O God! How many souls! The day of resurrection will reveal it! Help me ever to be faithful and abide by Thy everlasting truth! Live it, preach it, and rest on it in Death! Help me ever to point sinners to the Cross, and labour with success. Thy name be praised!" Of these meetings there were 2716 sermons and 620 lectures.

July 10th: "My wife returned from Scotland last Saturday, and lectured about her tour to the "International Convention at Edinburgh before a crowd of people in 1st church".

A printed sermon, entitled "*Vort største behov*" (Our greatest need) was sent to Her Majesty, Queen Sofie; to the Lutheran bishop, Mr. Bang, and others. Letters of thanks were received both from the Queen and the bishop, which I have kept. The Queen's answer was written by her secretary.

*Mother* came now and then on a visit to us. In July, the 17th, 1901, she was in Christiania during the visit of *Dr. Adna B. Leonard* and his son, the *Rev. A. W. Leonard*, and *bishop Vincent*, who came to preside at the conference at Hamar.

It was at this conference Dr. Leonard preached his wonderful sermons about the *Holy Ghost*. I acted as interpreter, and was so overwhelmed at times, that I could scarcely continue to interpret for him.

I worked a good bit those days in an attempt to write "The history of Methodism in Norway". I collected considerable material for the purpose. I also helped to issue a songbook for the "Epworth League". "Lærken" was the name we gave it.

Large meetings were held in Calmeyergatens missionshouse to raise funds for the poor. I took part in these. I also issued a small paper for the members of 1st church: "Vægteren" (The watchman).

May 12th 1902: *Lectured against the shows* in Oslo. They were a mixture of theatricals and concerts: awful performances at times of a *morally low type*, kept going by people, desirous of gaining money, no matter how many souls were ruined and lost, morally and spiritually.

I looked up these plases, saw and heard what was going on, and then gave an account of the whole thing. "God helped me! The press and others ridiculed me, but the more they ridiculed, the more they proved how straight the thrust was made. There was quite a stir in the city. Nothing has occupied the public mind of late, more than this violent attack". The lecture was printed by a Lutheran minister, and destributed far and near.

July 29th: "Bishop Mc. Cabe has promised me to deliver his renowned lecture on "*The Brigth side of Life in Libby Prison*".

In the report of the annual conference held at Fredrikshald, the statement may be seen in the list of appointments: T. B. Barratt, superintendent of *Christiania City Mission*. This then was a new start in my life!

## CHAPTER VII.

### *Christiania City Mission.*

As it will be seen, I made attempts to start a "*Central Mission*" ere this, but now I was enabled by the new appointment, to take over the work personally unfettered by any other work, and this time we gave it this new name.

On the 4th of Sept. 1902, I write as follows in my journal: "What made the conference of the utmost importance for me, was *the decision to start the City Mission.* I have long been praying and speaking about this, but now at last it has come to pass. I had been in doubt as to the best method of founding it — if it should be connected with some local church (in that case 3rd church), or if it should be worked seperately  I worked out the plan and the address to the conference, but after conversing with the presiding elder, I determined to try the first plan, and put this and a substitute before the conference at once, leaving it with the conference to decide what was best, trusting God for the outcome."

My "Appeal to the Conference" will be found in the journal. "Quite a storm arose when the idea of connecting 3rd church and the mission was presented, and at the same time considerable ill feeling toward the plan seemed to have filled some souls. However, after the speech by Bro. *Ole Olsen*, I arose and stated that I felt it as a call from God. My arguments and the earnest manner (even tears) in which I spoke, convinced all, that something must now be done, and even Bro. Ole Olsen turned round and spoke warmly for the plan: *"It must be settled now!"* A motion by Bro. A. Olsen, requiring the appointment of a city missionary, was carried unanimously. At the same time, it was decided *that I was not to receive any salary* from the missionary appropriation. That left me without salary and without furniture."

"The appointments were read on Sunday afternoon, so that Laura (my wife) did not get hold of the right end of the stick before she received my letter on Monday morning. This cut her up somewhat, as she was afraid that we would be left all in the dark. I cannot but confess, that as I stood by the side of the bishop as his interpreter, when the appointments were read, a peculiar feeling crept o'er me as I translated the words: "1st church—G. Rognerud—T. B. Barratt, City missionary." But this was what I had been looking forward to, and as the scissors of the cabinet cut the threads connecting me with my four years pastorate in 1st church, I dropped right into the work God has surely called me to perform."

"I had opened my bible when falling on my knees Sunday morning, and my eyes fell on the 20th Psalm. I read it through and was comforted and strengthened. It is hereafter to be *the Psalm of the City Mission*, and its watchword will be: *"For Christ's sake!"*

Laura was helped through. I telegraphed: "Impossible any other way, God lives. Furniture of 5th Church to be used at first", and stated that a collection had already been started for our income. I have still my letter to her, after the appointment. Just a few lines of it: "Darling! I only wish you had heard the bishop! (It was bishop Mc. Cabe). Your doubts would have fled. God lives, dear! As the bishop often said to me personally, and many others said the same, we shall have enough, more than enough!" The bishop himself gave me a check for 250 kr. He sent also a very inspiring letter to Laura, which I still have, and allowed me to start the following morning for Christiania, in order to

Bishop Mc. Cabe.

explain things, and "to my happy surprise, Laura and all the children (except Mary, who was out in town) were down at the station to meet me. They never looked more beautiful than that day! I was so happy, and *dear Laura had found grace to lay all on the Lord."*

In Calmeyergatens Mission Hall, *bishop Mc. Cabe* "continued the subscription for the City Mission, immediately after his sermon. It came like a thunderbolt, but more than 2000 kr. in all were raised."

*Thus the "Chistiania City Mission" was started.*

This was in the summer of 1902, and as I look back on those days, I must confess that the Lord was surely in it all. Whilst I write these lines, in the summer of 1927, I notice that 25 years have passed since that event in my life. I feel assured, that the "Christiania City Mission" was the brigde by which I was to be led into all the experiences of the Pentecostal blessing, and *as a result into the Pentecostal movement itself.*

It gives an idea of the king of work done, when we remember that the City Mission commenced it's meetings in a theater. Journal: *"On Sunday, the 5th of October, we opened the City Mission with a meeting in Tivoli theater.* We had intended to take the Circus, but this was not quite in order, so I decided for the theater. People were stunned on hearing it, as they least of all expected that the premises would be allowed my use, owing to my fierce attack on the "theater" (low class theaters) recently. My subject was: *Try Christ!* God gave me a real good time. Many wept, and the greatest interest was shown throughout the sermon and the service." *Bro. Nils Bolt,* my assistant, took part in the service. "One of the first to grasp my hand after the service, was *Mrs. Rinman,* the mother of the evangelist. She was delighted with the service, and said, that from that day forward I would stand on her list of prayer. "Even the well-known priest of the Lutheran Church, pastor Storjohan, was present."

The secular press wrote rather lengthy articles about the service, and gave their readers an idea of the plan of the new mission. One article had as its heading "*American*". The writer commences by saying: "We are becoming very American on various

Openair service.

lines, and the most American of us all is, without a doubt, the Methodist pastor, Mr. Barratt".

It was to be expected, that this new line of work would cause much ridicule and give some worldly writers, within the secular press, occasion to

In the Roccocosal (Grand Hotel) A meeting there.

make fun of God's work, but results proved that numbers of people were reached that way, who never visited church, or had any desire to become christians, and *many were saved* by these extraordinary means.

The meetings were held in concert halls, the Students Hall, Grand Hotel, theaters, in the open air, and wherever we thought it possible to *reach the masses with the Gospel*. The mission took up *philanthropic work* of various kinds, and little by little a band of faithful workers gathered about me. Concerts, of a religious stamp of course, were held at times in connection with some lecture or address, and we enlisted help from the various denominations, as well as from the Methodist church.

At times I visited other towns and held similar meetings there. Numerous accounts of the meetings will be found in the papers, both religious and secular, which prove the blessing these efforts were made to be by the good Lord. Extracts and cuttings are also to be found in my journal.

February 16th, 1903: *"Dear mothers birthday;* she is 73 years old to-day. God bless her and give her many happy returns of the day!"

Tuesday, 7th of April: "Just been reading *Dr. Torrey's* book on *"How to bring men to Christ."* He has the same views as myself in many respects. It did me *good* to read about the *Baptism of the Holy Ghost.* Meeting for boys at 6 o'clock".

Here again the views I had imbibed through good Methodist theology by well-known leaders, concerning the necessity of a *Baptism* in the Holy Ghost, was brought to my mind by this leader among preachers.

In *"Missionæren"*, nr. 13, an account appeared of the meetings I was called to take part in at *Trondhjem.* In large letters, the editor headed his article: *Pastor Barratt's work. The Christiania City Mission. Alliance meetings in Trondhjem. Hundreds of souls at the foot of the Cross."* This lengthy article gave a very sympathetic account of the City Mission and a vivid description of the meetings at Trondhjem.

At the annual conference of the Methodist Episcopal Church, I was again appointed as the bishop's interpreter, and gave also a lengthy report of the new "Forward Movement" within the Church. As it gives an idea of the spiritual needs of the City, and shows how we tried to meet them at that time, I give an extract of it here:

"C h r i s t i a n i a, (now Oslo), the capital of Norway, is beautifully situated at the end of the Christiania fjord.

The surroundings are very picturesque, and of late years the appearance of the city itself has been greatly modernised.

The last census taken shows a population of about 225.000 inhabitants. (This year 1927, there are 254,000).

It would take us too long to describe things of general interest within the city and its environments. That is not the object of this report.

We wish merely to give a report of the m o r a l and r e l i g i o u s  s t a t e of the people and explain the work we have lately started and mention some of its results.

The same may be said of Christiania as of most cities "it all depends on what you want to specify." Should I dwell upon the many institutions for the education of the people and in detail describe the many noble efforts put forth for the uplifting of the social state of the city, one would surely say, that Christiania was not in need of our sympathies, but claimed our highest respect. So many modern improvements have been adopted to meet the social wants of the people that the casual observer might possibly be surprised to hear that our City Mission was highly needed. This is nevertheless the case.

Everybody acquainted with the inner state of the city knows that the moral aspects are not so bright by far as is the case with many other parts of the country.

A chart has been prepared by Director Kjær in order to illustrate the moral state of the country.

In this it will be seen that Christiania is marked with a deep, grey colour, as compared with the ligther and darker parts of the chart.

The worldliness, vice and drunkeness of a great number of the population has become a cause of great distress to christians generally. One of the leading Lutheran ministers has lately stated that "Christiania is morally a sinking city", and the result is that, although much is being done to grapple with the increasing evil, thousands sink down in the whirlpools of sin and are lost.

Within the State Church, of the many fractions at work there, the "Christiania Inner Mission", is the strongest. Then again there are a number of "Free Missions" combating the evil, besides the Salvation Army. The Methodist Episcopal Church is represented by five local societies, two of which have only been organized within the last few years.

There are also a great number of temperance societies, as well as a purity society. Were it not for this the currents of sin would overwhelm the city entirely.

Every attempt, therefore, to stem the tide and promote the kingdom of God ought to be hailed with thankfulness.

Several years ago I raised the question within the Methodist church, if it would not be expedient for us to start a "Forward Movement" in Christiania.

The spiritual and social needs of the city were apparent to all, and the successful way in which the 'Missions" of the "Forward Movement" in England coped with the spiritual and social distress of the people there, convinced me that an attempt ought to be made.

The difficulty lay in the lack of means to start the Mission, and someone must needs take the responsibility of doing so.

This I was willing to do, provided the conference was ready to send me".

"The difficulties to overcome were many, but God gave strength and wisdom day by day.

It must be borne in mind that the conditions of church membership in Norway are different from those in America or even in England.

No one can become a member of another church here before leaving the State Church This has in thousands of cases prevented new converts from joining the Methodist Church. The statistics of the Meth. Church may therefore appear small, but the work done has nevertheless been deep and effectual. But this restriction has been, as it may be seen, an impediment to the work. Many Lutherans will not even attend services in a methodist church.

Then again we have the thousands who scarcely ever attend any church whatever, although nominaly members of the state church; and even if they would, there is not accommodation enough for them in the churches and mission halls. The want of places of worship in Christiania is such, that if all the inhabitants would attend Church simultaneously, about 200,000 would have to stand outside.

Besides this fact, we have to deal with the masses who hate the Church and the priest or minister, whatever denomination he represents.

How then are these to be reached with the Gospel of salvation?

It is not merely a question of how can a methodist

On the way to a picnic and service in the woods. The Boys brigade leading the van.

minister reach them, but how can any minister at all reach them and bring them to Christ?

That question strikes home to the root of this City Mission.

The difficulty of the question as to **membership**, we settle by not organizing a Church, but a Mission.

Then in order to reach the class of people, not generally touched by the Churches, we hire theaters, concert halls, **dancing saloons** and lecture halls. At times the attendance has been very great, and it may safely be said that the Mission throughout has proved a success.

All classes of people have attended the meetings and amongst them numbers, who never attend any church at all.

At our aftermeetings, and we have them whenever it is possible, we have prayed with hundreds of penitents since starting the Mission, many of whom we know rejoice to day in the blessed assurance of acceptance with God.

Many cases of great interest might be mentioned, but space does not allow of it.

It often happens that people, who have drifted into the meetings from mere inquisitiveness, have been so powerfully influenced by the Holy Spirit during the service, that they have been convinced of sin and sought salvation. They stand amongst our warmest friends to-day.

A young student at our Theological school, Nils Bolt, supported financially in his studies by Bishop Vincent and Baroness Langenau, has been my assistant.

My wife has also taken an active part in the Mission."

"Great enthusiasm is shown by all the friends and workers of the Mission.

The plan of organization adopted is similar to that authorized by the General Conference for the Epworth League.

There are seven departments.

The first comprises evangelical work: the second, social work, or work for charitable purposes. Aid towards self-help, temperance work, as well as work for the advancement of the moral state of the people; slumwork, and a special work for prisoners before and after their release from prison; work among factory girls and the like.

The third department is to spread good literature, arrange for reading circles and popular and instructive lectures.

The fourth department: Music, song, entertainment, etc.

Fifth: Work amongst the young people and children — Epworth League, Sunday-school, Boy's Brigade etc.

Sixth: Correspondance. Seventh: Finance.

All who join the Mission accept the following terms:

"By the Holy Spirit's help I will try to lead a life of personal communion with God and realize the christian principles laid down in the word of God; and to the best of my ability, promote the interests of the City Mission".

The position of the members to the Methodist Episcopal

Church will be similar to that of the Epworth Leaguers.

The great thing is to reach the masses and get the people saved. The objects of the Mission have therefore been framed thus:

Objects:
1.) To awaken and sustain a deep religious life amongst the population;
2.) help forward its moral and social state;
3.) promote the general culture of the people on a christian foundation.

The Mission is therefore based on a sure foundation and its work drawn up on broad and strong lines.

Our motto is:

### "FOR CHRIST'S SAKE!"

"Some were afraid that the Mission would weaken the other churches, but this has not been the case. It has stimulated them.

The work being so new, our funds have not been large enough to do more for the social department this year, and it must be remembered that the financial state of the city has never been so low and times so bad as now. But God has nevertheless helped us to meet our expenses, and we will trust him for the future."

Christiania, June 27. 1903.

Yours in Christ Jesus!

T. B. BARRATT.
Superintendent
of the Christiania City Mission

"The report of the *treasurer* was very interesting, and showed a wonderful sacrificing spirit on the part of our friends."

The Superintendent.

The interest in the Mission increased constantly and requests for me to visit other denominations and preach and lecture in their halls and churches became very frequent.

The *Dissenters* of Norway formed a "*Dissenterting*" (Parlament of dissenters), of which I was also elected a member.

The main object of this Parliament, was to take care of the rights of dissenters throughout Norway. It's mission has been greatly blest of God.

In 1903 I visited *Rome*. Our daughter *Mary* was there, studying music at Crandon Hall. It was a wonderful treat to see the old renowned city. "I preached here and there on the way forth and back in the various cities, through an interpreter." Then in November I visited *Stockholm*, Sweden, and God gave me a glorious time there. Crowds visited the services at the Methodist "Trinity Church", where *Mr. Åhgren* was pastor. The papers gave accounts of the City Mission work in Christiania and my last visit to Rome, as well as a report of the meetings in Stockholm.

In 1904 I visited Sweden again, this time *Gøteborg*. I was specially invited by the Epworth League there, and preached in the splendid Y. M. C. A., as well as in "Bethlehems kyrkan" and the Methodist church. I was asked to give an address at a meeting for ministers of various denominations, even of the Lutheran Statechurch, on the subject *"How shall we reach the masses?"* A very lively discussion arose, which resulted in the adoption of a resolution to the effect, that a plan for this kind of work in Gøteborg be moved and discussed at their next meeting.

In order to concentrate the work more fully and spread the truths that the City Mission endorsed and propagated, I started a new paper *"Byposten"*, which proved to be a blessing to many. The first number appeared in 1904, Saturday, 27th of Feb.

One of the sadest announcements that figured in one of its first editions was that of *Sussies* death:

"Our loving child *Sussie* (Sussanah Wesley Barratt was her real name) fell asleep to-day (the 3rd of May, 1904), 12 years old, happy in her Saviour". Sussies's death made a great impression on my mind and called forth some of my best songs, and stimulated me to work with still more ardour, if possible, for the Lord. She was a charming girl, full of love and faith in the Lord. Whenever we asked her "How are things going Sussie?" she always answered "Bare bra!" (only well). Her death drew my heart nearer heaven! There was something angelic about her whole being.

Not long after this my brother-in law and colleague in the church, *pastor Simon Haave*, passed

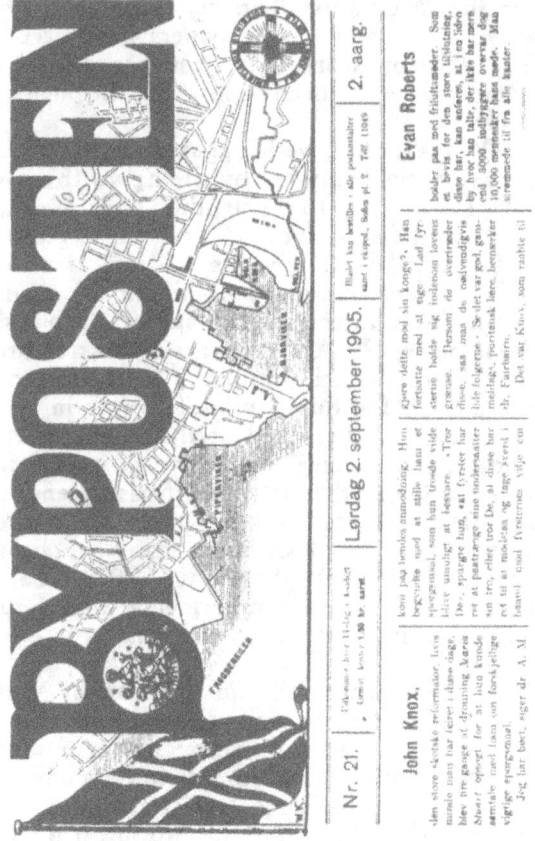

away. He was one of the most faithful workers in the vineyard, a real evangelist and soulwinner.

A letter from Bishop Vincent, at this time, will interest many:

Chautauqua, N.Y. July 2, 1904.

My Beloved Barratt!

I send you out of my heart words of sincere condolence in the time of your bereavement. Dear Sussie — so amiable and beautiful — snatched from your grasp! I feared it when I read your former letter. I foresaw the frost of death in the December brightness and delicacy of the lovely leaf. I wonder if God sends his own angels once in a while into human bodies, to have them live a while to shed on poor mortals the light of heaven! Then he takes them home again to fulfil some blessed ministry — perhaps on earth — watching, tending, guarding, helping those who loved them for a time. How wonderful are His ways! And how full of tenderness!

**Sussie.**

May you and your dear wife and children — and dear grandmother as well, — feel the consolation of Gods grace in these days of bereavement. And dear Haave — so good and faithful — he too has gone. My assurance of sympathy to his stricken family! — — —

What a good Bishop you will have in Bishop Burt!

Love to all who remember me,

Faithfully yours

John H. Vincent.

Bishop Vincents recommendation of *Bishop W. Burt* proved to be well deserved. In my notes on the conference held in Stavanger in 1904, I write: "The conference was one of the best I have ever attended. *Bishop Burt* presided, and a grand man he proved also to be. I knew him from my visit to *Zürich* last year, and through Mary, and my stay at *Rome*.

My assistent in the C. Mission, Mr. Bolt, was appointed pastor at *Trondhjem*".

A picture of mother and our first boy Tom.
Compare it with that of mother and myself as a boy.

"After conference I visited *Varaldsøy*, where my mother, and Louisa, my youngest sister, and her children, were spending their holidays. I shall never forget the visit to the old place, *after about 18 years absence*".

The work in the City Mission was constantly on the forward move. In making up statistics for 1905 I note that, from the time I commenced to hold meetings, I have in all held 7661 meetings, including 3669 sermons, 825 lectures, sermons, and lectures at festivals, besides after-meetings etc. These *festivals* are verry common in Norway, in all religious denominations. Besides coffee and cake, which is served after singing, prayers and an address, or sermon; those present have liberty to testify and bear witness to their Master's glory. In Methodist circles and the City Mission, the festivals generally winded up with an after-meeting and an altar-call. A festival of this kind might last for hours.

"*Byposten*" gave its readers a general view of the Revival meetings that were held in Oslo and elsewhere. For the first time I mention *Los Angeles* in no 8, but not in connection with the Pentecostal Revival (it was not as yet a reality), but as the seat of the general conference of the Methodist church. I little thought then, that it was to be *the starting point of one of the greatest revivals since the days of the apostles, if not the greatest!*

The meetings in Oslo were continuously being held in the various Halls and market places: thousands had been reached with the Gospel, who never enter a place of worship, and there were signs of revival not only in Oslo, but in the surrounding towns and country plases.

I was at this junktion that the now so well-known evangelist *Albert Lunde* came to Oslo. The largest Hall in the city was secured for his meetings — "*Calmeyergatens Missionshus*". This Hall had been erected by leaders of an earlier revival in the city. Albert Lunde, being a Lutheran, was even allowed to speak in the aristocratic church in Uranienborg. The evangelists *P. G. Sand* and *Modalsli* exerted also considerable influence in connection with the meetings. A great Revival was the result, in which numbers of souls were saved.

Much could be written about this work of God,

but I must return to my story. At present Mr. Albert Lunde has his own Hall in the city and one of the largest congregations. He is loved and respected by all, and his services are still a great blessing to the people.

My being a Methodist always made it difficult to some extent, to carry on the Mission work. Although I may fairly say, that during those days, I believe no one took greater interest in *Alliance-Work* than myself. I mean Alliance-work, without requiring its adherents to give up any ground that was dear to them. We were to meet on evangelical lines. I therefore took active part in the so-called „*Enhetsmøter*" (union meetings) and endorsed them very heartily in the "Byposten" and elsewhere. However, there always seems to be a feeling of doubt amongst leaders within the State-church, as to the purity of the motives of outsiders. They quite naturally expect, that wee seek to pick their sheep and build up a work which stands in opposition to theirs. This makes it easier for *Lutheran* evangelists to get hold of those, who are more favourably disposed towards the Statechurch. Although I had the purest of motives and sought to win souls for Christ, I stood now, not only as Methodist, but as the leader of a perfectly new organisation. I can therefore quite understand the prejudice and opposition that appeared at various angles of the work from several quarters.

Despite all handicaps, there was enough to do. Sinners were dying in their sins, and I felt that a deep, free work of God was necessary to reach these lost souls. So in the face of all prejudice and protests and even ridicule from many, I felt that time was short, and that I had merely to push forward. In an appeal, I prepared for English speaking readers, I was eventually able to state, that "*the Press* has now taken quite another position and writes very respectfully of the work done by the Mission.

Even *the free churches* and the *Salvation Army* show considerable interest in the movement, and *the Lu=theran "Inner Mission"* papers speak very favourably of it."

I commenced to organize the work on as broad lines as possible, by giving permission to join the mission without leaving State-church, leaving it to converts to decide, if they later on would join the Methodist church or not. The *law* in Norway does not prevent the formation of a Mission, but demands that all, who yoin other churches, shall leave the State Church. Here then I adopted the easiest method, at least I thought so, that would bind the new converts more effectually to the Mission. The Constitution of the Mission provided for the formation of a Board, consisting of members of the quarterly conferences within the Methodist church and the city mission.

At last the question arose in my mind, if we had not better *erect a large Central Hall for the Mission*, and continue the work out from this centre.

*But where was the money to come from?* My former attempt to raise money for the Central Church in Oslo on my visit to England, had been a failure, but could not *America* help us this time?

In 1905 the *"Byposten"* was crowded out at times with articles about the great *Revival in Wales* under *Evan Roberts*, and with accounts of the wonderful revival meetings in connection whit the *Torrey—Alexander Mission* in England. This had a great influence on many in Norway. Of course many of the other religious papers were full of it as well. Prayers were sent up: *Lord, send a great Spiritual Revival over Norway!*

The account of *"How Evan Roberts received his baptism in the Holy Ghost"* began to make people long to obtain the same blessing.

Large flaming headings in the "Byposten": *"Revival—Revival—Revival"* with a detailed description of the work of the Holy Ghost in England, and the Revival spirit that was burning in our own hearts, brought numbers of people on their knees before God, not only in Oslo, but the fire was spreading in many places.

A *letter* I wrote to *Evan Roberts*, dated Jan. 2, 1904 will be of some interest:

> Dear Bro. Evan Roberts!
>
> You will be surprised to receive these lines from one so far away from the scenes of revival in Wales, but it will interest you to know that we are following you and the great work God is doing in Wales. Oh, it's glorious! I wept for very joy when reading accounts of it by Mr. Ferrin Hulme and others in "The Methodist Times".
>
> We have had seasons of revival in Norway also, and at several of our meetings in various denominations souls are being saved, but the general cry is "Lord give us a revival the like of which we have never seen before! I started some midday prayer meetings a short time ago and our prayer subject was: "Revival over Christiania!" Those meetings were greatly blest and results were seen in more ways than one. Five of us sent an invitation last week, through the papers, to christians and ministers in all denominations, to join in similar meetings and pray for the same thing We had our first meeting on Monday at 12 o'clock. It was a real good meeting. Since then increased interest has been shown. The accounts I have given of the revival in Wales, have been and are still a means of inspiration to us all. I have already delivered two lectures to crowded meetings about it, and almost filled our City Mission paper with an account of it. Other friends are speaking about it, and one has also lectured about it. So you see there are friends far away from Wales, who rejoice with you in the glorious results you constantly witness, and which God to a great extent has made you the direct instrument of performing.
>
> Will you and your friends remember Norway and our work in Christiania? Join us in prayer for a mighty revival over this centre of the political, social and religious life of this grand old country. I have learnt to love this country and it's people. Came here from England with my parents when a boy five years old. We are now naturalized Norwegians. I passed through Wales about 11 years ago and took part in meetings at Cardiff.
>
> God bless you — more and more! Pray for me personally. I have often experienced the power of the Holy Spirit in my work as a minister, and now as leader of the Chri-

stiania City Mission, of the Meth. Epis. Church, but I want a Fuller Baptism of fire. Pray about it!
Yours in Christ Jesus<br>
T. B. Barratt.

This letter was, I am told, inserted in one of the Cardiff papers. It is characteristic of the work in Wales, that nothing is to be done, unless they are led *by the Spirit*.

One of Evan Roberts' friends and co workers sent me an answer to the above letter:

Dear Brother!

I have just read your letter and am led by the Spirit to send you a photo of that Holy man — Evan Roberts.

Praised be the Lord! The revival is Divine in it's origin and influence — praise God — it will spread over the whole world.

Pray for us. We are praying for Norway, Spain, America. etc. May the Lord bless them with the Baptism of the Holy Ghost, and your folks as well.

Yours in Christ Jesus<br>
L. S. Jones.<br>
Bapt. Pastor, Bromford.

None of us thought then *how* all these prayers would eventually be answered. The *Pentecostal Movement* is no doubt *the outcome of it all, Hallelujah!*

In the midst of all this, I decided *to go to America to raise funds for the new building,* which was to be the centre of the City Mission. I announced my decision to do so in July, 1905.

In September large *Farewell meetings* were held in Oslo. I took a short tour of the country first with my wife and our boy Tom, visiting Trondhjem, Kristiansund, Aalesund and Bergen, holding meetings everywhere. I then left Bergen for Liverpool, and proceeded from there to *New York.*

## CHAPTER VIII.

### In America.

Most excellent letters of introduction to all Methodists and christians generally, were given me by several bishops, and the Norwegian King allowed me to make use of his name in connection with the enterprise. The Hall was to be named "*Haakons—Borgen.*"

Bishop William Burt, wno was Bishop of Europe, wrote: "I take great pleasure in certifying that the Rev. T. B. Barratt is a member in good standing of the Norwegian Conference.

He has come to this country in the interest of the great work he is doing in connection with the City Mission in Christiania, which commands the admiration and hearty support of all christian people.

He is a man of excellent gifts, an interesting lecturer, a successful evangelist, and a fine musician.

I most cordially commend him to all our ministers and people, because of his personal worth and because of the great work which he so ably represents.

Let me intreat for him a cordial welcome to all our churches.

Brooklyn, 20—11. 1905.

William Burt.

Bishop John H. Vincent wrote: "I take pleasure in testifying to the efficiency of the Rev. T. B. Barratt. of Christiania. He represents in the Norwegian work of our church what Chaplain McCabe for so many years represented in the United States.

He preaches, he sings, he prays, he serves the people, he reaches the crowd, he brings men to Christ, and having a knowledge of the English language as well as the Norwegian, he secures the sympathy of all English-speaking people.

I bespeak for Mr. Barratt during his labours in the United States, the sympathy and co-operation of all good people of all the churches, for Mr. Barratt, represents the Holy Catholic Church.

Indianapolis, Ind. Nov. 11—1905.

John H. Vincent.

Bishop McCabe wrote: "Dear Brother! Your letter to hand. I do most cordially commend your enterprise of erecting a City Mission Building in Christiania, Norway, and I trust that you will have great success. I have been there and I have seen the immense congregations which it is possible to gather under one roof to hear the Gospel of Christ. I trust you will strike someone who will make this enterprise a possibility very soon".

Philadelphia, Pa. Nov. 3, 1905.
                                    Yours faithfully
                                        C. C. McCabe.

These and other recommendations inspired me with hope, and I trusted that *all* the churches would help me, and that it would be an easy matter to raise the necessary funds. On reaching America, I came across an advertisement: *"D'ont wait for something to turn up — turn up something."* There was a lot in that I thought, and in fact, it has been the red thread in my life. Perhaps I had made the mistake, that I had often been *turning up things in my own power*, and the time was at hand, when the Lord would teach me, that *he* wanted to say *more* about my plans, yea, that *he* had *a special plan for me, that was still hidden from view.*

My first step was to become acquainted with the preachers, in order to have an evening service in their churches and possibly a collection towards the City Mission.

One day, just after coming to America, I received a letter from Laura, stating that

### MOTHER WAS DEAD!

*Ah, that was a hard blow!* The influence of her life was great and will remain with me to the end. She was a wonderful Saint of God, who spread the Gospel truth in life and in deed. Loved by all who learnt to know her. When the friends heard me weep, they tried to comfort me. Burt, Leonard, Trelstad, spoke beautiful words of comfort, likewise Bishop Dowell. But God alone could give sufficient comfort. *And He did!*

It appears that she died the day after I came to America.

The great and influential paper "*The Christian Advocate*" wrote an excellent article about the City Mission, and I trusted it would have a good effect on the churches.

I visited several towns. In Chicago, I had several services amongst the Scandinavian Methodists. There I also heard *Dr. Torrey and Alexander,* as well as the pianist, *Mr. Harkness.* When there, the President of the Y. M. C. A, where *Albert Lunde* had formerly been at work for the Lord, asked me to conduct a series of revival services. In Chicago I also met the *evangelist Jones,* who had taken part *in the revival in Wales with Evan Roberts.*

In my letters to "Byposten", I wrote from *Minneapolis* words of encouragement to the friends of the City Mission at home, and explained to them how difficult it was to become known amongst *the American or English—speaking churches,* that everything takes time. I had good meetings in Minneapolis amongst the Norwegians, and went from there to St. Paul and other towns.

In agreement with the bishops and other leaders within the Church, I arranged to appeal to the ministers throughout the methodist church, to invite their members on a certain day to give *five cents* towards the Christiania City Mission. Of course it was necessary to work up an interest for this plan through the Conferences. *If that plan had succeeded,* we would no doubt have been able to build "Haakonsborgen."

From New York, June 19, I wrote a good bit about the *Holiness meetings* at Des Moines, and dwelt somewhat on *the subject of holiness and a pure heart.*

The Missionary Secretary, *Dr. Adna Leonard,* expressed his sorrow one day to me, because it seemed that the time we had chosen for my visit among the English—speaking churches was so unfortunate, for it was the year of the *Jubilee in India*, and much was being done to meet the wants of the people at San Francisco *after the fire* there. He thought that the next year would have been better for me. I wrote to "Byposten" on the 16th of June, 1906, *that I had already purchased a ticket back to Norway*, but just then a letter came from *Bishop Burt* stating, that if there was any chance of an opening among the English—speaking churches, then I ought to stay longer. I thought at first, that I had better take across to Norway and return again in the Autumn. Much would depend on the attitude the Bishops would take towards *my five cents plan*, but both Bishops Burt and Fowler desired me to stay longer. "Unless somebody is sick at home, *stick to your job*", said bishop Fowler. So I determined to remain, and right glad I am that I did not leave America then. This step was the cause eventually of my receiving *the Baptism of the Holy Ghost.* A blessing of greater worth than every cent in America!

I took my abode at *Dr. A. B. Simpson's "Missionary Home."*

The pastors in the Norwegian and English churches, who invited me to visit them, had shown me every kindness, and although I had not attained what I wanted, I felt encouraged to know, that neither they nor their churches, nor I myself, had lost anything so far *financially*, but that much blessing had attended the services and meetings held in the various cities where I had been.

A book that interested me and gave me new impulses was *"Finney's Life"*, and a book by *Dr. Hall* on the Central Truths of Christianity. It was a powerful appeal for orthodox theology. The first book was as a new chapter in the book of Acts.

About a year had now elapsed since I left Norway for America, and it was just a little beyond four years since the City Mission was started. I wrote the following, on Sept. 11, 1906: "What this year has been for me, God alone knows. He has taught me many things, and much of what I knew before has become a greater reality to me. One learns as long as there is life. What results the year will bring concerning the object I have in view, I cannot say. All is laid in the hands of God. *I have been a stranger amongst strangers.* I have had a good time among the Norwegian churches, and some of the English speaking churches have been very kind, but on the whole it has been a hard and difficult time from the commencement. Numerous ways have been tried, but the results hitherto have been enough to knock down the courage of the most hopeful man that is to be found — where he is I do not know. Yet the Lord has strengthened me with a wonderful courage, so that no sooner has one plan been crushed before a new plan was at hand. I have prayed and cried, and have been chastised in spirit and comforted, and then renewed the battle. Had it not been for the strong faith I have in the importance of this work, and that the Lord will still find a way out, I would go back home at once!"

In June I spoke at the *"Preachers meeting"* in New York, as the speaker for the occasion did not turn up. A vote of thanks was passed and a resolution, adopting my five cents plan, *with an appeal to all the pastors within the Methodist Church*, as well as the leaders of the Epworth League and Sunday' Schools, to stimulate all, both young and old, to give five cents towards Haakonsborgen, some Sunday in December. This resolution was signed by *George Adams, J. W. Campbell and G. E. Strobridge.*

I really trusted, that when so many ministers adopted this resolution, there surely would be an open door at last. But no! The good

Lord had something better for me in store than that, Hallelujah!

When praying I constantly felt the need of a still greater blessing over my own soul! I stood, and had from youth been standing, for Holiness and the Baptism of the Holy Ghost, and had no doubt often felt somewhat of the fire burning within, a touch of the unseen hand, but I knew there must be a still deeper work and a constant victory.

All the trials I had passed through during the last year in America brought me down—deeper down, before the Lord, seeking, praying, weeping in His presence, thirsting for a full baptism of the Holy Ghost—the experience itself, and not only the intense longing for it. What that really meant I was of course not aware of, but the Holy Spirit drove me nearer the goal, day by day, blessed be God!

Of course the work done for the coming subscription had some influence, and if I could have proceeded with it, there might possibly in due time have been a more favourable result financially, but my thirst for a greater spiritual blessing was now almost unbearable.

About this time I read of the Revival at Los Angeles. In "Byposten" (No. 20, 1906) I gave a graphic account of it under the headline: "Pentecost Afresh. Los Angeles is now visited by a revival, that reminds us of the revival described in Acts II."

I then gave an account of the marvellous outpouring of the Holy Spirit at the meetings, with the signs following. This account gave, no doubt, many a mighty shock in Norway when they read of it in "Byposten", but it prepared the way for what was to follow. In no. 22 I gave a detailed account of my own experience.

I dared to accept full cleansing on the last day of September (Sunday) at 5,30 o'clock. and exactly eight days after this, on the same spot, and at the same hour, I received a mighty anointing of the Spirit.

## IX.

*A mighty anointing of the Spirit.*

An account of this wonderful experience was sent to the friends at Los Angeles, whom I have never seen, home to my wife, to be inserted in the "Byposten" and other papers, to the "Christian Advocate" and to Dr. Adna Simpson, all to the honor of God. I evidently thought at first, that I had received the *full Pentecostal Baptism*, and gave my letters the heading "*When the Fire fell*". But, as stated at the commencement of the next chapter, this experience was only a "glorious introduction" to the *Baptism in the Holy Ghost and Fire,* received on the 15th of Nov., 1906. It was a foretaste of the baptism itself, for which I thank God. Comp. John 20, 22.

Many desired me to reprint the account, and I did so. It surely prepared the way, in the minds and hearts of many, for still greater things. The inner Power given me, by this mighty anointing, drove me to relate the account of it to numbers, who immediately began to seek their way to the *Cross* for full cleansing in the Blood of Jesus and the Fire from Heaven.

Here then is an extract of the account I sent around:

New York, Oct. 8th, 1906.

"Hallelujah! It took place yesterday, Sunday October 7, between five and six p.m. Praise the Lord, my heart is burning! It seems to me that I am the happiest man in the world; everything has become new, I am filled with peace and joy and love to God and man. Yes, indeed the Lord's ways are truly unfathomable. His leadings with me have always been most wonderful, and there has always been a cry in my heart, "Forward! Forward!" Ever since my serious illness over twenty years ago, there has been a constraining power in me to go forward.

The doctrine of Holiness has always been the dearest subject to my heart, and I have fought many a fight for it without having really had the experience myself. Many a time I have thought that I had received the blessing, but on account of not having been faithful, and partly because of fearfulness to testify of the grace I had received, I lost it again. Many a time I have been so filled with the Lord himself, my cup has overflowed.

And the time when most souls were saved, has been the time when I have been nearest God in faith and prayer.

There has been so much discussion on this subject of Sanctification which has only left bitterness in our hearts instead of holiness.

I think I told you in our paper about a wonderful blessing God gave me at Christmas time. I was reading a little about Mr. Moody, at the time when he met Mr. Moorhouse, and how he preached seven times from John three sixteen. As I read this the Lord's Presence filled the whole room, and my being was filled with His Love. Oh! it was glorious, but nothing to be compared with what I have experienced since.

After that I met some of the New Theologians, who are found in all denominations, and my spirit burned with indignation! I must say the Lord wonderfully undertook concerning the literature which fell into my hands, and the lectures to which I listened, and strengthened my faith in Biblical Truth, though it was brought out by them in a philosophical light. I have never studied the Centre of All — The Redemption — as I do now. Never have I rested more securely on the old foundation. Hallelujah!

From what I have written, you will all understand, that all my attempts to raise funds for "*Haakonsborgen*" have hitherto been unsuccessful. During the summer I did not even have the chance of speaking in the churches, excepting the Norwegian churches.

I understood, that the dear Lord was after — *me!* I had prayed by the hour for help towards "Haakonsborgen", until I became quite dumb and w a s o b l i g e d t o l a y a l l d o w n a t H i s f e e t. Then the Spirit took hold of me in a new way, and searched through my whole being. Not for a moment did I doubt that I was a child of God, had I done so, I should have gone into despair. I had experienced so much of His Grace and His Love to me, that I felt the slightest doubt would have been a sin against His Holy Spirit.

Oh! how abominable I was in my own sight, as I saw myself in the light of His Holiness! Over and over again I was humbled to the dust as I saw my own ambition, selfishness, and wilfulness, Oh! My Lord! How grieved His Spirit must have been!

I was now a silent listener, as the Lord prevented me from conducting meetings myself. I went from one place to another, attending meetings and hearing different preachers, and over and over again my conscience smote me so greatly that I was terrified, but He also comforted me. Praised be His Holy Name! As I am writing this, my heart is so full that I can hardly continue, but for the Glory of God it must be done. Perhaps some of those who read these lines, may be in a like conflict as I was. Beloved friend, Jesus will help you through, as He helped me, doubt not a moment!

Reading Finney's experience, was a great help to me in those days. I read his biography, with my Bible, open before me, until there was a great cry within me for deliverance. Some articles in Dr. A.

Simpson's Magazine were a great help to me, but the strange thing was, that I knew it all before, and had preached it many a time: yet though I had experienced so much, it all seemed new to me now, and I had to read it very carefully, line by line, word by word, often with tears, and intense prayer, on my knees, and often prostrate on the ground. Then I heard about:

### The revival in Los Angeles,

about which I wrote you. I immediately sent a letter to the friends over there, and told them about my conflict, but you know we never can find words to express the things that lie deepest in our hearts. At a meeting where Mr. Lyal spoke at Dr. Simpson's hall, I asked them to pray for me, *that my heart might be filled with the Spirit of God.*

However, what I first needed was to be cleansed in the Blood of Jesus, so that I could *believe* I was purified from all my sins. O, my dear friend, if you have been there, you know that this battle may be just as hard, possibly more so, than when you at first sought the Lord.

Sunday, eight days ago, after a long struggle on my knees, I took the bible to the window, and my eyes fell on something there, enabling me immediately to grasp full cleansing through the Blood of my precious Saviour.

This lasted until Tuesday: then a letter came from Los Angeles. I will let you have it here. It is a remarkable letter. I read it over and over again:

Los Angeles, Cal , Sept. 28, 1906.

**T. B. Barratt!**

Dear Brother in Our Lord Jesus Christ. Greetings to you in His name!

Your earnest letter touched our hearts; we are praying the full pentecostal baptism upon you! So that you may be equipped for His service as you never have been! God is on the giving hand — is ready to pour this precious baptism upon you, as soon as you are ready to receive it! There has to be a complete coming out, and leaving all for Jesus — losing sight of all but God — even the things we have done — our own experiences, theories, ideas even our own thoughts, and just letting God have His own precious way with us. After you have fully consecrated, and know God has cleansed your heart, then fast, and wait upon God. Keep yourself in a receptive attitude — and no matter what workings go on in your body, continually let and ask God to have His own way with you. You need have no fear while you keep under the blood — "Perfect love casts out all fear". Sometimes a wonderful shaking takes place, and some times the language comes at first, as a baby learning to talk. But let God have all — tongue, hands, feet — the whole body presented to him, as your reasonable service! When the Holy Ghost comes in, you will know it, for He will be in your very flesh. Be obedient on every line. Be nothing — that He may be all in all. We would be so glad if God should lead you to Los Angeles — many have come from afar, and have gone back with their wonderful pentecost. Hallelujah! We send you a sample copy of the paper, and will be rejoiced to hear from you again. I have lived in Los Angeles for about 12 years, and very many of my friends, those I have known for years, are getting their pentecost, and are thus ready to meet Jesus when He comes, and labor for souls as never in their life until that time shall come, or they go home to glory! Oh praise God forever! When we have this baptism, we are very different from what we ever were before — and we would do nothing to lose it. It fits us up for the stake, or whatever may come!

May God bestow this wonderful baptism upon you most speedily is our earnest prayer

Mrs. I. May Throop.

After having received this letter, I made up my mind that I would have the same blessing that is spoken of in Acts 2, 4, and that the friends in Los Angeles had received. I needed it both to live for God and to work for Him. Though I really had given up all before I was cleansed, still so many things came back to my memory from my past life, that I really felt sad, but I believed that Jesus had purified my heart "by *faith*" Acts 15, 9.

The heart searching prayers that went up to the Lord every day, were without any doubt, a result of the mighty influence of the Spirit over my mind and heart. I was to have gone here and there, but I had to give it all up: I also fasted somewhat. The Apostles fasted, and doubtless the first Christians did so too. Acts 13, 2. 3. Now and then to have a season of fasting does not weaken the body, it rather strengthens us. As regards "Haakonsborgen", I said to the Lord; "If you want this cause to prosper, then it will prosper, though men and devils oppose; and if you do not want me to have success in this work, then I do not care to have it. I only desire Thy will in this matter!" (This was before the cleansing). God alone knows what a burden then rolled off my heart! I read the word of God over and over again. Oh! how it helped me at this time — here alone, far away from loved ones and friends, shut up in my room with God only. I do not mention this to make the impression upon anyone that it is necessary to wait so long. There are many in Los Angeles who were saved, purified and baptized in the Holy Spirit, at the same meeting.

A thought struck me, that perhaps when I went back home I would be *persecuted* if I preached

*the full gospel in this way.*

I have never been timid as far as I know, but the s e l f within us does so like to be glorified, and unconsciously it enters into our very best and holiest service for God, but now they can say what they like.

*My all is on the altar —*

reputation (if there was any, it was absolutely undeserved) glory, energy, time, strength, ability, friends, all my loved ones, with great pain I took them one by one, and laid them again, but now fully, on the altar. What I was, what I might be, my plans (and God knows they have been many), my desires, my future too — God could send me, now, wherever He liked, to the smallest congregation in the country or to the largest! To China, Africa, Iceland, anywhere. He could let me continue the ministry I was in, or send me all over Norway, or round about the world! I was His for ever; and the dearest, the last I let go fully — my own life — He was also to have that!

Of late years I have often said that I was not afraid to die, but I wanted to live for the sake of my dear ones, for the church, for the salvation of souls, till I was spent. However, I had to say "Jesus, if thou dost want me to die, have Thine own way". The Devil tempted me, but I cried out to the Lord and said: "Even if I am sent to Hell, I will cling to the work of redemption", but it was very soon clear to me that Hell was not the proper place for me. I was His, my Saviour's, eternally.

All this I had experienced when I was pleading with God for a pure heart, and now, when seeking

### The Baptism of the Holy Ghost,

I went over it all again, but I had the assurance in my soul that all things were settled now. I was taken deep, deep, deep down — ground to powder. At times I said: "Jesus, tell mother and father, and Sussie, and the others home there, what I am doing". And He did so, no doubt. Heaven witnessed my conflict. It was God's Spirit that fought with me to get complete victory in my heart and life.

Saturday evening I attended one of the meetings. A preacher from *Wales* spoke, and I felt it was a greeting from God to me. He spoke about the Holy Spirit, and was filled and permeated by it himself. On Sunday I took part in the Lord's Supper in the little chapel there. *Pastor Wilson* conducted the service. In *Dr. Simpson's* Alliance work, numbers of all evangelical creeds take part. *Wilson* was pastor in the Episcopal Church. He had been saved through the Salvation Army, but still used the priestly garb of his Church. The organist was a soldier in the Salv. Army, and sat there with h e r uniform. Several other ministers were present. Behind the altar on the wall stood the inscription:

*Jesus only.*

And thus we melted together in H i m!

After the service I went upstairs to my room (I was staying at the Alliance House) and locked the door and remained there all the day, not even going down to lunch. I felt that something must take place, the blessing must come! I was so hungry! All within me was crying out to God for help. Had I received full light on the subject, I might have entered into the *full* Pentecostal experience. But I was determined to hold out. My heart cried out in mighty appeals to God. I thought I would keep the battle going, even if I did so in my own strength. This I soon saw was perfectly hopeless, but how often we keep battling, even unconsciously, in our own strength!

I had noticed, at times on Sunday, a remarkable warmth in my breast, but it left me. Whilst weeping Sunday afternoon, a little before 5 P. M., the fire came back to my breast. I hid my face in a towel, so as not to disturb the inmates next door, but it did not last long ere I shouted so loudly, that they must have heard me afar off, had it not been for the noise in the street. I was a while bathed in perspiration (They no doubt shouted aloud in the house of Cornelius — "loudly magnified God." Norwegian translation. Acts 10, 46). I could not help it; I w a s   s e i z e d  b y t h e  H o l y  P o w e r  o f G o d  t h r o u g h o u t  m y  w h o l e  b e i n g, and it swept through my whole body as well. Then I remembered the advice given in the letter from Los Angeles concerning the body, but I was not afraid — I was willing to die. In order to be sure that this was the work of God, I laid my hand on my pulse: The beat was as even as usual. I drank a glass of water, but the storm went on. I then got hold of Bro. Lyal, but could scarcely say a word when he came in. Then my whole body shook under the great workings of the Spirit.

Some will possibly believe that I was overtaxed after the long struggle. *No!* — I had been resting several weeks without holding meetings. I felt stronger physically than usual. Bro. Lyal did'nt know what to make of it. When he came in, I was lying stretched over a chair on the floor. He began to pray to the Lord for me, but I stopped him: "This is the Lord!"

"Yes, but you know brother, that the devil attacks people at times," he said.

"The devil is conquered ere this, my brother," I answered weeping, but sure of victory, *"this is the Spirit of God!"*

I had asked the Lord to give me the Baptism of the Spirit in such a way, that I would always be sure that it was not human feeling merely, or the work of men, but the supernatural power that touched me and went through my whole body, soul and spirit. Now I received the assurance that this *was* God's Spirit. He was filling the empty vessel.

*Br. Lyal* helped me up and asked me to lie down a while on my bed, but the work went on there just as mighty as before. Then he went down stairs and returned after a while in company with *pastor March* D. D, but then I was sitting on a chair and my whole soul was filled with the wonderful peace of God.

They were so delighted when they saw me.

We conversed together and thanked God, and I went down and took dinner at 6 o'clock. After that I went to the meeting. The Fire of God was constantly burning within. I felt as if I was the happiest man in the world. Everything was new — *everything!* The two men I spoke to, went immediately forth to be prayed with and gave their hearts to God. When I related my experience at the meeting there was great joy.

When I was struggling, before the anointing came, I thought of many of the dear saints in Norway, who many a time had been vexed by my determination to carry out my own will. I made up my mind that I would ask them all to forgive me as soon as I came back. I had often been hasty and ambitious and wilful. It almost seemed as if I could manage the devil himself, but God knows how foolish I was. Deep down in my heart I was really sincere and meant it allright, but my impetuous mind, which was sometimes subdued and under control, breaking out again, may have hurt many a one. I hope soon to see you face to face, and then to ask you personally to forgive me, but as my return journey has been postponed for some months, I must ask you to do so anyway. As I am writing and thinking of these things, my tears are flowing and my heart is lifted up in prayer to the Lord.

Oh, what victory God gave me, Hallelujah!"

Thus runs the story of the first mighty outpouring on my soul, on *the 7th of October, 1906.*

The letter goes on to say:

"I could not sleep for some time that night; the Spirit spoke and prayed and rejoiced within me.

The following day I went to see *Bishop Burt* at the office. Wherever I came I was obliged to tell people what God had done, and asked them if they were saved or baptized in the Holy Ghost.

Bishops, preachers, and people amongst all classes.
There was a preacher's meeting that day at the head office, and they immediately began to ask me to conduct meetings, although I had not told them of the blessing, and for some time no one had asked me to preach. "A reporter of one of the large papers is waiting for you, they said. "What does he want?" "You have asked to see him. No, indeed not," I said, with a smile. „I have not asked to speak with any reporter."

But there he stood. He had heard my lecture about Norway. "Well, if you wish to report anything, tell them, that the Lord baptized my soul yesterday with the Holy Spirit." He desired to know more about it, and I gave him a testimony at the same time about Jesus. I thought surely that I had received *the full Pentecostal Baptism*, as many do in our day, who have passed through a similar experience. To Bishop Burt I said: "I have packed my trunk and intend to leave for home with the "Coronia" to-morrow."

"No", he answered, "you must remain here until December: do the best you can, and return home by Christmas. Perhaps the Lord may still have a way, especially in connection with the five cents collection, in December. You have done, what you could, but you must bide the Lord's time. Fifteen bishops have promised to support the collection, and I will bring it up once more at the bishop's Board, so take the whole thing with perfect ease, trusting the Lord!"

"A minister who had attended the meetings last summer, met me yesterday. He rejoiced when he heard about it all. "You look 10 years younger," he said, "and have received of the anointing that remains!" And it will be sure to do so, *if I constantly rest in Jesus only!* Pray for me, dear friends, that it may be so, and that *the fire of God* may fall on all His servants, and upon all His church on earth, *and over dear, old Norway!"*

At the meeting yesterday, my sister (Mary) came in. I seldom see her; she was passing through the city, and rejoiced and wept for very joy when she heard about all this and saw me. When I met *pastor Trelstad*, I said: "This is not the old Barratt you see now brother," and related what God had done.

The days that passed by, after this gracious anointing of the Spirit, were a constant revelation to me of the love of God, such as I had never seen or felt it before. Everything seemed changed, although I had not as yet entered into the full Pentecostal glory. There was a constant peace within. At times the Holy Ghost was as a *fire* within me, reminding me of the indwelling Christ and His wondrous Love. I knew that Christ had taken seat in the Temple of my heart. My chief desire now, was, to glorify His Holy Name! I wrote in my Jornal: "The Spirit warms my heart when I get near anybody He wants me to speak to; all other experiences have been eclipsed by this great demonstration of God's power in my heart.

Just after the meeting, at which I first testified of the blessing, I went out on the street and had to speak to two men about it. So far, nobody has been annoyed at the testimony. I went straight for a group of young men on a street corner; some joked, but the message was respected, I believe, nevertheless. Some Hebrew drivers took it pleasantly; one felt no doubt inclined to joke, but his comrade corrected him. I asked a young man at a newspaper stand if he was a christian. "No", he answered, and "did not intend to be." He was a Hebrew. "Do you know the Hebrew's God personally?" "No." "But Christ will reveal Him to you," I said. He became very thoughtful when I left him. I met a catholic priest once on the car. He seemed surprised but interested with my story. "Are you a catholic priest?" I asked. "Yes», he answered, reaching out his hand somewhat reluctantly to take mine. "I'm a protestant minister," I said, "and received such a blessing last Sunday night." "How so?" "The Lord baptized my soul with the Holy Ghost, and since then I have been so blest and glad, it's bubbling over, so that I'm obliged to tell all that love the Lord about it." We had a quite conversation. He had just started reading his prayer—book, when I changed seats and spoke to him.

I passed by a wellclad gentleman on the street. My heart was burning and I knew I must speak to him. "How do you do Sir? Will you permit me to put you a question? Are you a christian? "Yes", he was. I told him my story, and we walked far down the street together. He was one of the officials of a "Reformed Church."

Young business men have been so interested to listen to my story. I came across two fine young gentlemen on Broadway one evening, and could not pass by them. "Excuse me, gentlemen, do you love the Lord?" They looked at each other, then at me, and said nothing for a few moments. The tallest of the two then looked heavenward, but the other asked "What do you mean?" There was my chance to give a short message. I've come across several catholics, and their answers were interesting. One big fellow, walking along smoking, held on to the point, that what a man had been from his boyhood, he ought to continue to be. He was a catolic. I had a good chat with him. On passing a stable a little further down the street, I saw several men standing there, and passed by, but had to return and, by way of introduction, asked if they cared to have a paper, presenting the chief person present with a "Christian Advocate". They were very polite; one of the men was a Dane, and a little bit tipsy, poor fellow. When he heard I was from Christiania, he said he had been there, that's how I found out he was a Dane, and spoke to him in Norwegian.

When I attended the first meeting of all the New York and New York East and Newark Conferences, at the Evangelistic Commission Sessions, I felt God wanted me to speak to the crowd. But how could I? The program was fixed — and these programs often shut out the Holy Spirit from the church. There are so many big men to do the work, that the Holy Spirit doesn't get a chance. As Bishop Fowler preached, I was relieved somewhat by saying "Amen!" now and then, but towards the close I thought I could have fainted under the pressure of God's Spirit to arise and speak. I remember before this that I felt anxious and almost trembled at the thought of facing a great crowd of American preachers, but now the Lord had filled me with a message of a special nature. Dr. Henderson was to speak after the Bishop, but before he could get a chance, I was on my feet and shouted: "Bishop — Dr. Henderson, will you give me a chance to speak, if you don't my heart will burst!"

I then went before them and told them of God's wondrous grace. It was nothing but God's Spirit that could have given me the boldness to do that, and I understand the message made a great impression and struck home. One minister said it was «the keynote of the meetings.» I don't know, but I was relieved and praised God for the chance and the grace given me.

Dear old Bishop Andrews spoke so beautifully to me after the meeting, and Bishop Fowler likewise. He said something like this: "You will be staying on now I should say?" He meant concerning my intended journey home. He thanked God for me: "*Praise the Lord!*" After Dr. Henderson's address, he (dr. H.) invited all the pastors round the altar. There was a great crowd, so that was soon filled as well as the benches around the altar. I could but immediately begin to thank God for H i s mercy to me, and then the brethren continued in prayer. I threw my arms around one of the brethren nearest me, and told him how blessed it was. "Praise Him!" he answered. "Ah, I do! my soul is full of it!" I bowed down to the floor, close by the rich Mr.—, who had given me 100 dollars the Saturday before towards Haakonsborgen. He had just given the opening address of the evening: I grasped his hands at the close, and he seemed greatly impressed. Somehow or other, the ice was broken, and there was scarcely anybody in that crowd but went about handshaking all over the Church. At "the Book Room", I suppose everybody knows about it now. In the stores and on the cars, God works through this poor vessel. Twice I have been constrained to shout out an invitation to Christ, on the cars. It's a new life, a well of blessing in my soul!

Sometimes in the night I have been awakened and the Holy Spirit has groaned and prayed within me for those I have spoken to, and I believe they will be saved. At the meetings to—day I wept like a child, as a song, describing the glorious victory of the B a p t i s e d  s o u l, was sung by a married couple. It just described all my struggle and victory.

When I came from the meeting I have just described, I heard a young man walking briskly behind me, and stopping short I asked him if he was a christian. "No", was the reply. Then we walked together right down to the elevated, where he left me. On the platform of the elevated I asked a policeman if he was a christian; gave my message and stepped into the car which had just come. But as he was going the same way, he stepped in too and took a seat by my side, where we conversed together. He was an Irishman. On leaving the elevated, I accosted two gentlemen and gave them a message. And thus the Lord's Spirit has been working. T h i s  w a s the kind of work I cared least of all to do.

When I went down to White Star Line Pier, to see dear *Bro Lyal* off, the old man at the ticket office, on the elevated platform, took a strange interest in me as soon as he saw me, and gave me his seat the few moments we waited for the train. He was a butcher by profession, but fared badly and had now taken that job. God gave him a message — In the car I got the conductor to sit by my side and gave him a message. As he rose at the station, another man took his place. He looked stern, but I put the question pointblank: "Are you a christian, Sir?" And he received the message very kindly. I gave him my card, and he wanted to know where I was going to preach, as he would "look me up".

Thus it has been going on. Wonderful life!

I have spoken to people before. Many thought I did too much of it then. There was surely a very deep desire in my heart to bring the people a blessing; but now it springs forth from a deep assurance, and a wellspring of love, and has much deeper effect, Hallelujah! Praised be God!

The Journal continues with descriptions of similar scenes. It seemed as if the Lord gave me quite a mission on the streets of New York. Some of these cases were very remarkable.

"Received a nice letter from Seymour, Los Angeles, yesterday. But now the victory is won, Hallelujah! Amen! God deepens His own work more and more!"

I did not know, even then, that a still greater blessing was held in store for me — the *full* Baptism in the Holy Ghost and Fire!

Sunday, 14th Oct.: "I attended the Missionary meeting at the Gospel Tabernacle in the morning; at which *Dr. Simpson* preached and the Missionary collection was taken. With the afternoon collection, it amounted to more than 70,000 dollars. I reckon Dr. Simpson to be one of the greatest preachers of our day.

In the evening I preached at *Dr. Byrts* Church at Brooklyn. He took me to the Epworth League first, in which I took part. There was general surprise at seeing so many present at that service and at the service in the Church. God blest His word wonderfully to many, I believe. The altar was filled, at the close of the meeting, with officials and members seeking the Baptism of the Holy Spirit."

Monday 15th: "I had a good time yesterday, just on the same spot, where Jesus met my soul the Sunday before, and at about the same hour. Glory to His name, Amen!"

The street work continues. Many touching scenes at times. Much writing in between. The Lord has helped me out of many financial difficulties also.

*Bishop Vincent* sent me some very interesting letters, after receiving the account of my experience. I have them still. He thought, that I had always had it. I pointed out as clearly as possible, the definite work done by the Holy Spirit now. He wrote many beautiful words, but I asserted nevertheless, that I had really received a definite experience, the like of which I had not attained before.

I had not been clear as to the gifts of the Spirit. I did not expect Tongues as a definite sign of the Pentecostal blessing, but the friends at Los Angeles wrote and said I must press on to get the gift of Tongues. In answer to this, I wrote: "I am willing to be anything for my blessed Saviour."

Oct. 23rd: "Am seeking the gift of

tongues and the other signs of Pentecostal Power, God in His mercy will give me."

24th.: „Have been praying all day. Ate no lunch, but intensely sought the gifts, renewing my vows, praying and praising God. Consecrating anew, although I knew no special hindrance — all belongs to Jesus! Have studied the matter again. Have felt the fire burn within often, but am expecting a renewal of the Baptism in conjunction with the gift of tongues and other gifts the Lord may send.

It surprises me, that I have to look so long in vain—as it seems. But God has His reason, of course! Oh may this seal of the Pentecostal Power soon be given me!"

25th: "I have rested well: I enjoy perfect peace. I know it was the great anointing on the 7th of October, but I want the finished work. In one sense never finished on earth, but the Pentecostal testimony or the seal (gift of tongues) to the power, and still more power! In looking back on my life, and in passing through in my mind's eye what Christ has done and is doing for me, I cannot but praise Him. Just fancy, it's a year to—day since I first saw America. What a marvellous year it has been!"

"1:30 o'clock: Still seeking the gift, but oh, what a glorious time I had with the Lord this morning. His very presence was here; the Holy Fire was burning in my soul, filling me with joy, as a cup running over, and glad Hallelujahs! Glory to His name! Amen."

"Heard *Gipsy Smith* last night at Grace M. E. Church. It was a most deeply spiritual meeting, and God gave him great power. I heard him in Hull, England, deliver his famous lecture "From Gipsy tent to Platform." He remembered me when we shook hands."

"I did not get the gift of tongues yesterday, nor have I received it yet to—day, but God is blessing me wonderfully. Praised be His Holy Name!"

"I have written to Los Angeles for an answer to some questions." Former letters told of persecution, even from the Methodists, but I was told that "the Holy Ghost only comes in when you come to an end of yourself." I still have these letters. The printed heading of each letter ran thus: "The Apostolic Faith Movement. Chas. F. Parham, Projector. W. J. Seymour, Pastor, 312 Azusa Street, Los Angeles, Cal." The letters were signed by G. A. Cook, Man. Ed.

They were delighted to hear of my experience. I quote a few lines of a letter:

"As I read your letter I could feel the Spirit moving in me thrilling me with joy and witnessing to the great work that had been done in your heart. May the Lord keep you in that state of grace and deep humility that you now enjoy. I told about your baptism before the meeting yesterday and great joy was manifested.

The speaking in tongues should follow the baptism. If you had remained under the power, until the Lord had finished, you undoubtedly would have spoken in tongues, not necessarily for use in a foreign field, but as a sign to you of Pentecost, the same as at the house of Cornelius and at Ephesus. Some go several days after the baptism before speaking, but unless you do speak, there is always a tendency to leak out — a leak-hole for the devil to tempt you. While we are getting a Bible experience, we may as well go all the way with Jesus and measure up in every particular. Many here have taken the stand, that speaking in tongues was not necessary, and after being highly anointed have claimed their Pentecost, but their power was limited and nearly all have seen their error and tarried until they spake in tongues. May the Lord bless and use you."

I also received a letter dated Nov. 2:

"Your letter of Oct. 26 at hand. We are joyed to learn that God is doing so much for you. Satan is not converted and is still in the business of perplexing God's people. He is very wise and cunning, and has many tricks to use that you nor I have not learned of. You must keep your eyes on J e s u s, and doubt not that God has begun a work that He is able and willing to finish. God has many lessons of humility and patience to teach us by witholding gifts and blessings that we seem to think should be always forthcoming. The more earnestly we covet a gift from God and the more we sacrifice to obtain it, the more highly we will prize it when it is obtained."

These letters had a great influence on my mind. I understood that there was a lack in my experience, but knew that God was willing to satisfy my every want. As I look back on those days of prayer and earnest pleading before the Lord, I understand that the Holy Spirit was teaching me great truths, little by little, but I had not received any teaching concerning the tongues as a special sign of Pentecost before, in the circles where I had hitherto been.

13th Nov.: Received the best news from home. My dear wife writes, the work at home is begun to blaze and God is giving a revival of grace as never before!"

14th Nov.: "Had a glorious evening all alone with Jesus last night! Oh, how sweet the Divine fellowship! G l o r y!" —

On the 15th of November I received the

*Baptism in the Holy Ghost and Fire,*

accompained with *tongues*, as the disciples on the Day of Pentecost in Jerusalem!

O h  w h a t  a  g l o r i o u s  a n d  w o n d r o u s  e x p e r i e n c e.  P r e c i o u s  S a v i o u r,  h o w  s h a l l  I  e v e r  b e  a b l e  t o  t h a n k  T h e e  e n o u g h  f o r  T h y  c a r e  a n d  m e r c y!  B l e s· s e d  b e  T h y  E v e r l a s t i n g  N a m e!  A m e n!

## X.

## WHEN THE FIRE FELL.

*Baptized in the Holy Ghost and Fire.*

An account of this experience, on the 15th of Nov., was sent home to Norway, to be inserted in "Byposten" and other papers, the day after the *Fire* fell. They had received the description of the former experience, on the 7th of October, and now I felt, that my friends ought to know the outcome of it all.

I did not speak in tongues on the 7th of Oct. as it will be seen. I had never seen anybody receive the Baptism in the Holy Ghost. This mighty experience, that was sought for and received by all in the first Christian Church (Acts 19, 2; 1 Cor. 12, 13), seemed to be quite unknown in the Christian Churches of our day, when I except some persons, of whom I had read and heard, and very few, even of them, ever spoke in tongues or wrote about them.

In Acts you find tongues mentioned, in connection with three of the great outpourings of the Spirit, related there, and in the other two cases, you are given to understand, that they were no exception to the general rule. But I had never seen the Fire fall, and knew very little about the tongues, before the news about God's mighty work in Los Angeles reached me. Had I received sufficient teaching as to this important truth, I might have, as Br. Cook said in his letter, have gone through with the Lord, until the tongues came, on the 7th of October.

How strange, that all these things should be so unknown to us. What a responsibility rests with the Church, that has laid aside this great blessing in lukewarmness and unbelief!

The Lord showed me nevertheless, through this break in my experience, that it is possible to receive great anointings of the Spirit, without speaking in tongues, but that if we receive the *full* Pentecostal Baptism, as they *"at the beginning,"* it will be a greater infilling, accompained with tongues, prophetic language (Acts 19, 6), loud praises (Acts 10, 46). — In the Norwegian version: "høilig prise Gud," that is: praising God loudly, but especially *tongues*, which *was to be the special sign of the new dispensation*, all the other signs having been found among believers before Pentecost. (Mark. 16, 16). I wrote therefore in my account home, that "it appears to me, that when I spoke in tongues, it was in connection with a power which was far beyond all that I had experienced before, that my former experience was a *glorious introduction*," to the

### Baptism in the Holy Ghost and Fire,

which I received on the 15th of November, 1906. I possibly made a mistake on the 7th of October, and disturbed the workings of the Spirit, by expecting help from others. At any rate I had to wait more than a month before the Power was turned on again, as it were, in an ever increasing degree, until I burst forth in tongues and loudly magnified God, in the Power of the Holy Spirit. This time nothing interfered with the workings of the Divine Spirit, and as a result, the same outward sign of the Spirit's presence was *seen* and *heard* as on the Day of Pentecost in Jerusalem, Hallelujah! I learnt also, that the change wrought in our lives, by the Holy Spirit, when we become the children of God (regenerated), was a different experience to the *baptism* in the Holy Ghost, when He *fills* us, and immerses us into His own being — body, soul and spirit. (1 Thes. 5, 23, 24; 1 Cor. 3, 16, 17).

My description of the Baptism was as follows:

«Many will be astonished and sceptical as to what I am now writing, but others will rejoice I am sure, and many will seek this blessing.

I waited about a week after having received the mighty anointing on the 7th of October, still looking for the manifestation of tongues, but nothing happened. Then I wrote again to Los Angeles in order to know, if possible, the reason why it did not come. They asked me only to tarry before the Lord in prayer, and He Himself would guide me. One day I spent twelve hours before the Lord to find His mind in the matter. O! How glorious it was, here in the quietness alone with the Lord, to tarry before Him.

How many things the Lord taught me then, and shed new light on my spirit. How precious His word became! Days and hours never to be forgotten. Over and over again, the enemy tempted me with the thought, that the manifestation of tongues was not for me. Once the presence of the devil was so near to me that I shook my fist at him in the Name of the Lord, though I did not see him. The reason why it took such a time was because *I doubted* whether I could receive the tongues, and the thought of such a strange thing taking place — that I should suddenly speak in an unknown tongue, this alone was sufficient to hinder the work of the Spirit in me. As some special manifestation in my jaws and tongue took place, my faith was strengthened, little by little, to believe that the speaking in tongues would soon be given me, and that it was already my privilege, only that I had to wait for the Lord's time, when His full power would possess me. However, the Lord did not mean this to take place in a corner. Wednesday evening I had to tell those, who sat beside me at table (christian friends), that I sought this blessing and would surely get it. Immediately a remarkable sensation passed through my whole body. I heard that a doctor's wife had arrived from Los Angeles, who had received the Baptism of the Holy Ghost, and the gift of Tongues. I called on her; I put my case before her, and asked her to lay hands on me, and pray for me. Immediately I had the same feeling in my speaking organs, only stronger than before. She sent me to a friend of hers, who conducted meetings in New York. She had recently received her baptism in Canada, according to Acts 2,4. I went to the meeting, and surely, if I had been as I was before, I would not have stayed but gone home again. You may be sure when the power of God falls upon people, old traditions and rules will not be followed exactly. Here was a movement and life which would not have fitted in with High Mass in a cathedral, but it would not hurt the cathedral, nor those who attend the services there, if this light and life should break in on them. The next morning I came again, and we had a wonderful prayer meeting, and I attended the evening meeting also.

When I think of it now, it seems strange to me that the Lord should take me to such a place of no reputation, to give me the greatest blessing that I have ever received in my life. It may be beneficial for some to notice, that I had to stop asking for tongues. The cry which now was within me was to receive

*the full Pentecostal Baptism, as the Christians of the Early Church received it.*

I specially mean, "accompained by tongues"; if not the gift of tongues, that remains, but as in Acts 10, 46. I was now prepared for the outward evidences of the Power, and not at all anxious, as many have been, because they did

not know what it was, and have therefore w i t h-
s t o o d *the Power of the Holy Spirit!*

There were not many people at the evening meeting, but G o d's  p o w e r was m i g h t i l y  m a n i-
f e s t e d. I asked the leader of the meeting, a little before 12 o'clock, to lay hands on me and pray for me. Immediately the power of God began to work in my body, as well as in my spirit. I was like Daniel, powerless under the Divine touch (Dan. 10, 8) and had to lean upon the table on the platform, where I was sitting, and slid down on to the floor. Again my speaking organs began to move, but there was no voice to be heard. I asked a brother, a Norwegian, who had often heard me preach in Christiania, and the doctors wife, to pray for me once more.

"Try to speak", the Norwegian said, but I answered, t h a t "i f  t h e  L o r d  c o u l d  s p e a k t h r o u g h  a  h u m a n  b e i n g, *He must make me do so by His Spirit!* T h e r e  w a s  t o  b e  n o h u m b u g  a b o u t  t h i s!"

When they were praying, the doctor's wife saw

### A Crown of Fire

over my head and

### A cloven tongue as of Fire

in front of the crown. Compare Acts 2, 3—4. The brother from Norway, and others, saw this supernatural highly red light.

T h e  v e r y  s a m e  m o m e n t,  m y  b e i n g  w a s f i l l e d  w i t h  l i g h t  a n d  a n  i n d e s c r i b a b l e  p o w e r, a n d  I  b e g a n  t o  s p e a k *in a foreign language* as loudly as I could. For a long time I was lying upon my back on the floor, speaking — afterwards I was moving about on my knees with my eyes shut. For some time this went on; then at last I sat on a chair, and the whole time I spoke in "divers kinds of tongues" (1 Corinthians 12, 10) with a short interval between. When speaking some of these languages, there was an aching in my vocal chords. I am sure that I spoke seven or eight different languages. They were clear and plain; and the different positions of the tongue, and the different tones of the voice, and the different accents, made me understand how different the languages were, one from the other. (Now, while I am writing this the Spirit works on my vocal chords and I have to sing). The most beautiful of all was the singing — when the inspiration reached its climax, I burst out in a wonderful baritone solo. I never heard the tune before, and did not understand the words, but it was a most beautiful language, so smooth and easy to pronounce. Those who were present and heard the whole thing, said that my voice was quite changed. I shall never forget how beautiful and pure the singing sounded. It seemed to me the rhythm in the verses and chorus, was as perfect as it is possible to be. Several times after that I sang songs, and to-day the Spirit has been constantly singing through me in a foreign language. I have recited poem after poem, that were given me instantaneously by the Spirit.

Now I am asking the Lord to give me the interpretation of the languages I speak.

This lasted till about four o'clock in the morning. There were nine persons present until 3 a.m., who can testify to the truth of every word I have written; some of them stayed till 4 a.m.

Once a great concern came over me, not for myself, but for others; my voice grew stronger and stronger; I rose up and spoke with burning zeal, till I felt the victory was won. It was surely a serious message that the Spirit gave me that moment. In that way I could sometimes speak in a strange language, and my voice grew stronger and stronger under this mighty power, until thousands of people could have heard me. (This was no doubt the prophetic gift).

**Then** the Spirit of prayer came upon me, when Norway, and my loved ones, and my friends at home, were laid so heavily on me, that I cried aloud under the pressure. Then all Scandinavia, the whole of Europe, New York and America, were laid on my heart, in the same way. Surely I have never prayed like that before! It was the Spirit Himself Who prayed through me, and «made intercession with groanings which cannot be uttered». (Romans 8.26, 27).

Sometimes I burst out in thanks to God for His marvellous grace towards me; prostrate on the floor I rejoiced, and praised my Saviour for His Love. Sometimes it seemed as if the veil were so thin, I could almost expect to see the heavens open over me. Glory! Glory! Glory! Oh! That I, unworthy as I am, should experience anything like this. Those few moments, except, when that serious message was given, my mind was restful and satisfied; such waves of God's love swept over me, that I wept, and sang in the Spirit.

Sometimes I have felt as if I were strong enough to cast a mountain into the sea. Now I understand the secret, how Samson and David got their strength! At 4 o'clock in the morning, I went to rest and slept as sweetly as a little child. I have related this marvellous work of grace to several already. Rested a little this afternoon, and then I took my gymnastics that I generally take every morning. I am happy and rejoicing in the Lord as never before.

I have entered into *details* in this account, because I understand that different questions will arise in many a heart, with regard to this truth. But, dear friends, *read your Bibles!* The unbelief of centuries, and the expositions of those who are not led by the Word of God, are no longer an authority in this matter.

If I could get this wonderful blessing, surely anyone can press on with boldness and ask the Lord to show them His will!

Dear Reader, press on, and get your soul filled with this Pentecostal power,

*if you are a Christian!*

Then you will be flooded with Divine Love! None but real christians can receive "the promise of the Father" (Luke 24.49). You need this fulness of Love; for the Baptism of the Holy Ghost is a divine "Baptism of Love", which enables you to

*love your enemies and bless those who curse you.*

Press on, press on *now!* Do not tarry a moment longer. Follow on, and receive the riches of your inheritance which Jesus has in store for you.

If you are not saved, dear reader, make haste. *Oh! Make haste!* Do not stay away from the Lord any longer! All these things are waiting for you, but you must go the right way. Flee from sin and receive Jesus as your Saviour, by faith. Do not try to put away sin in your own strength. When you come into contact with Jesus, it is *He* who works in you to will and to do that which you yourself are unable to accomplish. You will get

*a new heart.*

You will be born into the Kingdom of God by the power of the Spirit, and then the way will be open for you to go forward and, by the prayer of faith, receive the fulness and purity in your spiritual life which Jesus gives. Make haste! The time is short.

*Jesus is coming soon. Hallelujah!*

\* \* \*

After sending the above account to Norway, I continued to write in my Journal. The effects and results of this wonderful experience became immediately apparent to all.

Monday 19th Nov. 1906: «Saturday night

Bishop Burt.

was a remarkable evening, filled with great Power of the Holy Ghost. I have written to Los Angeles, Chr. Alliance paper, Bishop Burt, and others, about my experience of the gift of tongues. Several from the Alliance House attended the meeting Saturday evening. I have, in between, been at work on the street. Yesterday was the most remarkable Sunday I have experienced, I presume. It was spent at an "All Day Holiness Meeting (Palmer Anniversary) at Beecham Hill M. E. church. During most of the afternoon, I was under a tremendous pressure of the Holy Ghost and for some time could not stand erect. I was like a drunken man! Saturday and Sunday, I saw Miss — in a trance. The first time I have seen people in a trance. I am praying now for the gift of interpretation and healing. Glory to God for all His love and grace! Hallelujah!" (This proves, that we need not be in a trance to be baptized in the Holy Ghost and speak in tongues).

Nov. 21: *Bishop Burt* did not say anything about the gift of tongues, but counselled me not to dwell on the blessing I had received, but to go to work and reap results on the evangelistic field. I answered, that I of course could not think of resting on the blessing, as that would be building on *the effect instead of its cause.* He was so sweet, the dear, beautiful man! May God bless him!"

The effects of my Baptism however, were soon very apparent. Possibly my friends thought that I was under some unhealthy influence, and that a change of circumstances would do me good. The fact that *I had spoken in tongues,* instead of awakening thankfulness, caused consternation it would seem. I was advised at any rate, to take the first boat home to Norway. This then of course upset our plans concerning *the five cents* collection. And in fact this glorious outpouring of the Holy Spirit *had upset more than that,* as later accounts will prove. Haakonsborgen was gone for ever, but the Holy Ghost was come instead! Hallelujah!

The last record of meetings in my Journal was on the 10th of Sept., 1905: 3858 sermons, 827 lectures, and other meetings, including above 100 religious "fester". (Festivals). However, now the meetings became so many and at times lasted so long, that I gave up reckoning — the Lord knows all about it. My first sermon was held almost 26 years ago, on the 5th of Dec. 1880. I was now a little over 14 years old. The dye was cast, a n d I c o u l d n o t, a n d w o u l d n o t f o r v e r y l i f e, g o b a c k!

I wrote on Nov. 21 in Journal: "I must be guided by the Holy Spirit. I am happy and content with H i s wondrous will and influence, and whatever the r e s u l t s may be that follow, by being obedient to H i m, I take them in H i s strength, in the name of my blessed Redeemer"!

It seems, that the Lord had given me, to some extent at least, the gift of discerning spirits. I wrote under the same date the following statement: "At a meeting Monday evening, a s t r a n g e s p i r i t crept in during the testimony of some. It was in opposition to the Spirit God gave me. I cannot agree with the fleshly noise some make, and the wild jumps, as on a play ground I left the meeting with my sister, who by a strange coincidence happened to be present that evening. I rejoice and can shout my Hallelujah! with the rejoicing souls of Zion, but w i l d s c r e a m i n g is a different thing. While I condemn no one, we need not work side by side with those who allow the flesh to dominate, instead of the Spirit, excepting when we may lift them higher, or bring light to their hearts by the Holy Spirit. When I came home, and laid my head on the pillow, s u c h e x q u i s i t e p e a c e r o l l e d o v e r m y s o u l! God will keep me by His grace! Hallelujah!

Sunday 25th. Nov.: „The last week was re= markable in various respects. In the evening, on Wednesday, I met the missionaries, Mr. and Mrs. Meade, from Los Angeles, who were on their way to Africa again. I had been looking out for them some time, having through them entered into a clear understanding of the revival at Los Angeles. Thursday night we were at the Mission Hall, 250—14th St., and after that at the Hall on 40th St., between 8th and 9th Ave. Here six persons received the full Pentecost with tongues. On Friday evening we were invited to the home of one who professed to be seeking this blessing, but he and his friend sought controversy. The result of this, was my writing a pamphlet or tract on the subject, which Bro. Meade desired me to send to Los Angeles for publication."

Thus commenced the long battle I have been led to fight all these years on controversial lines, in addition to my evangelistic work.

Perhaps I had better give a few more extracts from the Journal, concerning my short stay in New York, after receiving the Pentecostal blessing. It was stated, that I was the first person to receive it in this way in that city, with the sign of tongues. God knows. But it was really a marvel, that my poor unworthy soul was made to participate in this wonderful blessing in this remarkable way. I do worship and glorify His Holy Name!

Nov. 25th.: "Last night a most powerful meeting at 40thSt. Mission. Many are seeking the blessing. During the night, I was awakened and began to pray for my wife and family, and my soul went out to God for His help in every respect; but I had not prayed long before I heard distinctly a voice say within:

*"Psalm 20; 121, 3."*

I arose and read 121,3 first, and then the 20th Psalm. Now I know that was God's message to me. The 20th Psalm is the Psalm of the City Mission. 121,3 is a part of the Psalm they sent by telegram on the 4th Anniversary of the City Mission. It suited my wants exactly, Hallelujah! He does all things well.

29th. Nov.: "Thanksgiving Day. Since the last entry, the Lord has been teaching me great lessons. I am just like a child starting in afresh. The Spirit has led me now to write a pamphlet: "Thoughts on Pentecost and the gift of tongues." The study has profited me greatly.

We have been having remarkable meetings at the 40th. St. Mission. Some have received their full Pentecost with the tongues. Last night was a glorious meeting. God is my eternal refuge and hope. He helps me in temporal affairs as well."

This then was the beginning of the Pentecostal Movement in New York — all these wonderful meetings there.

Dec. 1: «Excellent meeting last night. Yesterday afternoon I testified of my experience at the Gospel tabernacle. May God be honoured thereby."

Dec. 3: "Marvellous meetings yesterday. We have been attacked in the newspapers to-day, and I have just written an answer."

In the „*New York American*" stood a wild, so-called sketch of scenes, said to have taken place at our meetings, and an article, that clearly proved, that the author as well as the artist had no idea of what they were writing and sketching.

My time in New York was drawing to an end. The work on the street and elsewhere in that great city would have to be given up. The main object of my coming to America was not reached, and those who had the most to say, as yet, thought it wise for me to return home. Just a few cases from the streets:

I met with a little more obstinate case one day than usual. "Are you a christian, Sir?" I said, to a burly looking fellow, a business man evidently, just after a talk with another.

"What do you mean? — do you want to know if I am a church member?"

"No, not at all, but if you have given your heart to God?"

"How, what do you mean?"

"If you have opened your heart and life for Christ?"

"I'll tell you what my religion is — I believe in giving a square deal to everybody."

"That is, you serve them properly, I suppose?"

"Yes."

"And — in — love?"

"That's right," he said reluctantly, as he stepped behind me in the crowd and entered a store. But who knows how far these words may go? — God save him!

"Are you a christian, Sir?" I asked a young man about 27 years of age. He answered by asking: "Are you a religious crank?"

"No, Sir, I am not You don't call a man a crank do you, when his heart is so full, that he must try to do people good?"

"But it is a strange thing to ask a man that question on the street?"

"I know it is, but it is important nevertheless."

"I should say," he continued, "that each man ought to mind his own business."

"It's my business to save souls."

"My soul was saved long ago," he answered coldly.

"Then," I answered, "you will appreciate the question I put to you."

We almost were parted at the crossing then, but I put the question again:

"You will then, I should say, appreciate the question I gave you?"

"Of course," he answered, and we parted. I may never see him again, but I never feel irritated when opposed, for God keeps me calm and full of love to those I speak to. May they all be saved."

Dec. 8th: "If all is well, this is
*my last full day in America.*

Night before last, I was at Brooklyn, saying goodbye to friends. Last night we had our farewell service in 40th St. How wondrously strange, that my *"finish up"* in America should be in that little humble place, among those humble friends! —

How different to all I had thought or hoped for! — and still, this was what I rejoiced in mostly, this was most in harmony with the new life and power I had just experienced — for *God* was there in a wonderful degree! We felt His presence and comfort and light and power,

*Hallelujah!*

I have been busy winding up, of course, for the sail to—morrow with the "Campania." All the Los Angeles folks were going too (those intending to start as missionaries), except Mrs. Leatherman, who was going to Palestine later on.

How much I have learnt these days, Praise God! Finished yesterday a tract entitled "*A word to church members!*"

Sunday 16th. Dec.: "I am now on the North sea. I left New York on the 8th. To—day I held a service onboard, and got the Swedish friends present to testify and lead the singing. God gave us a great and good time. On our arrival at Hull yesterday, I got permission to speak to the emigrants in the large waiting Hall. There were several hundreds there, and God gave me a message that was received with appreciation by that motly crowd of Scandinavians. Oh, what swearing and cursing, and drinking and card playing, I have heard and seen on this tour!"

So now — New York and America were behind me, and a world of events before me! God alone knew what was coming!

## XI.

### Back again in dear old Norway.

*The Revival breaks out in Oslo, and other parts of Norway, in Sweden, and Denmark, England, Germany, Switzerland, and other countries.*

In the „*Byposten*", I had kept my readers as well informed as possible concerning the turn of events in America; and related how the revival was gaining ground in the face of all opposition, and the wonderful results of this mighty outpouring of the Holy Spirit. Souls were being saved and sanctified and filled with the Holy Ghost, as on the Day of Pentecost. Marvellous healings and miracles were seen almost every day, and the revival spread from town to town, and although the devil did his outermost to stop the work, God was in it! so it spread far and near. The attacks and cartoons in papers, savage attempts to break it up, only proved the means to awaken more keen interest in the work. Hallelujah!

And now I was in Norway once more. What would be the results there of my new stand, and how would my old friends take it?

I was determined, nevertheless, to be led by the Spirit in all things, whatever might take place.

In No. 1 of "Byposten" for 1907, the first article had as its heading:

"*Vækkelsen utbrudt i Christiania.*"

(The Revival has broken out in Christiania)

It points out, that the Revival has especially affected the christians. Meaning thereby, not the formal christians, but those who seek holiness and a deeper life in God, as the Spirit intends, through them, to awaken the formal christians and people of the world, by a mighty revival of grace.

The article describes the full Pentecostal baptism, and states: "There are now already more then 16 persons, who speak in tongues in this city. Several of them sing in tongues, and nearly all have spoken propheticly in the Spirit, prayed in the Spirit, and some have even been in a trance and seen things that are unspeakable. (2 Cor. 12,4) The prophecies are already being fulfilled here in Christiania in a wonderful manner, and they will be perfectly fulfilled, as soon as we fully believe the Lord.

It's not more than eight days since (Dec. 12, 1906) the first meeting was held in the large Gymnasium, and there has transpired so much in this short time, that we can only stand still and thank the Lord for His unspeakable grace towards us.

From the very first meeting, a mighty power has been resting on our hearts—the Power of the Holy Ghost! We cannot bind Him to any special plan for the meetings. There is no decided program, save as the Spirit Himself decides."

A description of the meetings follow: "Here, as in Los Angeles and in New York, the mighty, joyous *"Pentecostal—Hallelujah!"* is often heard. Yesterday the throngs stood quite close to each other in the students hall, making it almost impossible to stir. Of course many were inquisitive, and hoped to hear the tongues, or see some other demonstration of the Power of God; but there are hundreds of God's people now, seeking a clean heart and the Baptism of the Holy Ghost, and many unconverted souls are seeking salvation. Hallelujah!

This is but the commencement! This

power of the Spirit is for all God's people, and not merely for a certain denomination."

I state that several of the Methodists, the salvationists, and members of other denominations, have commenced to seek the blessing.

The remarkable thing is how rapidly the Revival spreads over Norway. The Lord had surely prepared the way for it. It caught like fire in dry grass. Instead of looking up the people, they came to us. Crowds thronged the Halls we used. They were by far too small to receive the hungry hearts that tried to come in. People came from far and near. Numbers were baptized in the Holy Ghost and took the Fire with them back home.

It was really wonderful to see how the Holy Spirit led on His own work! It would require several books, if I was to restate the accounts of the development of the Revival in detail, as it appeared in „Byposten" and elsewhere. However, I will still try to cull some of the most important items from the Journal and "Byposten".

March 27, 1907: "Since my last entry, I have passed through some of the most strange and glorious experiences of my life. The papers, religious and secular, have been kept busy. Great opposition has met the movement, but it proceeds victoriously, nevertheless, for God is in it! Hallelujah! The Swedish, Danish, Finnish, American, German, and English papers are writing up the matter, and now I believe my prayers that wonderful night in *New York* are going to be heard. This Revival is going to sweep all over Europe, Glory to God!

How many meetings I have had, I cannot say. I have two, sometimes three a day, and the meetings last up to four or five hours at times. The work is spreading all over the country. Of course I've a lot of correspondance, besides all the other work, but God knows what work He has given me to do, and knows how to stay and help me. — There is no retreat to be sounded, no backing out of this, and I don't wish to — God is my joy and strength eternally, Hallelujah!"

I was surprised to see the interest for the Revival here in other countries. Ministers and evangelists came from the neigbouring lands in Scandinavia, as well as from England and Germany. One of the first to visit us was the *Rev. Alex. A. Boddy*, vicar of All Saints parish, Sunderland, England. He came, not only to see the revival, but also to get a blessing for his own hungry soul. Ever since his visit he pressed me to visit his church, God willing, and assist at the meetings there.

Well, the Fire continued to blaze, and numbers were blest. Also at first there were not a few ministers of various denominations, seeking their Pentecost. In "Byposten", 16th Feb. 1907, I have an article taken from a Swedish paper, stating that the Revival had commenced at Skøfde, *Sweden*, through the influence of a young man, whom I learnt to know when in New York. A lady had spoken in tongues in Stockholm, and another young man, a Norwegian, had commenced in Arvika. It's rather amusing to note, that the correspondent lays stress on the fact, that those speaking in tongues seem to be "*of a sound mind.*" He scarcely expected it.

Surely one of the most astounding proofs of the down—grade state of religious life in our day, is, when God does something real, several editors, physicians, and even ministers, try to prove that it must be the result of miserable nerves, or some hypnotic influence. Ah, there are even those who, now, as in the days of Christ, say it's all the work of demon power. They know not the risk they run!
— — — those who speak and write thus.

Of course I can well understand, that people unacquainted with the workings of the Spirit, when the Divine Power is demonstrated, as is the case here, may at first stand aloof, and not be able to understand all the movings of this Mighty influence. Yet that does not give anyone the right to condemn a work, that proves to be such a blessing to thousands.

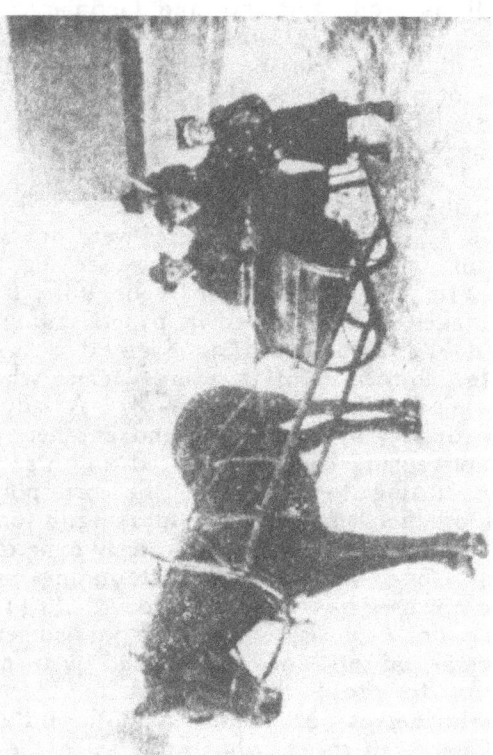

The Rev. Alex. A. Boddy and the writer in a sledge, just below the Palace.

March 4: "In the Turnhallen (Gymnasium) yesterday, the Rev. A. A. Boddy preached." It of course awakened considerable interest to see an English clergyman in our midst, especially when it was sounded abroad that he was seeking his Pentecost.
I commenced to travel here and there, in

addition to the work in Oslo. Everywhere the Holy Fire of the Spirit influenced the crowds that thronged the churches and Halls. God's people were baptized in the Holy Spirit, sinners were saved, and *Christ* glorified. Hallelujah!

In "Byposten" for April 6, I note that *Pastor Paul* from Germany, had come to see the Revival. He is well known because of his connection with

Pastor Paul

the Holiness-Movement in Germany. He spoke at our meetings and was made a blessing to many.

"Requests for prayer began to flow in to our meetings from Switzerland, Russia, New Zealand, South Africa, England, America, Sweden, Finland, Denmark, Iceland, Germany; ministers, Lutheran priests, and others were desiring our humble prayers for themselves and the churches they represented."

The "Byposten" became the centre, as it were,

of all the news from the various parts of Norway where the Fire fell, and brought news constantly from other parts of the world, wherever the Movement came.

On April 20th, a notice appeared in "Byposten" to the effect, that restrictions had to be made concerning the crowds that thronged the meetings. Many came after the sermon, only to see t h e a f t e r- m e e t i n g, and were therefore quite unaffected by the sermon; they came merely to criticise or make fun of the work of God. We guarded against this.

At times, the whole meeting became an "aftermeeting." The Power was so great that I could not preach, but had merely to move about and lead the seekers, praying with them and instructing them.

In the month of May I received a letter from pastor Boddy, who was then in England, that two persons had received their Baptism there, and had commenced to speak in tongues. He had not as yet received the Power himself. The F i r e w a s, t h e r e- f o r e, f a l l e n i n E n g l a n d in the same way as on the day of Pentecost. More was to come!

That month I visited SWEDEN. Crowds attended the services I held in *Stockholm*. "How strange it is to think, that it's exactly three years ago since I received the telegram from my wife, whilst here in Stockholm, that our precious little girl, *Sussie*, was sick and near death's door. Oh, how many wonderful experiences I have passed through since then!

Here in Stockholm, the Movement has commenced in two Baptist Churches, and has met a terrific opposition, even from many christians. However it is wonderful to see how the Lord blesses the people that attend the services." I held meetings in the Baptist churches "Elim" and "Tabernaklet", as well as in the M. E. Church,. "St. Paul", and finished up in the large c i r c u s.

I also visited *Upsala*, and preached in my friend, *pastor Ahgren's, church*. About 100 students were present. "It's easy to see that the Holy Ghost is at work," Bro. Åhgren said, during the meeting. After that I visited Gøteborg, where great crowds attended the meetings, with the same results as elsewhere. Hallelujah!

This was m y  f i r s t  v i s i t  t o  S w e d e n, after my return from America.

Reports were constantly coming to the "Byposten", from various parts of Norway, describing the wonderful workings of God's Holy Spirit.

From Sweden, I went to *Denmark* and commenced to work in Copenhagen.

The first meeting was held in "*Golgatha*", the Meth. E. Church, where Bro. Christensen was pastor. On the 10th of June, 1907, I wrote: "T he F i r e  h a s  f a l l e n  i n  G j e n t o f t e  a n d  C o p e n h a g e n,  H a l l e l u j a h!" A lengthy account of the work of the Holy Spirit in that city follows: I was obliged to take to the large "*Konsert-Palæ*", because of the crowds that attended the services. Ministers from Germany came, and longed to see the same work of grace in their own country.

I received a letter from *India* just then, stating that the Fire was falling there, and an earnest request to pray for that great country, was sent to the "Byposten".

I note that there was no attempt on my part to bring to the front any controversy on the general subjects, t h a t  h a v e  d i v i d e d  c h r i s t i a n s  i n various fractions. In fact I attempted for some time to guard against any definite step on those lines, merely preaching the great evangelistic truths in connection with the Revival. I had not as yet seen the necessity of W a t e r-B a p t i s m, and tried, if possible, to form a U n i o n of all interested in the Pentecostal work.

Two of our sisters went to *Germany*; and not long after I received a letter, stating that t h e  F i r e  h a d  f a l l e n  i n  G e r m a n y. This letter was inserted in one of the June numbers of "Byposten" in 1907.

On July 27, I wrote an article as to "my attitude toward the annual conference of the Methodist church." It contained my report to the Bishop and members of the conference. I explained how the Lord had led me since I returned from America; and pointed out very clearly, that I could not in the future be bound to any definite plan; that this might even sever me from the City Mission I had loved and worked for, as the invitations were constantly coming from all parts of the country, as well as from other countries, to come and conduct evangelistic meetings. I felt, for the time being, that my work ought to be on the Evangelical Alliance plan as much as possible, attempting to meet the wants of as many as possible, no matter where the call came from. Still I hoped that the Conference would not lay down the City Mission, as it could, if led aright, be of "immeasureable benefit to the religious life of the City". I thanked the Bishop and Brethren for the fellowship of past years; for all the love shown me and all forbearance with me, since I was a young man; and requested the prayers of the Conference, trusting God's blessing would, in rich measure, rest upon the church I had belonged to since childhood.

I could with difficulty suppress my tears as I read my report, but I felt that I was on the way God would have me go.

The Bishop spoke some very kind words, and the result was, that I was severed, by my own wish, from the Conference-membership, although I was still to remain as a member of the church.

The two sisters, who had commenced to unfold the banner in Germany, visited also Switzerland, and the result was, that I could write in "Byposten", Sept. 7. 1907: "The Fire has fallen in Zürich, Switzerland."

In every country where the Fire fell, it spread to different towns and was followed with the like blessed results. Especially so, in Sweden and Denmark and Norway.

I again visited *Denmark* and had some glorious meetings there. This time my family was with me, and remained there until I went across to *England* from Denmark. I was not a little anxious about this tour to England at first, but the Lord made it clear to me that I was to go.

Not long after this, Bro. Boddy issued a "Leaflet on Tongues," with the following heading:

## «TONGUES IN SUNDERLAND».
### *The beginnings of a Pentecost in England.*

"How can we sufficiently adore the Loving Master Who has begun to visit us now in England, in Sunderland.

On Saturday, August 31st, 1907, my dear brother Pastor Barratt, arrived across the North Sea. We had been praying for him specially ever since he sailed from Copenhagen on Thursday, and God gave him a beautiful voyage and brought him in six hours before time. Hallelujah! What rejoicing there was at our "Waiting Meeting" that night, when it was found he was actually in our midst. I soon found he was still the same after all his months of storm and service; manly, peaceful, rejoicing in the Lord, humble and yet strong for God.

On the night of Sept. 1st, three who were seeking Him entered right in and went right through into Pentecost with the sings following; to encourage others, God allowed them to be dealt with very tenderly. (Strangely enough they were all from one house, though not related to each other).

I had a talk with one a few days later and found that the Holy Spirit had done a real work. She thanked God so humbly and so lovingly that He should have come to her. She was passing through deep waters,—and had difficulties, yet she felt that, while God was removing all earthly helps, He had done far more for her by coming Himself.

The Lord then dealt with two friends who came among us about a month before, and who have been helpers together with Him in this place ever since—both working and praying: not waiting only, but ready to accept any work He called them to (this is a point I think many should note).

The place was almost filled with glory that Sunday night, as the first words came slowly from a prostrate from stricken down by the overwhelming power of God. From the commencement, the Lord interpreted word by word deliberately.

**Worthy** is the Lamb!
Jesus **IS** victorious, Glory to God!
Praise Him! PRAISE HIM!! **PRAISE HIM**!!! Jesus says, "Be loosed." They shall speak with Tongues.

**I am coming soon.** (3 languages seemed to be spoken).

\*

The next evening, as the sister who spoke in tongues so wonderfully, testified to the larger meeting that her Pentecost had come, the Gift of Tongues was (involuntarily) witnessed to as God took possession and sang in the spirit, and spoke, and interpreted.

Soon others began to receive. The Heavenly Anthem was heard now as two or more in wonderful tones—prolonged cadences—sweet bell-like tones, were adoring the Lamb. Every day now others are entering in. Visitors arrive from distant places to share the blessing. From London, Llandrindod, Clifton, Eastbourne, Leith; Lydd, Halifax, Stockport, Brighton, Heathfield, Brixton, Ilkley, etc., they come.»

I arrived in Sunderland, according to the Journal, "the last day of August." On writing a fortnight after this, I state: „As I look back on the wonderful work *God* has done during this time, my heart is full of praise and adoration. About 17 have spoken in tongues and others are very near receiving their full Pentecost. Glory to God for His mercy!"

We meet the same case here as in other lands, that many step in and obtain their Pentecost before others who have been seeking, for some time. The reason is this, that the former, who take things more simply than the latter, become as babes and accept the blessing by *Faith*. "The last shall be the first" is a truth, often spoken in this respect. It is very humiliating for those, who have sought the blessing for weeks and months, to see new converts step in and rush right on to Pentecost at the same meeting; but God is in it. The "waiting" hearts will nevertheless thank God when the blessing comes, that He kept them waiting so long. There are lessons to learn, that will help them wonderfully after the *Fire* has fallen.

Some extraordinary scenes have taken place. The Power of God has been demonstrated in Pentecostal glory, Praise His Holy Name!"

"It's remarkable to see and hear the wonderful change that comes over people when they get their Pentecost. Instead of the timid voice and demeanour, their whole appearance and method of testifying is changed. Those, who have never dared to say a word at the meetings before, become bold and fearless, and testify to the saving, cleansing, and baptizing power of *Jesus*, with burning hearts and bright shining faces. Oh, those transformed faces! — how they cheer you and draw your mind homeward! Almost all, who have spoken in tongues hithertoo, have received the interpretation at the same time, very often sentence by sentence, or word by word. The joy of some has been inexpressible."

A song much used in Sunderland, was the one I wrote in America, just after my baptism:

### On the hilltops.

I have reached the sunny hilltops of Zion,
I have left the dreary valley behind!
Now I never fear the roaring old lion!
All in Jesus now I find!

Chorus! Hallelujahs roll and thunder on from peak
             to peak,
While the Sun shines, while the Sun shines!
O, what glory! What a vision!
It's for all who seek,
To the hills of perfect love!

Oft I sought this wondrous blessing—but never
Did I gain this glorious summit before,
Now I'm here to be with Jesus for ever,
And His majesty adore!

Oft my all seemed on the altar, and Jesus
Spoke so sweetly to my languishing heart,
Oft I fought in burning zeal—until Jesus
Took me here with Him apart.

Now my heart is all on fire with His glory,
Songs of joy and worship burst from within!
Oh, that all would hear the dear, dear old story,
Of His power to save from sin!

I wrote several small pamphlets concerning Pentecost when in England, and Bro. Boddy spread them by the thousand.

Oct. 10th.: "The meetings are going on as usual. The papers are alive with the Movement a l l  o v e r  E n g l a n d, it seems. Received a letter from one gentleman, a proprietor of a "Palace of Amusements", who was converted by reading the accounts in the daily papers"

13th.: "Heard yesterday, that *Pastor Paul* has received his Pentecost". In the London "Daily Chronicle", an article appeared. It gives a good idea of the perfect absence of spiritual insight. It reads thus:

*Revival wonders. — Old and young "speak in tongues". — Alleged healing. — North=Country stirred by strange signs.*

I wonder if his grace the Archbishop of Canterbury has heard of the Rev. Alexander A. Boddy. Does he ever, I wonder, mount the watch-tower of his episcopal stronghold at Lambeth, and peer out towards the North, where the coal god sends up black incense to the ungrateful heavens, where unlovely Sunderland sits groping to the light through dirt, depression, and — I had almost said — despair? I wonder! If he does so, the strange things I have heard in Monkwearmouth to-day are but stale tidings, though they have left me helpless in a tangled skein of dreams and visions. At least I can make nothing else of them, so I pass the story on for the calmer, cooler consideration of London.

Sunderland is in the grip of a religious revival. It is not an ordinary revival, though it is accompanied by some of the more commonplace phases of—dare I say?—hysteria, which made such a strange figure of Evan Roberts in Wales. To reduce most of the phenomena with which I am about to deal to their lowest common denominator: there have been groanings and grovellings, visions and tears, laughter and visions.

But, on what I must accept as reputable authority, there has been something else besides. According to the Rev. Alexander A. Boddy, the Vicar of All Saints, Monkwearmouth, Sunderland, "More than 20,000 people throughout the world are now so filled with the Holy Ghost that they are speaking in tongues." Of these, Mr. Boddy informs me, about twenty are to be found in his parish—even more.

### CURED BY THE SCORES.

Step out of the train and ask the first man you meet who Mr. Boddy is. The man will look you up and down with a queer smile. "Boddy? Oh, ay! Yon queer chap at Monkwearmouth — the faith healer?" Then he smiles again. I write in no spirit of irreverence. I am assured that there are scores of people walking about these streets to-day, who speak of wonderful cures. The vicar's own wife is one of them.

Young men tell of visions, in which the Christ has appeared. Children start up in the parish hall, where the revival meetings are held, and after undergoing what are described as "fierce spiritual ordeals", chatter in strange language, variously recognised as Chinese, Hindustani, Norwegian, and what not.

Said, "unemontional" matrons are taken home to bed o' night «drunk» with ecstatic joy. Boys and girls, after the strange Pentecostal baptism, start up and sing in sweet, silvery, unearthly voices.

There are messages and manifestations. Old feuds are patched up. The wrong is made right: the sick are made whole—all in 1907, in Sunderland! This on the testimony of the Rev. Alexander Boddy, once a solicitor of the High Court, now the evangelistic leader of a mining population.

### EVAN ROBERTS OF THE NORTH.

There is another figure in the strange landscape: the Evan Roberts of the present, movement, Pastor Barratt, Cornishman, naturalised Norwegian, a. dreamer if you will; a madman if you like; but the heart and soul of a religious movement before which others pale.

It is just, a month ago since Mr. Boddy, having heard of the Pentecostal phenomena that were shaking the Norwegian churches, went to Christiania and saw—what? "Meetings held in an upper chamber; a very bare low mission-room at Torvgaden; boys and girls around me, from, say, seven to twelve years, of age, seeing visions and speaking in tongues, as well as older people.

"A bright lad cried out in intense vehemence with his eyes shut: Oh, I see the House of Satan thrust down, and down, and now the hosts are entering heaven! Oh, they are going to shut the door, and some will be too late! Oh, Jesus, Jesus! Then off into unknown tongues, and a few minutes later he was just a simple Norwegian boy again".

\*

In this strain he continues. "Hysteria", "queer chap", "dreamer", "madman if you like" — — sweet epithets are they not? But they show up the spirit, and the whole style of the writer: unsympathetic, misinterpreting the real facts in the case.

Still, one sees, that something was stirring! That God was at work, even if His work was misunderstood by many. Thus it was in the days of the first christians!

Several extracts from the papers might be quoted, that give an idea of the stir the Revival was causing in the North of England. Here are some of the chief headings in Thomsen's Weekly News: *Extraordinary revival scenes.* "*Gift of Tongues*" at Sunderland: Persons speak in unknown languages. A local pastor explains the Phenomenon" Another paper: "*The Gift of Tongues.* Amazing revival scenes in the North of England." Another: "*Receiving Pentecost.* Strange revivalist scenes. Vicar's child talks Chinese." North Mail: "*Utility of the Gift of Tongues.* Pentecostal services at Wearmouth. Young man's testimony."

These are just a few. One paper notes correctly, that "visitors from London, Llandrindoh, Clifton, Eastbourne, Leith, Lydd, Halifax, Stockport, and in fact from all parts of the country, have flocked to hear the revivalist". It states, that I was "deluged with invitations to conduct services here, there, and everywhere." Another paper makes the same remark, that invitations came in "from all parts of the United Kingdom, but the calls were so numerous in Norway, that he must go back."

I was obliged to write a very serious letter to the Rev. —, one of the great religious leaders in England, because of the way in which "he slighted the work of God in Germany." I stated that he had made a great mistake. This was "the old time revival of the Apostolic times."

The Farewell meetings at Sunderland

were very touching. One Brother testified, and said how sorry he was that he had lost the first five weeks of the Mission, owing to prejudice and not knowing better. His daughter had been saved at the meetings lately. A Salvation Army Brother praised God for the blessings he had received at the meetings; also a colored gentleman from London. I then had to take the time needed for some words of farewell and encouragement. After that I invited all who would meet in Heaven, to gather around the table. It was an affecting scene. We clasped each other's hands and sang and prayed together. The vicar thanked God because I had "honored the Blood, and honored the Bible".

Other testimonies were given. A number of friends went from the meeting to see me off. Mrs. Boddy remained behind with the seekers. On the Station platform, we sang songs and hymns until the train came. Then Bro. Boddy, and about twenty others, accompanied me to *Newcastle*, etc. etc.".

"I do thank God for that delightful stay in Sunderland, and for the results of the Mission, extending far beyond the boundaries of Sunderland.

\* \* \*

Thus the Fire commenced to fall in Sunderland, England, in 1907.
This year:

*1907,*

is one of the greatest years of my life, and whenever the Pentecostal friends in Scandinavia speak of the Revival, they generally measure it with the blessings of 1907. That dates the glorious commencement of this great and Heaven-sent revival in Europe.

*All Glory to God!*

## CHAPTER XII.

*The tour to India.*

*Visiting several European countries, Palestine and Syria. Conferences in London and Sunderland.*

On returning home from England, I found the H o l y   F i r e burning with more intense heat than ever. Wonderful things took place, but all this gave of course the opponent of all good enough to do. Satan did his very best to undo and prevent the spread of this work of God, and many — sad to say, e v e n o f  G o d ' s  o w n  p e o p l e—took stand with the ungodly against it!

But the Fire could not be quenched, praise God!

At the commencement of the year, I received an invitation to visit India. I have still the letters sent me by *Mr. A. N. Groves*, who arranged the whole thing, and from *Miss Maud Orlebar*, and from *Mr. Max Wood Moorhead*.

The letter from Bro. Groves was dated 8th January, 1908, and read thus:

> Dear pastor Barratt,
>
> I am unknown to you by sight, and it is not probable you have heard my name; but these are days in which news travels fast. We have been greatly interested in this corner of the world through reading the account of God's dealings with you in "WHEN THE FIRE FELL", and of hearing of the recent Mission you were led to conduct at Sunderland at the request of Mr. Boddy. We have been stirred, I believe by the Spirit to write and ask if you have had your thoughts turned at all to INDIA and it's many missio-

naries, occupied in giving the Gospel to the heathen, though often hungering for spiritual food themselves? Some hundreds of these missionaries, from need of change, weakness of body, or inability to visit Europe, collect at the Hill Stations of South India during the hottest months of the year — from 15th. March to 15th. June—and are then free from work, thus affording unique opportunities for addressing them.

During the past year, the intense interest was taken, in Coonoor, in the so-called Pentecostal Movement, owing to the visit of Mr. and Mrs. Garr from Los Angeles, California, U. S. A., and I regret to say, much bitterness has been engendered; but we believe there is an honest, deep, desire in some, for spiritual blessing. If the Holy Spirit should move you to leave your work at home for a period, and come out here for March, April and May, or longer, there would, we feel sure, be blessing, and in regard to funds, it will be a privilege to us to guarantee all expendes incurred".

He then gives an idea of the best route to take.

"I am not a missionary myself, but only a planter, though taking much interest in missionaries and their work".

Yours in the Lord,                     A. N. Groves.

After putting the matter before the Lord, I determined to go to India and sent a cable, by request of Mr. Groves, to that effect. He wrote on receiving it:" It has made our hearts glad this morning to receive your cablegram from Christiania". He prepared the way for me by sending the following "Circular Letter" around to the missionaries and other friends in India:

It has been laid upon the hearts of a few of God's children, for some time past, to wait upon Him in prayer for the provision of a suitable instructor in the truths connected with the so-called Pentecostal Movement—one who has known by experience, and not theory alone, that the Holy Spirit is able and willing to work in these latter days as He undoubtedly did in the early days of the Christian Church—and He has graciously intimated His approval, by opening the way for His servant, Pastor T. B. Barratt, of Norway, to come out to India in March, when we hope an opportunity may be given for many missionaries and others coming up to Coonoor for the hot season, to hear for themselves and bring to the test of scripture the truths taught by His servant, who has since 1906, when he received the baptism of the Holy Ghost, had a seal put to his ministry in Christiania and other towns, which no sincere believer can dispute. May The Lord put it into the hearts of His people to come together in the spirit of the Berœans, as indicated in Acts. 17: 11; and to believe facts when demonstrated by The Holy Ghost, as in the case of Cornelius and his friends (Acts. 10: 46). Meanwhile let us continue much in prayer that God, and He alone may be glorified through this visit.

Coonoor, A. N. GROVES.
February 1908.

I felt it rather keenly to have to leave the family again for such a long tour; but my good wife encouraged me, and said "there could be little joy in remaining at home, when the Lord desired us to go elsewhere."

I passed down through Sweden, Denmark, Germany, and Switzerland, on the way out, holding meetings all the way. I started from *Brindisi*, with a splendid boat, that took me to Port Said. Here I met the "S. S. India", and continued to Bombay.

I stayed somewhat at Rome, when in Italy, looking up things of interest, and spoke at a meeting for young people in the M. E. Church there.

This tour gave enough of interest to write about to "Byposten", and accounts of the whole journey — to and from India — appeared, both in this paper and in other publications, with many illustrations.

From Sunderland came word to the effect, that Bro. Boddy had started a Pentecostal paper:

"*Confidence*".

This paper was the first of its kind in England, and for years the back stay of the Pentecostal Movement in Great Britain.

Mr. *Max Moorhead* met me in *Bombay*. I found that meetings were arranged for me there, and the attendance was such, that I prolonged my stay there three weeks.

However, the devil was at work, doing his best to quench the influence of the meetings held. An anonymous writer sent *a bundle of lies*, concerning me, personally, to all the missionaries. But the lies were so vile, that one of the missionaries said: "the *spirit* in this circular, proves the falsity of the attack." A pamphlet, written by a German Minister "Satan among the saints," and articles by Mrs. — in "The Christian," were broadcast among the missionaries. I wrote an answer to the German ministers malicious attack: "Satan among the critics," which proved to be an eye-opener in many cases, and broke the influence of his false statements. Numbers commenced to seek the blessing in Bombay, and Christ was glorified, Hallelujah!

Several evil—minded persons tried to make the people believe, that the revival at *Mukti* had nothing to do with the "Pentecostal revival". But the following letter, sent me by *Miss Minnie Abrams* (Pandita Ramabai's right hand), will prove how false this statement was:

"Just a few lines to bid you welcome to India, and state that we are praying for blessing upon Bombay.

You will meet much opposition, as the "**Pentecostal-Baptism**" is not pleasant to the flesh. Even beloved children of God, because of ignorance, have stood foremost in this opposition against the Lord. Be not therefore surprised, if you find your way entrenched.

The Lord has again commenced to pour forth His Spirit here in Mukti, for which we praise Him. We would be delighted to come to Bombay, but are fighting a great battle

## AND ANOUTLINE OF MY LIFE

here, and will help you with our prayers. The Lord will bless His work there and keep man hid away."

Yours in the Lord,

**Minnie T. Abrams.**

At one of the meetings in Bombay "my soul was filled with such power and blessing, that I burst forth in tongues. The interpretation was given by

On the way up to Coonoor.

Miss Gardner. Just then I heard a voice within me, saying, in the English language:

*"Jesus is coming soon!"*

Friend are you ready for His coming? T h e d e v i l never exhorts us to prepare for the coming of the Lord!

The cry from Coonoor, to h u r r y u p, made it necessary to break up the meetings in Bombay and start for the mountains.

It is impossible to give a detailed account of the meetings here. Missionaries from several Missions attended the services. *Bro. Groves* had arranged everything satisfactorily. The "Drawing Room meetings" proved a great blessing. Of course the battle went on here, as well as at Bombay. Numerous

Mr. and Mrs. Groves.

attacks were made against this work of God, but the *Holy Spirit* led us on, and not a few of the Missionaries received *a full Pentecost*, Glory!

Meetings were also held amongst the heathen. I had different interpreters, and God's blessing rested on these meetings in a wonderful way. *Bro. Joshua*, who was my interpreter on the public Market-place, had himself been baptized in the Holy Ghost eleven *years before this.* No one could therefore accuse him of having any connection with the Pentecostal-Movement then. He received his Pentecost eleven years before I visited Coonoor. He was at work on the Malabar coast, and wished to speak to the people in their own language. After much prayer in the woods, he came to the Conference, and God's Spirit fell on Him. He did not commence to speak the language he wished to; but he spoke in "tongues", and that with such violent force, that many were afraid. They had never heard anything like it. It lasted half an hour.

People asked him why he spoke that way, and he told them what he had asked God to do. "Oh, that's no good. Those days are passed. They belonged to the apostolic times, not ours. You have been side—trapped, and have received something wrong, instead of what you asked God to give you."

How strange that christians, the moment something happens that they are not able to understand, immediately ascribe it to the influence of evil spirits. As if God, our Heavenly Father, had changed His mind since the Days of Jesus, and had commenced to give H i s children a stone instead of a loaf, a serpent instead of a fish, a scorpion instead of an egg, a n d a d e m o n i n s t e a d o f t h e H o l y S p i r i t! (Comp. Luke 11,9—13).

T h a n k G o d, *He* i s e v e r t h e s a m e l o v i n g F a t h e r!

"Have you spoken in tongues since, Joshua?" I asked.

"Yes, often. When I am very happy in the Lord, and pray to Him, then it comes quite naturally."

Ah, it's the same old P e n t e c o s t a l p o w e r! — with similar results, Hallelujah! Bro. Groves took me around to the various tribes here and there, during my stay at Coonoor. The scenery was magnificent; and the heat, of course, not so intense as down on the plains.

We received word from many parts of the world, that the revival was sweeping on, and mighty things were being done for the Master.

Not long ago, I received a letter from one of our missionaries in India, Bro. Arthur Cornelius, who had been at Coonoor this year (1927) and had

The Missionary Home at Coonoor.

met one of the old missionaries there. When he heard that Cornelius was from Norway, he asked if he knew me. "Certainly, I belong to the church of which he is pastor; he is also the president of the Missionary Society that sent me to India." When the old man heard that he burst into tears. "T h e r e" said he, pointing to a spot by the harmonium, in the Hall where they were standing, "there I received my Pentecost, when he was here!"

It did my heart good to hear it.

The wife of *Dr. Franklin* (Sweden) was also one of those, who received her Pentecost then. Her husband, at present the leader of the Missionary work among the Pentecostal friends in Sweden, wanted the Baptism, but would not have the tongues, (according to his own statement, when in Norway, the last time), so the Lord left him without the Baptism as well, until he was willing to receive

Mrs. Franklin.

it in the Lord's own way. He then received a full Pentecostal baptism, Hallelujah!

My stay in India lasted from the 3rd of April until the 15th of August, and I heartily thank God for the opportunity He gave me to visit the friends there. I learnt much concerning the missionaries and their work, and saw what God can do when His Spirit is accepted, and influences, and fills His people.

Before leaving India, I felt that I m u s t visit *Mukti.*

After a short stay at *Calcutta,* where meetings,

blest of God, were held in St. Andrew's — a Scotch Presbyterian Church, in the Y. M. C. A., and the Bon Bazar Baptist Church, I went to Bombay, staying at the Alliance Missionary Home, of which *Miss Orlabar* was the Superintendent, and went from there to Mukti. The work here is well known to all; I need not therefore describe it. *Mukti* means S a l v a- t i o n. And here I witnessed the blessing of Salva-

Dr. Franklin.

tion, flowing in deep, broad currents, through these saints of God.

One morning I spoke to 1200 of these young women. I had a splendid interpreter, and God's blessing rested on the service. They gave me Luke 10, 21, as a greeting to the friends in Norway.

What p r a y i n g I heard there! Simultaneous **prayer.** You should have seen those Heaven--turned faces! — and heard hundreds of Spirit-filled women pray to God at once! The praying was kept up until the time to disperse was at hand. Then they marched out in classes, but the praying still went on, until the last class was gone; and when I looked around there were still some of them lying prostrate on the floor, praying and speaking in tongues.

I remember reading the report of a correspondent of the Press, who had visited Mukti. He confessed that, although he could not explain it, 'he could testify to the fact, that he had heard these Indian girls speak in several of the dead languages and others, although they themselves had no knowledge of them.

A temple in South India.
(Cut out of the rock).

I determined to visit

*Palestine*

on the way home. A little book might be written of what I saw and heard in this old centre of the Jewish and Christian world. However, word had reached me from SYRIA, that *pastor Mygind*, who was a Missionary there at that time, desired me to stay at their Mission a while. When there, the Spirit fell on longing souls. I conversed with the people about the l a t t e r  r a i n. They know the effects of it in the natural world, but they little thought that G o d  h a d  p r e p a r e d  a  l a t t e r  r a i n  i n  t h e  S p i r i t u a l  w o r l d as well.

When the Spirit fell, and the sound of t o n g u e s was heard outside, people rushed to the windows and looked in. The windows were full of faces, and they all asked inquisitively: „W h a t  i s  t h i s?" This reminded me of the Day of Pentecost. There were some very remarkable cases. One young Syrian girl, certainly spoke in several languages; she prophesied in the Spirit as well, and all present understood that this was the power of God. I have scarcely ever seen such an influence of tongues o n  t h e  c r o w d, as in this case.

Sick were healed, and as a result of it all, the outpouring of the Spirit at S c h w e i f a i t gave us hopes of a similar outpouring over the whole of Syria.

However, I had to return home.

I visited *Italy* again, and *Switzerland*, and attended a Conference in *Germany*, and proceeded to *Denmark*.

Here the renowned actress, *Mrs. Anna Larsen*, became interested in the revival. Her Drawing—room was opened for a meeting, which was attended by numerous actors and actresses, representatives of the Press, and leading men in the city. This meeting was reported in the Press in a very sarcastic way, but one of the leading actors wrote an article, putting things in their right shape, speaking highly of the address and thanking Mrs. Larsen for opening her Drawing room for meetings of that kind.

Later on Mrs. Larsen became soundly converted; left the theater; and is to day the wife of *Mr. Sigurd Bjørner*, the leader of the "Apostolic Church" in Denmark.

From Copenhagen, I went to Gøteborg and held meetings in Torghallen. I lectured also on "The 20th century Revival" in the "Tabernacle."

### Back again in Norway.

I found the Revival spreading here and there in the face of all opposition. Surely the powers for evil did their best to destroy this glorious work of God!

It was next to impossible to rent one of the larger Halls in Oslo for meetings on my return. Mr. Nordkvelle was willing to let me have the use of his hall, but dared not advertise me as a speaker, as that would imply that he would lose his hall.

I was still working much on Alliance principles, and tried to bring our people into that way of thinking, trusting that the good Lord would be able to combine all these severed hearts, so that we might love each other and work together on broad, evangelical lines. Numbers of those, who had joined our ranks, were come from different denominations and Missions, and I myself was still not ready for Water baptism.

The "Byposten" was filled with letters and articles and accounts of the work, not only in Norway, but from every part of the world. I held meetings in Torvgt. 7 and in Møllergaten 9, where groups of friends were found, as well as in the surrounding towns. Every now and then the Spirit gave me a new song or hymn, and they were sung among the friends.

On April, I was again in Sweden and Denmark. Went from there across to *London*; became acquainted with *Mr. Cecil Polhill*, who for years supported the Movement. I also met *pastor Niblock*, and took part in several meetings. The Holy Spirit was in our midst and greatly blest the word spoken. In May we had a very successful Conference at Zion College, with representatives from various parts of Great Britain, Germany, Norway, Holland and elsewhere. It was indeed a glorious Conference, full of blessing and spiritual power. The great truths of the Gospel were brought forth in Pentecostal strength.

After this, an excellent Conference was held at *Sunderland*. Several of the speakers at the London Conference went direct to Sunderland, to take part in the Conference there.

Whilst in England this time, I again visited Devonshire and Cornwall, and looked up *Albaston* and other places of interest from my boyhood.

After this, I returned to London and held several meetings there. I visited *John Wesley's* chapel in City Road; ascended his old pulpit; sat down on one of the old benches from the "Foundry"; looked up his grave, and the graves of Bradford, Oliver, Adam Clarke, and a number of the old nethodist preachers. It gave me indeed some very touching moments to walk amongst the graves of these holy men! I had read about their deeds and life work, . . . . . now they were beyond the vale! Then a few days later I went with Bro. Niblock to *Smithfield*, where they burnt the martyrs, in former days. After that, I visited *John Bunyan's* town—*Bedford*.

They had all done the work assigned to them, and then passed over the line to their reward! Lord, help us to walk in Thy footsteps, and be faithful, even unto death!

## CHAPTER XIII.

*The tumults in Copenhagen. Mrs. Anna Larsen (Bjørner).*

*False attacks again on the Movement. Møllergt. 38. Methods of organization. "Maran ata". "Korsets Seir" in different languages. Bartlemans visit.*

There was a good bit of travelling, after my Baptism in New York. The Lord would have me, as we have seen, visit several countries; but at last I was called to settle down and build up a Pentecostal assembly in Oslo, by the grace of God, and the assistance of good and faithful men and women, who were fully devoted to this great and glorious work.

In 1910, we gave "Byposten" a new name: "*Korsets Seir*" (The Victory of the Cross). The old name suited more the City Mission work, but the new name coincided more with the new state of things. The paper had grown in influence and represented the Pentecostal Revival, not merely in Oslo, but throughout the country. It has this name still, and has constantly stood for Gospel truth and the special truths that have been the watchword of the Pentecostal revival. It has collected and spread the good news of the work done throughout the world, by the workers within the Pentecostal Movement, especially amongst the Norwegians, and has had to battle for the truths entrusted to our care, time and again.

The work with the paper has of course taken much of my time, but I have felt that God called me to use pen, as well as tongue, in this great warfare.

I was called to visit Denmark and Sweden every now and then, and even Finland. In *Denmark* the "y o u n g  s o c i a l i s t s", as they were called, attempted to break up our meetings; the tumults they caused were very violent at times; the methods used were wild and unseemly. We kept the police outside at first, but were obliged to send for help at last.

The City Press had been guilty of false and untruthful statements concerning our meetings, and depicted the whole movement in the most uncharitable terms. They made fun of the whole thing, and showed to a nicety how far off they were from a clear understanding of r e a l  c h r i s t i a n i t y.

The "young socialists" cried and screamed, cursed and swore at me, threw chairs from the gallery, tore down the pulpit, and behaved like madmen at times. But in the midst of all this, s o u l s  w e r e  s a v e d, and several in their own midst were pierced by the word of God. One of their leaders gave his heart to God, and is at present a minister in America.

The fact too, that two actresses from the same theater, *Mrs. Anna Larsen* and *Mrs. Lewini*, were saved and had joined the movement, was too much for them. Could it be possible! They determined to be avenged in some way or other, but God gave us the victory, and at last several of the leaders of these young men came to me personally and asked me to forgive them. They saw their mistake, and said they had misunderstood the whole thing. So whilst windows were smashed, and wild scenes were transacted by these young rationalists, the Lord gave me grace to s t a n d  f i r m  o n  t h e  o l d  r o c k, and gave me some of the greatest victories I have had.

There were papers too, of considerable influence, that w a r n e d  people a g a i n s t  all these awful attacks by the socialists. *"Telegrafen"* wrote: "Under general circumstances, it is quite correct that the police act as civilly as possible, but when the crack of revolvers is heard, then it's time to strike hard, and now they *must* strike hard, before it is too late.

The revolver-bullet that smashed the window of the meeting-place last night, might easily have struck a person present, and that is to drive things too far, for the sake of pastor Barratt and Mrs. Anna Larsen».

The paper stood up for *"Freedom"*, and stated that "people must have a right to hold meetings without being prevented by a mob."

Mrs. Anna Larsen wrote also some very able articles in the leading papers, and her name and pen have always been respected, even by the greatest opponents, and are so to this day. Accounts of her conversion appeared in the most influential papers, and considerably checked the tempest that had arisen against the movement.

The secular Press was very busy during the first years of the revival, and that in all lands. One would have expected, that the people in so-called "c h r i s t i a n" countries would have some idea at least about the deeper things of God, but the moment God commenced to work, it was easily seen, that there is a tremendous difference between formal christianity and the real thing!

I corresponded last year with Mrs. —, a leading holiness leader, and others, and tried to show them how unfare and false their attacks have been against this Movement, and pointed out the danger of using their influence thus, against God's own work. Although I received very kind letters in answer to mine (I have them still in my keeping), there was nothing said to dispell or recall the false influence of former attacks.

How awfully sad! — —

Here then were dear people of God seeking in real earnest, and with the purest of motives, the necessary P o w e r to live holy lives and devote their all to the Master — and when the Pentecostal Power was sent, and the results were seen, as in former days, then some of the leaders of holiness movements stepped in, and — because they were not used to such demontrations of Power — denounced the whole thing, and even condemned it as the work of demons! What awful blindness!

It shows that the Lord is able to lead some people—leaders of influence — a good way, and then they suddenly stop and are not willing to be led further!

Mrs. —, in her letters to me, appeals to the *future,* and hopes that time will decide all. Almost 20 years have passed since this correspondance, but I for one, and I know there are tens of thousands besides, am able to say, that t h i s P e n t e c o s t a l  b l e s s i n g  h a s  p r o v e d  t o  b e  o f *lasting* w o r t h. We would not go back to our former state of living, but feel that the waters of this glorious river are constantly getting deeper! In the Autumn of this year (1927), it will be 21 years since the Fire fell on my longing soul in New York. I have surely had good time to turn back, but the blessed Lord is constantly leading me forward, and thousands are rejoicing to-day in the same blessed experience, in various parts of the world. The Movement is gaining ground, and has the same signs of God's approval, as the Pentecostal Revival in the days of Peter and Paul. Hallelujah!

Those, who are not willing to acknowledge their mistake and recall their awful condemnation of the work the Holy Spirit has wrought, will one day see the wrong they have done, and the evil influence they have exerted, in preventing thousands of God's own people from seeking the Pentecostal blessings! However these blind attacks have evidently broken the influence for good, that these leaders of the people formerly exerted, to a great extent. Thousands have lost confidence in their leadership!!

I commenced to hold meetings in

## MØLLERGATEN 38

in 1910, and wrote in my Journal on the 5th of September: "I have now rented Møllergt. 38, which will no doubt be a centre for our friends in the city, as well as for our many friends outside the city."

And so it was!

This step was to be of lasting influence and a great blessing to the cause of Christ! The hall belonged to a Temperance Party, but we could make use of it as often as we cared to.

Over the platform, we placed, in large words, this now so well-known and often used sentence:

"KRAFT TIL LIV OG TJENESTE FOR JESUS"

(Power for life and service for Jesus). When I was out travelling in Norway or in other countries, the Lord sent some evangelist, a brother or sister, to lead the meetings. I had at first to divide my time to some extent between Norway and other countries in Europe. Revival campaigns and conferences called for the help, God enabled me to give them.

In 1911, I collected about 600 "psalms, and hymns, and spiritual songs," for use at the meetings, not only in Oslo, but all over the country. We gave it the name of

## "MARAN ATHA"

(1. Cor. 16, 22). This collection of songs and hymns has been a great blessing in the work.

The book is even in use amongst some of the Norwegians in America. The oppourtunity was thus given me of publishing several of my own songs and hymns, and I thank God for the blessing they have been to many! I also translated several of our most well-known English hymns. I have hitherto not been able to collect and print the music for more than 300 songs: it takes time and money. However, the h y m n b o o k, as well as "K o r s e t s   S e i r", have proved the means of uniting the friends, to a great extent, throughout the whole country, for which we praise *God!*

In 1911, when in FINLAND conducting meetings, I also visited *Russia*, and had some meetings in St. Petersburg. There was such weeping at one of the meetings there after my sermon, as we went down on our knees. G o d   w a s   s u r e l y   i n   o u r   m i d s t, H a l l e l u j a h !

When in Finland, I issued "Korsets Seir" in the F i n n i s h language. It's name was "R i s t i n   V o i t t o". Bro. B r o f e l d t did the translation work. It appeared also in the S w e d i s h language: "K o r s e t s   S e g e r", and I was almost on the point of issuing it in the Danish language. I had already sketched the title page.

In 1912 *Pastor J. H. King* visited us, and was made a great blessing in our midst. He stood fully for the whole Pentecostal truth.

In "Korsets Seir" No. 12, 1912, I give a lengthy account of

"*The Evangelical Mission in Møllergt. 38*",

and the doctrines we preached there. This was also spread as a pamphlet. I   w a s   s t i l l   n o t   b a p-t i s e d   i n   w a t e r. The lines drawn up, were built much on a l l i a n c e - l i n e s.

I attended the C o n f e r e n c e   i n   E n g l a n d in 1912. This was the f i f t h Conference in England among Pentecostal friends. I again visited Finland, and had glorious meetings there. Praise God! A delightful visit was paid to Hardanger and *Volheine* also that summer!

In 1913, the authorities in Russia gave me permission to issue "Korsets Seir" in the Russian language.

We were also visited in Oslo that year, by *Bro. Frank Bartleman*, who was one of the first leaders of the Pentecostal work in Los Angeles.

Mr. Frank Bartleman.

As I had to leave for Sweden and Finland, my wife became his interpreter. Numbers came to hear him, and the Lord blest his visit greatly. Hallelujah!

## CHAPTER XIV.

### Pastor Lewi Petrus.

*Baptized in water at last. I leave the Methodist Church. The new assembly in Møllergt. 38. Opposition from former friends of the Movement. Ridiculed by the world. The victory on our side.*

In my journal (16th of June, 1913), I find the following statement concerning *Pastor Lewi Petrus:* "Bro. Petrus has recently been expelled, both he and his church, from the "District Union" among the Baptists; and this step has now been sanctioned and confirmed by the conference at Eskilstuna to the effect, that it not merely implied expulsion from the Union, but also from the Society of Baptists as a whole."

The especial reason assigned was, that he had allowed other christians, to partake of the Lord's Supper. They were baptized since believing, but not baptists. However, behind this act there was evidently a definite feeling of ill—will towards the Pentecostal Movement.

Of one thing I am assured, and that is: if the Baptists had known what would have been the outcome of this act, they would have hesitated and asked the Lord more about it.

Numbers of baptist ministers and baptist churches have since then left the Baptist Society and joined the Pentecostal Movement, with the result, that in no country, I expect, do we see the movement so fully and ably led on to victory as in Sweden. The progress made in this country is simply wonderful!

The Lord allowed the Baptists to make this mistake. He is always longing to bring his people forward towards greater heights, and make them more useful in His service. And now the Pentecostal Movement in Sweden is a settled fact, with which all have to reckon. Able men from s e v e r a l  d e- n o m i n a t i o n s  have joined the churches, and

Pastor Lewi Petrus.

others have been saved from the world an raised up as leaders in their midst. Remarkable revival scenes are constant being witnessed throughout the whole country.

My good friend, *Bro. Petrus*, who on his stay in Oslo came in contact with the Movement, is one of the principal leaders in Sweden: loved and res= pected throughout Scandinavia! The church he re=

presents has a membership now of about 2500, and the crowds attending the meetings, have made it necessary to take steps towards the erection of the largest church in Stockholm. The site is purchased; the architects are busy; and the money is flowing in. Hallelujah!

They have their twentieth jubilee this year (1927), to commemorate the commencement of the Pentecostal work in Sweden. Books, by well-known professors in Sweden, have been written about the Pentecostal Movement, more or less colored by Lutheran or liberal views; but at present a very able historical work, by *pastor G. E. Søderholm*, is being published. The first part contains 623 pages, and is already printed. Bro. Søderholm was a minister in the Lutheran church, but was brought into connection with the movement, and is now one of its chief leaders.

The work in Sweden has been very fortunate, as to leaders. Besides the above mentioned men, we might mention the poet and author, *Mr. Sven Lidman*, who in company with Bro. Petrus, is the chief editor of their paper „*Evangelii Härold*", (The Evangelical Herald). The work is constantly spreading over the country. Hundreds of young men and women attend the bible schools for evangelists, and a very extensive missionary work has been done.

Then we have pastor Friis, Dr. Franklin, pastor Alf Gustavsson, pastor Hedeen, and a great number of competent and Spirit-filled men. Dr. Franklin has especially the Missionary Department supervision.

### *The Water—Line.*

The Lord had considerable difficulty with me concerning water baptism. The strange thing is, that I could not see it before; but when I remember, that even the Lord's disciples did not see the necessity of leaving Judaism, with it's creed of circumcision, although they were Baptized in the Holy Ghost, I feel somewhat comforted.

I never could accept the Lutheran view of baptismal regeneration for babes. I saw the falsity of that doctrine from my youth, and had many a battle with the Lutheran priests on that line. However the Methodist doctrine, that children, although born in sin, were under the B l o o d, and therefore belonged to the kingdom of God, was very clear. The conclusion then was this: if they r e a l l y belong to Christ, they ought evidently to be baptized.

I defended this position, even after I was baptized in the Holy Ghost, with great energy. Numbers of my friends went across the water—line, but I stood firmly on this old theory until the year 1913.

This standpoint gave me considerable influence with people, who still clung to infant baptism. My good wife was clear on this point. She had not been baptized when a child, as her parents belonged to the "Lammerske bevægelse", a group of godly and holy men and women. When she became a Methodist, she was baptized, b u t  n o t  b y  i mm e r s i o n. She defended the Baptist view however, whenever I brought the matter up in private. No doubt the attitude I had taken towards this doctrine, had much to do with all my attempts to c r e a t e a u n i o n between the friends of Pentecost. However, I was thoroughly honest and kept up the battle, s i m p l y  b e c a u s e  I  b e l i e v e d  t h e  M et h o d i s t  v i e w  w a s  p e r f e c t l y  c o r r e c t.

At last I determined to study the subject again, no matter what the outcome might be. The w o r d o f  G o d  w a s  t o  b e  m y  g u i d e,  a n d  t h a t a l o n e  That settled the matter. I read through a very elaborate Methodist treatise on the subject, which especially tried to p r o v e t h e  n e c e s s i t y of  i n f a n t b a p t i s m, but when I had worked my way through it, I was through with infant baptism as well. T h e r e  w a s  n o  p r o o f  f r o m the bible that the apostles really practiced infant baptism, and I found it impossible to hold on to statements by church Fathers, who often had a different opinion on such an important subject as this.

I saw my way clear, and the very moment I saw it, I acted accordingly.

I was in Sweden when this step was taken, and took part in a conference at Ørebro. Here pastor Ongman had for years stood for a freer line within the Baptist Church, and had been greatly used of God.

He was a good preacher, and felt at first greatly interested in the Pentecostal Movement. However, he never left the Baptists; no doubt, to some extent, afraid that the large Bible-school for evangelists at Ørebro, through which he exerted so much influence in Sweden, would be excluded from working within the Baptist Church.

I asked Bro. Ongman if he was willing to baptize me, but unless I joined the baptists he could not do so

I then asked Bro. L. Petrus, if he was willing, and as I was a traveller in a foreign country, he decided to do so, although I would not join his church at Stockholm (Acts VIII, 36—39). To prevent the act from appearing a protest against the baptist friends in Ørebro, whom we were visiting, we determined to go to Stockholm, and there on the 15th of Sept. 1913, my wife and I were baptized by Bro. Petrus. She did not consider the baptism she received by sprinkling in the Methodist church, sufficient, as immersion is the only biblical way.

This step has proved to be of very great importance in our lives and work. Of course many of our old friends, when they heard of it, were surprised. They knew that I had advocated infant baptism so warmly. Many left us and severed their connection with the Movement on that account, but if I ever was convinced of anything, I was convinced of the correctness of this step I had taken. I could stand on the word of God with perfect confidence, and would not be bound to old man—made forms and doctrines any longer. Praise God for ever!

My good wife was always vigilant and as active in the work as the home life would allow her. The Lord gave us eight children; two were now in Heaven, Laura and Sussie. Mary, our eldest child, was a graduate of the Musical department of the International Institute at Rome, and had received her diploma from the Conservatory of St. Cecilia. She has since then become one of the most well—known and efficient pianists in Scandinavia. Then came Esther, Solveig, Tom and Alexander.

In my Journal (Oct. 6, 1913) I write: "The congregation in Møllergt. 38 has already commenced to attain a more solid form. Many consider the place to be their spiritual home. My wife stands in their midst, even if I am away (unless she now and then accompanies me), as the mother of the assembly, and prays for and loves the great crowd that flocks together there."

And this great crowd of people, that thronged the place, made it clear to us, even then, that we must have a larger Hall!

In 1913, I again visited *Switzerland*. We had wonderful meetings at *Zurich*. *Pastor Voget* from Germany, *Bro Bartleman*, and others took part in the meetings. *Mr. Steiner* was my interpreter.

The Revival had made constant progress, although the opposition had been very violent. Groups of friends were already found in *Wadenswil, Horgen, Seeback, Scolieren, Kloten, Rümlang, Wejaco, Stadel, Dieszenoofen, Wigoltingen* and *St. Gallen*. The conference at Zurich proved a great blessing.

"Monday, the 17th of Nov. 1913, I performed my first baptismal rite. Four sisters and one brother were baptized. The act took place in St. Olafsgt. 6, as we as yet had no baptistery in Møllergt. 38."

I received a letter in Nov. this year, from Mrs. *Anna Larssen Bjørner* (she was now married to Mr. Bjørner, Denmark), in which she relates some of the results of an address she had been invited to give the students in Copenhagen. The subject was: "What I have experienced as a christian." About 700 students were present, and judging also from the reports in the secular Press, the address had exerted a mighty influence on all present. Mrs. Bjørner says in her letter: "As I described my wonderful experience at the home of *Mrs. Mollerup,* and said: "This is what Jesus calls the Baptism of the Holy Ghost," we suddenly heard a crash, and saw that a young student had fallen to the ground, as if he was struck by lightning. He rose again shortly and stood with his face to the wall, but the unexpected break in the address was very remarkable. I had received a few cards to distribute among my friends, so that 20 praying, mostly Spirit filled persons were distributed among the 700 students, and we felt, that the Spirit of God had the meeting in His keeping. We had been praying a whole month, that souls might be saved then."

She then goes on to say: "We have just had a visit by a young theological student, who has lately heard *professor Amundsen,* one of the most learned theologians in Denmark, state, as he spoke of the gifts in Paul's letter to the Corinthians: "The tongues we have heard in Zinnsgt., and Colosseum of late years, are surely the same as those heard in the days of the apostles." And again: "The tongues are not a proof of the healthy character of the movement, but of it's power." This latter statement is rather strange, as it naturally follows —

that if there is great spiritual power in connection with the tongues, and that was what the professor meant, then surely the movement must be of a h e a l t h y  character!

The professor related a remarkable case to the young students.

At Holstebro a meeting was held against the Mormons. None of the speeches seemed to have had any influence on the people. Suddenly, *pastor Morten Larsen* fell down from his seat on the floor with a great bang, and remained lying there. He was as heavy as lead, but suddenly he rose up and went direct to the pulpit, and held a sermon with such power and authority, that it cut the people to the marrow and bones, and an unbelieving journalist present said, that he saw a bright light encircle the preacher's whole being. Mr M. Larsen said, when relating the circumstance later on, that he had never experienced the like of it. He came to the meeting to listen, and had nothing to say; then G o d  gave him words to speak, and this marvellous power and authority."

Pastor Larsen belonged to the Lutheran church, but especially to the "g r u n d t v i g" group.

*I leave the Methodist church.*

Although my connection with the annual conference was severed soon after my return from America, I still remained a member of the Methodist church; but as the events rolled on in my life, it became apparent to all, that I would have to leave the church, as well, and words to that effect appeared in the methodist paper ("Kristelig Tidende"). I therefore sent the following letter to the Editor:

Nordstrand, 12—4—16.

Dear Bro. Torjussen!

The reason why I have not left the church before, is this: I have felt in the depths of my heart, that I have been so warmly knit to you all, and have loved you all, so that it has been very difficult to take this step fully. Now I am driven to do so by the circumstances that have arisen. Although my view concerning the form of organization is different from what it used to be, I still believe in the guidance of the Spirit in our work. I have sent the following letter to—day to Bro. Hessen, pastor of 1st church:

Dear Bro. in the Lord!

As we are on the point of organizing our assembly in Møllergt. 38 on other lines than those commonly used in the Methodist Church, it will be necessary for me to notify that I must leave the Church.

I do so with a feeling of sadness, as there are so many precious reminiscences, that bind me to the Methodist Church, where my forefathers have stood, and where I myself have received so many blessings and have laid down the most of my life's energy, and where I still believe I have quite a number of warm-hearted friends. However the Methodist Church does not give us any right to organize an assembly according to the plan we have adopted, and as I therefore will be at variance with its discipline, I am fooced to leave my membership there.

This implies also my dear wife and our two boys, Tom and Alexander. Solveig and Frances desire also to join us. Mary and Esther are at present abroad.

With fraternal greetings, and a hearty thanks to you for good cooperation and the spirit of fraternity.

Your Brother in Christ.            T. B. Barratt.

At the same time I wish to thank you Bro. Torjussen, and all my colleagues in the Methodist church for the spirit of love shown me. I leave — not as your enemy, but as your friend and brother in the Lord!

Fare well!

Barratt.

Several of my friends thought that I had left the church the day I was baptized, but my old love to the friends there, and the fact that I knew, according to the scriptures, that all the first christians belonged to one or other of the christian assemblies, and as I found no other denomination that suited me, I remained where I was, until we ourselves became an assembly, according to the Scriptural pattern.

My old colleagues still meet me, as well as the younger pastors within the Methodist church in Norway, in the spirit of love and friendship.

### The new assembly in Møllergt. 38.

Step by step, the good Lord led me on. I saw clearly, that the work I was called to perform, must be guided by the rules laid down in the New Testament; but it was easier to see it, than to do it. I had been trying to work on Alliance lines, then we formed our "Mission" in Møllergt. 38. Christians must be members, I felt, not merely of a "Mission", but of a christian assembly. I knew this was the Lord's way, but how could it be effected. Would the friends of the mission be willing to take a step further? At any rate, God's word must be carried into effect. Whatever the outcome might be, I had to lead the people aright, on New Testament lines! Articles in the "Korsets Seir" prepared my people for the change, as well as several talks on the matter.

In my Journal, I write as follows: "June 26: Last night we met at our

### first meeting of the assembly

in 38, and it was organized with more than 200 members, according to the plan already accepted." The new assembly was therefore started as such on the 26th of June, 1916.

However, we must not forget all the preparatory

work done, that collected and bound the friends together as o n e  p e o p l e  in Christ Jesus.  Hallelujah!

The lines were drawn up clearly; and now, unfettered by anything, we had merely to go ahead and trust our Lord and Saviour, building up a Christian assembly, on t h e  s a m e  p r i n c i p l e s  a n d  l i n e s  a s  t h e  f i r s t  c h r i s t i a n s,  w i t h  t h e  B i b l e  a l o n e  a s  o u r  s u r e  g u i d e.

Immediately other assemblies sprang up here and there in the country, and the work began to show a more solid front.

*Opposition from former friends of the Movement.*

No sooner had we made a start in the right direction, than a tremendous warfare commenced against us, and it has been kept up by many unto this day.  People, who would h ave nothing to do with the teaching of the apostles in this matter, accused us of "a c t i n g  i n  t h e  f l e s h." We were working on "m a n—m a d e" lines, and were "s i d e- t r a p p e d" by the devil, etc.  They did not see, and many of them do not see it yet, that t h e i r  o w n  a t t a c k s  w e r e  t h e  o u t c o m e  o f  a  c a r- n a l  m i n d!

Not only this, but their chief leaders b e g a n  t o  o p p o s e  t h e  d o c t r i n e  o f  t h e  b a p- t i s m  o f  t h e  H o l y  G h o s t, teaching that every christian w a s  baptized with the Spirit — it took place in regeneration.

This has had a great influence on many, even amongst those who had received the blessing. However, we have taken a decided stand in this respect of late, especially a s  r e g a r d s  m e m b e r s h i p, not allowing any to remain as members, who do not fully believe the doctrines of the B i b l e, both in t h i s and in every other respect.  We have lost several members in our own assembly on this account, but this step has been a blessing to the work. New members are constantly coming, who are willing to go all the way with Christ!

It may be truthfully said, that the real Pentecostal assemblies have been strengthened during the battle, and the truths we have advocated have a firmer grip on the people generally now, than ever before!

For years we have been antagonised by the world, ridiculed, scorned, and made the laughing stock of ungodly men and women; the secular Press has derided us and spread lies and evil reports; but little by little the truth has been unfolded, and numbers see now, that this movement must be the same old glorious movement that started on the day of Pentecost in Jerusalem!

I see now why I went through all those deep and wonderful experiences in New York, in 1906! The Lord was preparing me for this work. I have had to wage a very hard battle at times, but my spirit has not been embittered. I have felt and knew for certain all the time, that my blessed King and Master was with me in the fray. I have had to use the sharp edge of the sword many a time, but I have been able to do so in the spirit of love. I thank God for His wonderful mercy and grace, Hallelujah!

I settled down more and more in Oslo to build up an assembly on the grand old truths of the Bible, and I felt that the Lord would prove, in the face of all opposition, that this work was of Him. I was assured that he was able, even in our day, to build an assembly of water- and fire —baptized christians, in the midst of an ungodly city, surrounded by the evils of our modern life, by thousands of formal christians, by people filled with envy and the desire to prevent our progress; to build a living assembly of Godfearing men and women, prepared to meet the King when He comes to take away His Bride, — and he has done it! Praise His Holy Name for ever!

## CHAPTER XV.

*Divisions. Before the Judgment-Seat of Christ. Norway's Free Evangelical Mission to the Heathen. Wigglesworth. "Utsigten". Sick and restored. Home-life.*

When I came from America and the revival had come into full swing, many at last closed their doors against us. But there was a group of friends that opened their doors, and we were very thankful to see this fraternal spirit. However as time slipped by, the stand was taken by leaders of this group, that regeneration was the same experience as the baptism in the Holy Ghost. They also began to fight against the formation of local churches. Besides this, the views promoted concerning holiness were not always healthy, the doctrine being preached, that "we have everything in Jesus, and need not therefore seek holiness or the baptism of fire, as a special and personal experience — we have it all in Christ!"

Of course it became impossible for me to adopt such erroneous ideas, and the result was, that a long battle has been waged concerning these doctrines, between us. I fully believe, that we have proved by the word of God, that there is, both theoretically and experimentally, a great difference between regeneration and the baptism of the Holy Ghost; that the local churches must be organised on biblical lines; that Christ has surely made provision for the salvation of all mankind, through perfect cleansing in the Blood, and a full Pentecostal baptism, but that we must, *each one of us personally*, go the bible way, and seek these blessings for ourselves! It's one thing to have money in the bank, but unless we make use of it, we may die, even as the poorest.

I tried long to effect a combination between the diverse elements among us, but to no good. Everywhere, I agitated for a *Union* between the Pentecostal people. I wrote once: "The Evangelical Alliance system has done a lot of good, but this revival ought to lead its friends a step further, and unite us, as at the commencement of the Revival, as

*One people!* —

no matter what views we may have concerning water baptism, or any other doctrine, as long as we hold on to the evangelical truths, and are determined to preach and practice them. We will not be able to reach the mark, by expecting that people will act in direct opposition to their consciences, but by finding a way by which we may, with a free conscience, worship God together and work for the furtherance of the kingdom of Christ."

No one can say, therefore, that w e  h a v e  n o t  t r i e d  t h e  a l l i a n c e - l i n e!

I was in real earnest about it, and hoped, that it not might merely be a spiritual union, but a real Pentecostal Union among the friends of this worldwide movement.

I did not know t h e n, what a difference the

*Water-line*

would make in my own life! In fact, christians lay by far too little stress on this blessed institution! In a country like *Norway*, where *Infantbaptism* is practiced so extensively, it often means a good bit to follow the Lord in this respect and throw the m a n - m a d e  s y s t e m s aside, and join those who dare to face public opinion and take "b e l i e v e r 's  b a p t i s m".

Although the water-line has made several things clear to most of us that we did not see before, it must also be remembered, that the revival brought together people from various denominations, and several of these have again adopted some of their old views, although they hold on to the doctrine of a full Pentecost. This has led to several

### Divisions!

Various doctrines and forms of organization have been adopted by friends of the Pentecostal Movement in several countries. They stand for the Pentecostal Baptism, with the signs following, and most of them agree as to "believer's baptism", but other doctrines and systems divide.
I a m  r e a l l y  s o r r y  f o r  t h i s !
But it has been the case with *all* revivals, from the days of the apostles until our day. Paul complained about it; and it has given outsiders enough to write and talk about!

One of the saddest divisions arose, when Mr. and Mrs. Larsen Bjørner (Denmark), joined the "Apostolic Church" in Wales. They still retain most of the doctrines that have been characteristic of the revival, but have accepted the teachings of this church concerning the apostolate, and Mr. Sigurd Bjørner was appointed "apostle" of the assemblies in Denmark.

Bro. Lewi Petrus and myself, have not been able to accept this appointment a s  b e i n g  o f  t h e  L o r d. It has therefore severed  o u r  work from that of our Danish friends, who have joined the "Apostolic Church".

However, it must be remembered, that other Pentecostal assemblies, similar to ours in Norway, and the Pentecostal assemblies in Sweden and Finland, are springing up in Denmark, that have nothing to do with the "Apostolic Church".

Looking at all sides of the question, I have found, that, although there m u s t  b e  a  f u l - a l l o w a n c e  f o r  b r o t h e r l y  l o v e  a n d  f r i e n d - s h i p between *all* who have received the baptism

From left to right: Bro. L. Petrus (Sweden), Mrs. Barratt and the writer (Norway), Mrs. L. Bjorner and her husband (Denmark). This photo was taken some time before the division in the Holy Ghost, the greatest influence for good will be attained, when those, who fully agree in the faith, *stand firmly united,* and labour for the truths they believe the Lord has entrusted to their care.  Greater results are reached then, as divided minds cannot easily work together!

Before *the Judgment seat of Christ* one day, each one of us will have to give an account of our stewardship.  Some have built on the foundation — *Christ,* with gold or silver, some with costly stones, but others with wood, hay, stubble. However, "each man's work shall be made manifest; for the day shall declare it, because it is revealed by fire; and the fire itself shall prove each man's work of what sort it is. If any man's work shall abide which he built thereon, he shall *receive a reward.* If any man's work shall be burned, he shall suffer loss; but *he himself shall be saved,* yet so as through fire." (1. Cor. 3, 11—15).

This applies especially to the *doctrines* advocated and the systems advanced and promoted. Many will suffer loss for false teaching, although they themselves be saved as through fire. "Just as a builder, whose building, not the foundation, is consumed by fire, escapes, but with the loss of his work," (Alford) "as the shipwrecked merchant, though he has lost his merchandise, is saved, though having to pass through the waves." (Bengel). This then does not refer to the Last Day of Judgment, before the Great White Throne. (Rev. 20, 11).

May *God* in His mercy melt all the Pentecostal friends together, yea, every child of God — into *one great army!*

But I was obliged to give up the Alliance-line in our work within the new assembly in Møllergt. 38. We had even allowed friends, who were not baptized, to become members, but experience has taught us, that there must be a real agreement between the members of an assembly, as to doctrine and methods of work. Most of those, who were not baptized, when admitted as members, have since then taken baptism. Those, who were not willing to do so, have been required to leave the assembly.

*The assembly in Møllergaten 38.*

The Hall in Møllergaten 38 had about 700 seats, but proved from the first, to be far too small for the crowds that came to the meetings. It was a comfortable Hall, and numbers of souls still look back on "old Møllergt. 38" as their spiritual birthplace, and the Holy of Holies where the *Fire of Heaven* fell upon them. There the sick were healed, and Christ honoured in our midst, *Hallelujah!*

Oh, what wonderful blessings God showered down upon us at times! It was not to be wondered at, that the devil did his best to raise a barricade against all this, but it was to no avail. Old friends might leave us, some, on whom we relied, might fall away from the Lord; God's own people might doubt as to the reallity of our experience; the ungodly might make fun of us; many might curse and swear, and pronounce their worst anathemas against us, some of our own midst might prove to a nicety, that they were carnal minded and sought their own glory, but amidst all failings and schisms, and in spite of the many difficulties that met us — we emerged from it all with greater faith in God, with more love to our fellowmen, with a more intense desire to glorify God, and experienced daily, that the Blessed Redeemer was faithful to *His* word. He never left us, but led us on, step by step, to *victory, Hallelujah!*

The assembly in Møllergt. 38 was the "*Mother-Assembly*" of all the Pentecostal assemblies in Norway. As such, it stood in the minds and prayers of our friends round about the country.

When the world said we were "insane" and made people "insane", thousands blest us and sought

Møllergaten 38.

our advice and prayers. They knew the work was of God!

At times I was called to visit *Sweden* and other countries, but little by little I had to settle down to a definite pastoral work in this assembly, for the work was constantly growing and called for all my energies and physical and spiritual strength.

I also kept up my work as editor of "Korsets Seir", and do so to this day. Every now and then, I have been called to write articles in defence of the Pentecostal Movement in other papers as well, and have issued several pamphlets and books, that might bring people some spiritual blessing. I felt that I must make as much out of my life, and bring as many souls to the Lord as possible, and let *Him* build up a live Pentecostal Assembly in Oslo.

I have also felt my unworthiness, my inability to do anything, except as the good Lord Himself gave wisdom and strength, but I praise Him for His constant love and guidance! To *Him* belongs all the honour and glory!

We appointed elders within the assembly, and the assembly elected me as their leading elder and pastor. (Titus 1, 5).

Besides this, we appointed deacons (1. Tim. 3, 8) and deaconesses. In the Norwegian translation, the term used for deacons and deaconesses is *"Servants of the church"*. This is also the term used in the revised English version, concerning Phebe. (Rom. 16, 1). Then again we divided the assembly into *"prayer-circles"*, and appointed a leader for each circle.

All these groups have separate meetings to discuss the problems that arise and prepare propositions, for the decision of the Assembly. The leaders of the "prayer-circles" have work similar to that of the class leaders in the Methodist church. He, or she, becomes the right hand of the pastor. The spiritual, temporal, and physical welfare of each member, is laid to some extent on them.

The "s e r v a n t s" of the assembly (deacons and deaconesses) work together, and take special care of the t e m p o r a l interests of the assembly. At times it becomes necessary to hold united meetings for all these groups, before questions of vital importance are laid before the assembly.

A s s e m b l y-m e e ti n g s are held every Monday evening. These meetings have been of great importance to the work. The pastor has an opportunity to address the members of the assembly, as it were in their own home. New members are received, and twice a month we have "breaking of bread", or the Lord's Supper. Here the members feel free to testify of their experiences, and most marvellous testimonies are heard at times. Every now and then, the Spirit makes use of the gifts He has bestowed on the assembly. Tongues with interpretation, prophesies, revelations are heard, and God has revealed Himself in our midst, comforting, exhorting, and guiding His people, Hallelujah!

Then again we have a live *Sunday=school,* with Bible-classes, and during the week special *classes* for the religious training of the children of the members of the assembly, as the children of dissenters in Norway need not attend the classes for religion in the public schools.

*Mission-work* has taken a prominent position in our assembly. In fact it may be said right here, that the general interest shown in mission-work, by the Pentecostal friends a l l o v e r t h e w o r l d, is one of the supreme facts, that proves the *divine* character of the Movement. It is doubtful, if there ever has been done so much for the evangelization of the heathen, through any religious revival, in the same s p a c e o f t i m e, since the days of the apostles. I mean now, of course, taking the Movement as a whole, throughout the world. The burning interest for the *salvation of the heathen,* shown by these *Fire-baptized* christians, has given, even the strongest opponents of the Movement, an object-lesson, as to the validity of the revival.

In Norway, in order to combine our energies and reach out as far as possible, we started

*"Norway's Free Evangelical Mission to the Heathen".*

O u r  a s s e m b l y has, ever since this mission commenced, been connected with it. However, we had commenced Mission-work among the friends of the Movement before this.

Our two first missionaries were *Miss Dagmar Gregersen* and *Miss Agnes Thelle*. They went to India.

We raised funds through "Korsets Seir", as well as at our meetings, for these sisters, and for *Bro. Engstrøm*, who had received a call to India. He was engaged to *Miss Dagmar Gregersen*, and the wedding was held in India in 1910. They started the "Banda-Mission". We helped *Bro. P. Gulbrandsen's* and other work in China; *Bro. Leonard's* work in Jerusalem; and *Miss Thelle's "Bilaspur-mission"*, as well as a mission in South Africa.

In 1915 a Missionary-Convention was held in Oslo, and all, who "desired a m o r e  c o m b in e d  M i s s i o n a r y  w o r k", were invited to take part. It resulted in the formation of *"Norway's Free Evangelical Mission to the Heathen"*. The writer was elected President of the first Council, *Bro. M. H. Sæther* Treasurer, and *Mrs. L. Barratt* Secretary.

The other Missions: "Banda", "Bilaspur", could not accept the rules of the new Council and left us. We were very sorry for this, but felt that t h e c o m b i n e d  a c t i o n  o f  a  c o u n c i l would be more efficient than the divided work of missionaries without this help. Time has proved, that this is the case. If all had stood firmly united, we would certainly have done far more than we have been able to do.

We must nevertheless thank God for the results of our Missionary work. Every Summer we have a Missionary Convention. It has always stimulated new interest in the Missionary cause, and the reports have shown, that, in spite of all difficulties, we have constantly been making headway.

The assemblies have not been requested to send representatives to this Convention. This Missionary Union is not therefore an o r g a n i z a t i o n in that respect. However, numbers of pastors and evangelists, as well as friends from all parts of the country, attend the Convention, and look forward to it as a great event, every year. The work of the Council, which is elected annually, at the special meeting of the Council, is to awaken interest in our Missions, raise funds, give advice to the missionaries, and work for their support; but the whole system is built and upheld by f a i t h.

The question has been raised lately, as to the advisability of holding a Conference for the whole country, with r e p r e s e n t a t i v e s from all the assemblies. The Conference was to comprise, not only the Mission cause, but the Home Mission as well, and other objects o f c o m m o n i n t e r e s t, without interfering in any way with the i n d e p e n- d e n t r i g h t s of each assembly.

However, at present the Missionary work has a very prominent position amongst the Pentecostal friends, and will certainly continue to maintain it; although it is quite natural, that other things of interest, crave our attention as a people, especially the H o m e - M i s s i o n evangelistic work in neglected parts of Norway.

During the Summer of 1915, when the Annual Conference of "N. F. E. Mission to the Heathen" was held in Stavanger, we were also able to celebrate its

*10th Anniversary.*

The meetings attracted much notice, and proved a great blessing to the Missionary cause, as well as a great uplift for the Pentecostal Movement.

Mrs. Laura Barratt.

Mrs. Barratt gave up her position as Secretary some years ago, which has been very ably filled by Mr. Ivar M. Witzoe (druggist). Mr.

M. H. *Sæther* has been the T r e a s u r e r of the Council, from the commencement.

We have at present stations in *China, India, Congo* and *South-Africa*; four stations in all, with about 30 missionaries. During the first 10 years, about 430,000 kroner had been raised for the Missionary cause.

Our friends in Sweden are able to show greater results, as far as the number of missionaries and subscriptions are concerned, but there are more people in Sweden, and the Movement there, has not had so many doctrinal schisms to battle with as in Norway. Still we thank God, that we have been able to do a little for the dark heathen lands, where our missionaries are working, and pray that the results may be greater than we at present can see.

Our work in *Møllergt. 38* proceeded v i c t o r i - o u s l y year by year, praised be God! In the various towns and country-places in Norway, new assemblies sprang up and unfurled the Pentecostal banner!

Our Hall was by far too small to accomodate the crowds that desired to attend our meetings. We appealed to the Inner Mission (Lutheran) in order to obtain the use of the large Mission-Hall in Cal meyergt., but they were too partial, and would not let us have it, not even on special occasions. This was much to our disadvantage when *Bro. Smith Wigglesworth* visited us. He visited not only Oslo, but other towns as well, and everywhere great crowds attended the services. However, we made considerable use of the "Turnhal" (Gymnasium).

Of course the papers attacked the meetings, and they did it in their usual way, by giving a false construction and statement of what r e a l l y h a p - p e n e d. It was at any rate very easy to see, that the revival was sweeping over numbers of the people. Mighty scenes of grace — the Holy Spirit was poured out upon the saints, souls saved, sick healed, Christ glorified — were witnessed at every meeting. I often meet people to-day, who thank God for those wonderful meetings and for the healing they received.

In Sweden, the same glorious scenes were witnessed. Bro. Wigglesworth's visit caused quite a stir in the Swedish Capital.

Bro. Smith Wigglesworth.

### "Utsigten".

A friend of ours had me to join him in purchasing a property on Norstrand, with the object in view of using it as a "Home of Rest", but "Utsigten" never became a "Home of Rest" in the way we had expected. The economical difficulties that arose in connection with the last war, made it impossible. I used part of it as our home for some time, but sold it eventually. It was during those days, that *I became very ill.* I held out in the work as well as I could; preached regularly and trusted the good Lord to help me out, but every renewed attack weakened me considerably.

I suffered from hardening of the arteries, the doctor said. The friends prayed for me; Bro. Wigglesworth, and other leaders within the Movement as well, and I prayed much myself, but it seemed as if I was constantly going down the hill towards the grave. However, I was prepared for any emergency. In fact I began to feel, that it possibly was the very best thing for me to get away *Home* — to the everlasting glory of my Heavenly Father, and see my Saviour face to face.

But at last the Lord heard the thousands of prayers, that had been sent up on my behalf. Little by little I regained my strength, and I may truly say, that I have never had more work to do than the last few years, since I recovered. I have been kept strong and healthy, although of course the years are creeping on, and I have now filled my 65th year. Meetings almost daily have filled the program, and several sermons a week, but *God* has given strength!

### Health-Methods.

It has no doubt been of some importance, humanly speaking, that I have obstained from alcoholic drinks all my life. Since I was in America, I have also discarded tea and coffee. Of course I never smoke; my *body* is on the altar, as well as my soul. I feel, therefore, that I must try to keep it in as good trim as possible. I have followed "Møllers System" every morning, more than twenty years. These morning exercises have proved very beneficial to me.

I do not mention this to "make myself over righteous", but I advise all, young and old, to remember, that our *bodies* are also to be t e m p l e s of the Holy Ghost, and we must therefore renounce everything, that does not profit us, and adopt such methods and modes of living that will enable us to devote ourselves as much as possible to the Masters service.

At the same time, we must remember that t h e Holy Fire from Heaven must permeate both body, soul and spirit (1. Thes. 5, 23; 2. Cor. 6, 16; 1. Cor. 6, 19) and that we are unable to do anything satisfactorily unless *He* gives wisdom and strength!

I praise God for years of sweet communion with my Saviour, and for the presence of the Holy Fire from above!

## *Home-Life.*

My home—life has been a great stronghold for me during all these years. My good wife has been a wonderful help through the struggles and battles I have had to meet. Her prayers have strengthened and upheld me, and, in younger days especially, she took quite an active part in the work. She does so still, as far as her strength and time permits. Gifted with a heaven—born sagacity, and filled with the one desire to see the work of the Lord prosper, she has been a pillar of strength by my side. God bless her!

We have had some hard family trials to pass through of late. Our daughter, Frances Barratt, as formerly stated, has left us. She died on the 26th of June, 1925. She was born onthe 19th of March, 1899. About 11 months later, *Tom*, our eldest boy, died, on the 3rd of May, 1926, the same day Sussie died, but just 22 years later.

But we know where they are now. *Jesus* has taken them! Deep waters surrounded us those days! But God gave our hearts daily comfort.

They are all three — *Sussie, Frances, Tom* — resting in one grave, in Nordre Gravlund (Northern

Frances.

Cemetry), but it's only the dust that rests there, their spirits have gone on before us to Paradise!
Our children's children are growing up around us. The group next page, was taken a few years ago:
There are five of them now. It almost makes me believe I am getting old. But I cling to the promise: "Thy youth is renewed like the eagle!"

Tom.

Stephan and Esther Due, and Jakob Lange.

## CHAPTER XVI.

*We leave Møllergt. 38. Our New Hall.*

*Old friends passing away. Spread of Pentecostal literature. 10th Anniversary of the Assembly in Oslo. Invitations to visit America again. Review.*

The other day (July 29. 1927), when sitting in my little "Ford", waiting for my wife, who was looking about the market—place, the following words began to form in my mind, so I wrote them down. Here they are:

*Soon* the Heavens will glow and brighten
As the radiance of our King,
Flashes forth as beams of lightning,
Whilst the Hosts of Heaven sing!

Crowds of souls have long been waiting
For this Day of Liberty,
When the Power of Death will vanish,
And the Saints are ever free!

What a meeting! — when God's people
Meet their Saviour in the skies!
Clad in white — immortal, glorious!
Filled with *Life* that never dies!

Time is short, the *Day* is coming,
When our Saviour will appear;
Words of warning daily reach us,
Words of comfort and of cheer!

Work and spread the Glorious Gospel,
Save the dying, heal the sick;
If you wish the lost ones rescued,
Oh, for Christ's sake then be quick!

Lavish on us, Lord, in mercy,
Of Thy wondrous love and grace;
Keep us perfect, keep us holy,
Till we see Thee face to face!

The last meeting our Assembly held in *Møllergt. 38*, was on Monday, the 14th of April, 1924. Let me quote what *Bro. Ludv. Bratlie* wrote: "A wonderful peace pervaded the meeting. Each one of us thought about the glorious times we had been blest with there. The wonderful victories we had obtained. The many souls that had been saved. The crowd, that had been baptized in water and the Spirit. I fancy I still can see the many uplifted hands of the children and young people, at the Sunday—school meeting the day before, who had found their precious Saviour. However, a feeling of sadness crept oe'r us, as we acknowledged the things that had not pleased God in our lives. Our shortcomings! But God let us know clearly through the "gifts", that all was forgiven, as we bowed down before Him and acknowledged everything. He renewed His promise, that H e would go with us and bless us in the future, as He had done in the past. The joy felt, b e c a u s e  w e  w e r e  n o w  t o  h a v e  o u r  o w n  H a l l, was imprinted on the face of each one of us. We had indeed great reason to rejoice; we moved from "good to better".

During the Easter season in 1924, which is kept in Norway as sacred as Sunday, yea even more so, we entered our *New Hall* in St. Olavsgt. 24. The property purchased by the Assembly, was situated in a very central part of the City. It cost a

The New Hall: Filadelfia.

good bit to turn the large fabric in the interior, into a suitable Temple for religious services, but Mr. Boye was a very competent architect, and the Hall, as it now stands, is the next largest in the city (The Mission Hall in Calmeyergt. being larger), and is a very bright and attractive Hall, seating about 1500 people, and can no doubt accomodate about 2000.

Great crowds took part in the dedication services. Not only ministers and friends of the Movement in Scandinavia, but ministers and leaders within the various denominations in Oslo were also present and spoke words of good cheer. This fact shows a turning point in the opinion of many. During the years that had passed, their eyes were opened to see that *God* was with us, and although they could not fully accept our teachings in every respect, they had at least to respect us and even love us, as God's own people. Even the s e c u l a r  p r e s s showed tokens of respect, and has often done so since.

This new Hall was the Assembly's o w n property, and was to become our n e w  s p i r i t u a l h o m e in the very heart of Oslo; and f r o m  t h i s c e n t r e, the good Lord h a s  p o u r e d  o u t  b l e s-s i n g s  o n  t h o u s a n d s  o f  s o u l s, H a l l e l u j a h!

It has been touching to see the great number of men, that often attended the meetings. We have preached *the Gospel of Jesus Christ*, but t h a t had enough in it to attract these men, who generally never put their feet inside a place of worship — and not a few of them have been saved. The Power of the Holy Spirit has been at work! Young and old have flocked together to hear the Old Glorious Gospel of Salvation through the Blood of Jesus! The Fire has fallen on the Saints; many of the sick seeking help, have been healed, yes, there have been many cases of wonderful healing, through simple faith in the Word. Numbers have been baptized in water, and the Assembly has been strengthened and upheld by the grace of God!

The *sacrificing spirit of the Assembly* has astonished many. People thought it impossible for us to purchase such a large property and transform a good bit of it into a tempel for the Lord, but the friends did it, and have held out, paying off the debt with great strides. Of course we wish the whole debt was paid! Who will help us? Besides this, we would like to reconstruct a part of the building, making it larger and still more practical than it is. We need also a good organ. Perhaps some of the readers of this book will help us? We will then be able to develope the work in many ways that we are prevented from doing now, but we know that God will open the way for us in every respect in the future, as He has done it in the past.

### The Home-call.

Several of our faithful and God-fearing members have been called home since the work began, and are now hid in glory yonder. The results of this mighty outpouring of the Holy Spirit, will never be fully known here. But we rejoice to know, that our labors have not been in vain in the Lord! He has reached out His hand and done a mighty work! We are only V e s s e l s—and very weak vessels. The only strength and power that has enduring influence, is that given us by the Holy Ghost!

One of our old friends in Denmark, Mr. Plum, who from the first was greatly interested in the Pentcostal Movement, passed away on the 6th of Sept., 1923. He published the well—known *"Kirkeklokken"* (The Church Bell), a Holiness paper, that has been a great blessing to thousands, not only in Denmark, but throughout Scandinavia. He also published many most excellent books, tracts and pamphlets, and did a lot of good. We have helped to spread these books in Norway.

*Spread of Pentecostal literature.*

My wife and I published the *"Korsets Seir"* and several books and tracts, through our own private publishing office, but we felt, as the work grew, that it would be more satisfactory if the Assembly took over the whole busi-

Mr. Thv. Plum.

ness. This was done on proper terms, and the results have proved that we acted wisely in so doing. We fell more free to agitate for the spread of our Pentecostal literature. The hymnbook *"Maran atha"* and the songbook for Sunday—schools, *"Stjernen"* (The Star), which I published, were included in the transfer, as well as „Korsets Seir", but I was to remain Editor as long as the good Lord will allow me.

He has helped me also, during the last two years, to write some new books: "*Verdens midtpunkt Jesus*", (The centre of the world—Jesus) "*Mrs. Mc. Phersons liv og virksomhet*", (The life and work of Mrs. Mc. Pherson) "*Forvandlet, eller en drøm, som burde bli til virkelighet*", (Transformed, or a dream, that ought to be realized) "*Ledetraad i Guds ord, for ungdommen og nyfrelste*", (Directive Lines in the Word of God, for Young People and New Converts) and this book "*When the Fire fell*" etc.

The first mentioned book has received a very hearty welcome in the religious Press, for which I am very thankful, as it stands for the Central truths in the Bible, in opposition to the Modern and Liberal view. The second is doing a lot of good. "*Transformed*", relates, in descriptive form, the story and work of the Pentecostal Revival, and gives the readers, through the discussions that arise, an idea of our teaching and aims as a people. "*Ledetraad*" is in fact a Catechism, with questions and answers. These books may possibly, later on, be translated into the English language.

Our people are being stirred up of late, to work for the spread of Pentecostal literature, as they, by that means, are able to reach thousands, who have false ideas about the Pentecostal Movement, or possibly are living in the world, without God and Hope!

A few days ago, another song was given me by the good Spirit:

> *Constrained* by Love, I plod my way
> Through earth's great harvest field,
> And scatter seed on every hand,
> Whatever it may yield.

The *Lord* gives Life where ere the seed
May fall on willing ground,
My business is to scatter wide
The treasures I have found!

*Live* Christianity deals out
With wise and lavish hand,
The Gospel truths, that kindle life,
And joy in every land!

My heart is full and running o'er
With joy celestial — free!
Constrained to sing, in anthems sweet,
Of this great Liberty!

It is the *Spirit's* song, within
Each cleansed and Fire-filled soul;
He honours Christ — proclaims with Power:
*Salvation free* — to all!

*10th Anniversary of the Assembly in Oslo.*

Our Assembly held it's 10th Anniversary in 1926, in the new Hall. The various reports from the leaders and treasurers of the several groups within the Assembly, were very satisfactory. God had indeed done a great work during these 10 years.

Of course we must remember all the preparatory work done, before the Mission became an Assembly. Almost 10 years passed by since my return from America, ere we took this step. And now 10 years had again passed by, but as we looked back, we had no reason to regret the step taken. Both spiritually and financially, the Lord has been our stay and glory, Hallelujah! His Spirit was still in our midst. Pentecostal signs were prominent, and Christ glorified. Blessed be God!

Since this Anniversary we have been led on in the same track, always looking forward and expecting still greater things!

In 1923 *pastor Stephen and George Jeffreys* (England) visited us.

Their visit was a great blessing to us all, and judging from the letter we received from Bro. George Jeffreys, they had themselves been greatly blest during their stay in Norway.

In *England*, the Pentecostal Revival has made mighty strides during the last few years. Praised be God!

And now, God willing, I visit America

Stephen Jeffreys.    George Jeffreys.

again, in company with my wife. One of our Norwegian pastors on the West Coast, *Bro. Joseph Ystrøm*, has done his utmost to get me to come, to visit the Scandinavian assemblies in America. It is really marvellous to think, that numerous Norwegian, Swedish, and Danish Pentecostal assemblies are to be found in America now, besides all the American assemblies, and when I was there last time, the Fire had just commenced to fall! Surely the Lord has done great things.

*The Rev. Robert A. Brown*, New York, who is

pastor at the "Glad Tidings Tabernacle", has also invited us. He was present in 14th St., New York, when *the Fire fell* in 1906, and has since then been on a visit to Norway with Mrs. Brown.

Calls came also from other American Assemblies, even from Canada. I asked the Lord about all this, and expected Him to lead me. Now it really seems that I may, after the lapse of 21 years, re-visit New York, and see the work God has wrought there and elsewhere, during that time, through the Pentecostal Revival.

During my absence *Bro. M. H. Sæther*, one of the elders of our Assembly, will take charge in my place and carry on the work in company with the elders and other workers.

God willing then, we start with the "Bergensfjord" on Friday, the 30th of September.

I may perhaps see the place

*where the fire fell*

in 1906, on my longing soul! What remarkable years I have passed through since then!

*Review.*

It will easily be seen from this *"Outline of my life,"* that there has been a constant development regarding my views of Scripture Truth, especially concerning the Bible's statements about *the Baptism in the Holy Ghost and Fire*, and as a result, this has greatly influenced my character and methods of work. I wish the development of character had been fuller and richer, but I am comforted by the fact, that there is, as our beloved brother Wigglesworth puts it, *"no stop on this line."* I feel very definitly, as I look back over the way I have wandered, from the first streak of day, until the present moment, that *God* has been my stay and my delight, and I thank Him for all His goodness and paternal care, for all His wonderful mercy and grace!

I remember once, as *Bishop W. Burt* was standing within the Communion Rails in the 1st M. E.

Church, Oslo, shaking hands with the friends and bidding farewell for the last time, that my wife and I joined the crowd and bade farewell with him. As he grasped my hand he said: *"Come back!"* — those were his last words to me.

But how could I?

I had parted with the church in a friendly way, and the experiences I had passed through made it impossible to go back!

I still love every God-fearing methodist, and all God's people, but it seems that the Lord Himself has been guiding my steps year by year, and now it is impossible to retrace them and return back to my former position.

Anything of real worth, found in the doctrines of the Methodist church and other churches we have, as a people, praise God! And to this, comes the added blessings that God has been pouring out over the world through the Pentecostal Movement. We all feel that there is still much land to take in, but as we go forward, obedient to Bible-truth, the Holy Spirit will give us the Victory! Hallelujah!

Dr. *Michael Neiiendam*, Copenhagen, has lately issued a very interesting historical work on *"Frikirker og sekter"* (Free churches and Sects), and has in this dwelt at large on the Pentecostal Movement. He is by far more sympathetic than several other outsiders, who have written about this subject, but as he discusses my personal experience in New York, he seems to have the same idea as the Swedish professor *Linderholm*, who thinks that the Baptism was the result of a *"psychical depression"*, because I was not able to raise the necessary funds for Haakonsborgen.

It is true, that the Lord used this means to some extent, to drive me nearer Him in prayer, but, as it will be seen from "the outline of my life" in this book, *I had for years been looking forward towards a greater spiritual experience!* My mind was clear, my motives pure, and my physical strength was in no way impared. My nerves were in perfect order, but the Lord brought me to the point, where I found that my *inner life* and my whole being *must* be permeated with the Holy Spirit, no matter what the cost might be! Of course it is difficult for people, who have never been influenced that way, to understand it. Personally I had no pecuniary want. I was really sorry that so little interest was shown for "*Haakonsborgen*", but my soul began to long intensely for the blessings from the Eternal World — and then God met me!

I would not, after testing this experience during 21 years, exchange it with anything else in the world, Hallelujah!

What saddens my heart at times is the fact, that I have not made more headway, after receiving so many blessings. I have at times allowed my strong feelings of justice carry me too far in my judgment of others. I have, I'm afraid, spoken too severely now and then, and grieved the Spirit, but He has always been at hand to admonish and make me seek forgiveness of those I may have hurt unnecessarily. Of course the Spirit drives us at times to condemn sin in its manifold forms with severe and strong words, but we need much grace to see to it, that it is the Spirit's voice and not give the flesh an opportunity.

My constant prayer is, that He may lead me on towards greater heights and still brighter visions of His mercy and grace, and keep my motives pure, always *under the Blood!*

As regards *the Movement generally,* there have of course been made many mistakes; and men, on whom we relied, have fallen away in the thraldom of sin and the world. Many, of whom we expected much, have stuck fast in the old forms and systems prevalent here and there, but this has always been the case in all revivals.

When you use the broom on a road, a good bit of dust will be whirled up, but you are nevertheless able to make the road look brighter and cleaner. It's just the same experience, realized in a great Revival. However, it's of little use to make much ado about the dust that some whirl up, be thankful that God is making the road brighter and cleaner!

One of the greatest objections to the Revival has been our teaching concerning tongues and the spiritual gifts, as well as the various manifestations that have accompanied it, but history, and especially the Bible, proves, that these manifestations and gifts of the Spirit have always attended, in some degree at least, the greater outpourings of the Holy Spirit.

This book is not the place to discuss the matter, but we believe that the arrows launched against our teaching concerning the Baptism of the Holy Spirit, and the Signs following, have been *broken against the rock of Truth!*

One thing must be borne in mind, and that is, that *the Gift of tongues* was an entirely new sign, connected only with New Testament times. All the other gifts spoken of by Paul, had been practiced in the Jewish church before the outpouring of the Spirit in Jerusalem. Even the disciples of the Lord practiced healing and worked miracles before that wonderful Pentecost in Jerusalem, but none of them had spoken in tongues. Even the gift of Prophesy had been in use among the Jews, but not the tongues. *Christ had especially reserved this gift for the Christian Assembly.* (Mark. 16,17.)

However, let no one think, that *we* consider this outward sign and gift to be our chief experience. The fact that is of greater importance, is the presence of the *Holy Spirit Himself within!* And wherever He reigns supreme, *Jesus is glori-*

*fied!* — not only in our hearts, but in our words, lives and actions!

This then is what *all* God's people need: *A mighty outpouring of the Holy Ghost!*

Then sinners will flock to the Cross of Jesus and accept *Him* as their Saviour. The sick will be healed, the poor receive help, and God's people will use all their strength and ability in the evangelization of the world, trusting the workings of the Holy Spirit! There will arise, in the midst of all christian denominations, a

*Pure and Holy and Spirit-filled People,*
r e a d y   t o   r e c e i v e   the   King   at   H i s   a p p e a r a n c e !

O, may the Spirit soon fall on *all* God's people, as the floods of the Latter Rain!

> The *Blood* of Christ has opened wide
> The way to Heaven once more;
> T'was closed by s i n, but now by f a i t h
> We enter through the door!
>
> O, longing soul, by sin oppressed:
> List to the Spirit's call!
> The Blood of Jesus takes away
> The stains of Adam's fall!
>
> The m o m e n t faith lays hold on Christ
> And His redeeming power,
> Deep wells of *Life* burst forth within
> And life's sublimest hour!
>
> Claim n o w the Blood-bought Victory!
> Step in by faith and live!
> *Christ died for thee* — that settles all,
> Believe! — tis His to give!

*Greetings to all,* who love the Lord Jesus Christ, and await His coming!

• • •

Since the above was written, Mrs. Barratt and I reached New York, having landed on the 10th of

October. Although it was somewhat stormy a few days, I held some meetings on-board.

On the 12th, the Norwegian friends, with Pastor Arne Dahl at their head, arranged a very hearty "Velkomstfest" (reception) for us in Brooklyn. Scandinavians crowded the hall: flowers and a hearty greeting awaited us from Pastor and Sister Brown: and a delightful, fraternal spirit pervaded the meeting. Numbers of Norwegians were present to bid us welcome to the States: some having, ere they left Norway, been members of our Assembly at Oslo; others I had met on my journeys through Norway and Sweden; and again, there were several who remembered me from my last visit. We felt quite at home at once, and I received a renewed assurance that the good Lord had planed this visit to America.

Pastor Robert Brown had already invited me to preach at a special

*Revival Campaign*

in the "Glad Tidings Tabernacle". The services, were to last from Oct. 10th—30th.

Naturally, I felt a good bit anxious about this as I had not preached in the English language for years. The Lord helped me, however, and at the very first meeting, I spoke over the *Radio* to hundreds of thousands, besides the great crowd that filled the Tabernacle. I had never done this before. Just before leaving Norway, I sent a radio-greeting to thousands of my friends there; but this was my first experience of *preaching* through radio to the people.

Pastor Brown has made arrangements with a Broadcasting Station, to broadcast his Sunday afternoon song-service and sermon to thousands and thousands of people in the States. Numerous proofs of the blessing this modern method of spreading the Gospel has been to the listeners of Radioland, are being constantly received.

A delightfully free and gracious spirit pervaded the services at the Tabernacle, from the very first; and at every meeting — we saw the hand of God prevailing. Sinners were saved; backsliders reclaimed; God's people cleansed through faith in the Blood, and filled with the Holy Ghost.

Glad Tidings Tabernacle.

Sinners came forward to the altar, generally; while seekers for the "Promise of the Father" crowded together in the minor hall below, and with hands lifted towards heaven prayed in dead earnest for the blessing — *and the fire did fall*, Hallelujah!

We closed the campaign last night (the 30th) and as I look back at these blessed days in the Tabernacle, my heart is filled with gratitude and thanks to God for His Grace and Mercy towards us.

Time and again I was called upon to help fill out the program of the song-service, by singing and improvising on the piano.

I surely felt thankful to be able to glorify God also in this way.

The Lord gave me a tune to the song on page 210, and a chorus which runs thus:

Spread the news at every corner,
*Hurry up!* the *Day* is near;
Soon the *Heavens* will burst asunder,
And our Saviour will appear.

While crossing the Atlantic, the Lord gave me another song, and a tune to it. Here it is:

Deeper than wells.
Clearer than bells,
Are the Words of life;
Stronger than Death,
Heaven-borne breath,
Lives above the strife!

Perfectly free,
Resting in Thee —
C h r i s t, my all in all!
Cleansed through the Blood,
Grace like a flood
Breaks through every wall!

Routes every foe —
Mountains must go!
Christ remains supreme.
Who can define,
Love so divine?
'Tis our greatest theme.

Heavenly Light,
All my delight;
Guide me all the way!
Nothing like Thee.
Satisfies me,
Lead me day by day!

T'will not be long,
Ere the glad throng,
Hears the trumpets blast!
Angels draw near,
Christ will appear,
Takes us home at last!

The interest, at the meetings in the Tabernacle, was intensified by the fact that Brother Brown was present at 14th Street, New York, in 1906, when the *fire fell* (as stated on Page 219). Brother Brown came from Ireland, and I from Norway, but a Norwegian, Brother Vinger, took us both to this little Mission on 14th street. At that time, Brother Brown was also a pastor in the Methodist Church. However, at one of the meetings in Glad Tidings Tabernacle, he stated that he did not receive the Baptism then, but was hungry and longing to break through.

The lady, who conducted the Mission at 14th street, in 1906, was also present at several of the meetings in the Tabernacle. Her name is Mrs. Haycraft, formerly Miss Williams. She had conducted meetings for about two months, when we came there in

1906. The day after the *fire fell*, she had received orders to move. The meeting had lasted too long: but God had wrought what He had intended to do in my heart, Hallelujah! *The fire was come!* Our Sister conducted meetings at this place about a week

Pastor and Mrs. Brown.

longer, after which the Mission was moved elsewhere.
It was Mrs. Brown, who started the definite work for the Pentecostal Movement in New York, not long after I had left for Norway. Her former name was Marie E. Burgess. Later on, Brother Brown attended her services and received his bap-

tism there; and now they have been united for years in the great and wonderful work that has its center in "Glad Tidings Tabernacle", from which blessings are radiating to thousands and thousands of hungry souls all over the states, and especially in New York.

\* \* \*

Since the Campaign in New York I have taken part in various Campaigns in Brooklyn, Chicago and other towns.

*"Nordisk Tidende"*,
the large Norwegian paper in Brooklyn, has spoken very favourably of the work God has done during the past years through this great movement.

My good wife and I intend, God willing, to visit several states, during our stay in America, and preach this glorious Gospel to both English and Scandinavian-speaking congregations, trusting that God will bless His own Word to the hearts of those who attend the services.

**GLORY TO HIS HOLY NAME!**

For Product Safety Concerns and Information please contact our EU representative  GPSR@taylorandfrancis.com
Taylor & Francis Verlag GmbH, Kaufingerstraße 24, 80331 München, Germany

www.ingramcontent.com/pod-product-compliance
Lightning Source LLC
Chambersburg PA
CBHW071234300426
44116CB00008B/1030